THE COMPLETE ILLUSTRATED WORLD ENCYCLOPEDIA OF

ARCHAEOLOGY

D1340944

  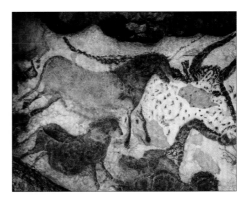

THE COMPLETE ILLUSTRATED WORLD ENCYCLOPEDIA OF

ARCHAEOLOGY

A REMARKABLE JOURNEY AROUND THE WORLD'S MAJOR ANCIENT SITES FROM STONEHENGE
TO THE PYRAMIDS AT GIZA AND FROM TENOCHTITLÁN TO LASCAUX CAVE IN FRANCE

HERMES
HOUSE

CONTENTS

INTRODUCTION

Archaeology has never been more popular than it is today, with a proliferation of TV shows devoted to it and archaeological tourism now responsible for a sizeable slice of the economy of many countries, such as Egypt, Mexico and Peru.

Archaeology is a truly vast subject, encompassing everything made or done by humans, from the first known stone tools about 2.6 million years ago up to events in recent history. The whole world is available for study to the archaeologist, barring wars or natural disasters, from mountains to jungle, from remote islands to big cities and from deserts to shipwrecks. Few fields of learning can match this geographical breadth and chronological depth.

This book will take you on an enthralling journey back in time and to different cultures and landscapes. The first section looks at the lives and work of many of the great archaeologists – the men and women whose commitment to uncovering the secrets of the past has brought us face to face with our ancestors.

The second part of the book focuses on some of the world's greatest archaeological sites and finds, exploring the civilizations behind them and the story of their rediscovery and excavation.

The archaeologists

The names of archaeologists such as Hiram Bingham, the discoverer of the lost Inca city of Machu Picchu, still seem to epitomize archaeology's spirit of adventure and unstinting quest for knowledge of the past.

The foundations for the professional and scientific archaeology that is practised today were laid in the 19th century by a group of amateur scholars – clerics, lawyers, teachers and doctors – for whom curiosity about the remote past became an abiding passion.

The early days of archaeology brought a succession of intrepid, often colourful scholars and adventurers. Among them were Arthur Evans and

Above A gold necklace from a spectacular collection of pre-Hispanic jewellery found in Tomb 7 at Monte Albán, in Mexico, discovered by the great Mexican archaeologist Alfonso Caso (1896-1970).

Above The British archaeologist Sir Mortimer Wheeler (1880-1976) at work on the well-preserved tessellated floor that he discovered on the site of the ancient Roman city of Verulamium, near St Albans.

Heinrich Schliemann who afforded the modern world its first glimpse of the Minoan and Mycenaean civilizations. There were also early Egyptologists, such as Giovanni Belzoni and Auguste Mariette; Max Uhle, the father of South American archaeology; and Augustus Pitt Rivers whose meticulous approach to excavation helped to put field work on a more professional footing. Early milestones include the decoding of the Rosetta Stone by Champollion in the early 1820s.

The first true professional archaeologists began to emerge in the early 20th century. Their pioneering work led to many significant breakthroughs: Alfred Kidder's excavations at Pecos, New Mexico; Dorothy Garrod's studies at the Palaeolithic caves of Mount Carmel; and, in 1922, perhaps the greatest discovery of them all – the tomb of Tutankhamen in Egypt's Valley of the Kings by the English archaeologist Howard Carter.

As the 20th century progressed, archaeology became primarily a field for highly qualified specialists, who had access to new and ever more sophisticated techniques for dating, excavation and survey. The new wave of archaeologists made significant breakthroughs in many subject areas and in every corner of the world. The groundbreaking excavations of several generations of the Leakey family in Africa, for example, have had a significant impact on our understanding of the origins of man. In Peru the tireless dedication of one woman – Maria Reiche – ensured that the Nasca lines were brought to the attention of the wider world.

Other great landmarks of modern archaeology include the decipherment of Linear B by the English scholar Michael Ventris, Kathleen Kenyon's important discoveries in the Near East and the Russian-born Tatiana Proskouriakoff's pioneering studies of the Maya.

The sites

In a book of this size, it is impossible to do more than provide a brief glimpse of some of the myriad important sites and finds from around the world. Any period or region of the globe could easily fill several such volumes. The sites that have been selected will, however, provide a unique insight

Below An aerial view of the immense temple of Angkor Wat in modern-day Cambodia. In recent years, radar data has enabled archaeologists to detect hitherto undiscovered areas of the vast Angkor complex, which are otherwise inaccessible because of poor roads and uncleared landmines.

into many of the world's great archaeological treasures – from the Temples of the Far East to the cave paintings of Europe and from the enigmatic cities of Mesoamerica to China's incomparable Terracotta Army.

This fascinating journey begins in Africa, from the pyramids of Egypt in the north to the prehistoric caves in the south. Next comes a sample of some of the ancient sites of the Middle East, including some of the world's oldest cities, such as Uruk and Susa.

The sections on Europe and the Mediterranean region reveal spectacular finds, including the Anglo-Saxon ship burial at Sutton Hoo in England and the Ulu Burun shipwreck off the coast of southern Turkey. The great sites of the Far East stretch from Harappa in the west to Nara in the east, while the Easter Island statues are among the jewels of Oceania. The vast continent of the Americas is represented by sites as diverse as the Viking settlement of L'Anse aux Meadows in Newfoundland and the magnificent royal tombs at Sipán in Peru.

That new exciting discoveries are still to be made in many parts of the world is a certainty. Large parts of Africa, for instance, remain practically untouched by archaeologists. And advances in science mean that archaeologists can now extract more

Above A family shrine (*lararium*) found in the House of the Vettii in the ruined city of Pompeii. Excavations have brought us face to face with a remarkable Roman city frozen in time since the 1st century AD.

information from less material – for example, a single fragment of a pot can be dated, analysed for its constituent materials, its firing temperature, its decorations and even, from traces on its inner surface, what it used to contain.

Another constant trend in world archaeology is that the dates for the origins of different phenomena, such as the invention of pottery or the cultivation of plants, keep getting pushed further back, while the place of origin may also move around as new discoveries modify our understanding. This is one of the many reasons why archaeology is such a compelling subject – new discoveries such as The Iceman, found in the 1990s in the Tyrolean Alps, can turn up unexpectedly and radically alter our cumulative picture of the ancient world.

This timeline presents a selective list of significant milestones and events in the history of places and civilizations featured in this book.

500,000 BC	Far East	* Peking Man, a skeleton found at Zhoukoudian, may date back to this time
130,000 BC	Africa	* *Homo sapiens sapiens* develop as a species
50,000 BC	Oceania	* The first stone tools in Lake Mungo, Australia, are made * Some of the rock art at Dampier may date back to this time
13,000 BC	Europe	* The people of Mezhirich in the Ukraine build shelters out of mammoth bones
5500 BC	Africa	* 5500-2500 Saharan rock art is created
5000 BC	Far East	* Mehrgarh in Pakistan has become a prosperous town and centre of industry
4000 BC	Middle East	* The Uruk society reaches its height in the 4th millennium
	Far East	* Harappa in Pakistan is an important centre of the local Harappan Bronze Age culture
3300 BC	Europe	* The Iceman found in the Ötztaler Alps lives around this time
3100 BC	Middle East	* Development of proto-Elamite script begins at Susa * The Sumerians develop cuneiform in the late 4th and early 3rd millennia
3000 BC	Africa	* 2975-2950 Distinctive dynastic mastaba tombs are built at Saqqara and Abydos
	Europe	* The first monument at Stonehenge in Wiltshire is constructed
2700 BC	Africa	* Djoser (ruled 2668-2649) commissions Egypt's first stone building
2600 BC	Africa	* Khufu (ruled 2551-2528) built his Great Pyramid at Giza, the site of many later monuments, such as the Great Sphinx
1700 BC	Far East	* Foundation of the Shang Dynasty in China
	Mediterranean	* The New Palace at Knossos is built by the Minoans of Crete in the 16th century
1500 BC	Mediterranean	* The Mycenaeans of Greece come to prominence
1400 BC	Africa	* Tutankhamen (ruled 1333-1324) is interred in the Valley of the Kings
	Mediterranean	* A Bronze Age ship sinks off the cape of Ulu Burun in Turkey in the 14th century
1300 BC	Africa	* Ramesses II (*c.*1290-1224) builds the twin temples of Abu Simbel

800 BC	Mediterranean	* 776 The alleged date of the first Olympic games at Olympia
	Europe	* Central Europe is inhabited by the Celts
700 BC	Mediterranean	*The first temple at Delphi is probably built in the 7th century
	Europe	*The Celtic kingdoms of central Europe begin to show Mediterranean influence
	Americas	* Occupation begins at Tikal, a Mayan city in Guatemala
600 BC	Middle East	* Construction of Persepolis begins under Darius the Great (ruled 522-486)
500 BC	Mediterranean	*The Temple of Zeus at Olympia is constructed
	Far East	* Rich burials of horse-riding nomads begin in the Altai mountains of Siberia
	Americas	* Construction of the Great Pyramid at Cholula begins
400 BC	Middle East	* 330 Alexander the Great destroys the palace at Persepolis
300 BC	Far East	* 210 Qin Shi Huangdi, the first Chinese emperor, was buried with over 7000 life-size terracotta soldiers
200 BC	Mediterranean	* Eumenes (ruled 197-159) built the Altar of Zeus at Pergamon * 146 Carthage is destroyed by the Romans
AD 1-100	Mediterranean	* 64 Nero constructs the Domus Aurea after a fire in Rome * 79 Mount Vesuvius erupts destroying Pompeii and Herculaneum
	Americas	*The Moche culture emerges in coastal northern Peru
AD 500	Americas	*The Central Mexican city of Teotihuacán reaches its height in the 6th century
	Europe	*The burial mounds at Sutton Hoo are in use from the late 6th century
AD 600	Americas	*The Ancestral Puebloan (Anasazi) Indian society flourishes in Mesa Verde
AD 800	Americas	* Occupation begins at the Mayan city of Chichén Itzá
AD 1000	Americas	* A group of Scandinavians settle at L'Anse aux Meadows in Newfoundland
AD 1350	Oceania	* Shag River Mouth in New Zealand is occupied for about 50 years
AD 1400	Americas	*The Chimú are conquered by the Incas and the assimilation of their culture greatly influences the course of Inca civilization
AD 1700	Oceania	* HMS *Pandora* sinks in Australia's Great Barrier Reef in the 1790s
AD 1800	Americas	* 1876 The Battle of Little Bighorn takes place

ARCHAEOLOGISTS

'It was a thrilling moment for an excavator, quite alone save his native staff of workmen, to suddenly find himself, after so many years of toilsome work, on the verge of what looked like a magnificent discovery – an untouched tomb.'

HOWARD CARTER

The following chapters chart the lives and achievements of archaeologists such as Howard Carter – shown in the foreground of this photograph taken in 1923 – who have changed the face of archaeology and our understanding of the past.

FOUNDERS OF ARCHAEOLOGY

During the 19th century, adventurers and antiquarians realized that the secrets of the past, both treasure and knowledge, lay beneath their feet. A cast of sometimes colourful, mostly self-taught amateurs populated archaeology in those years. Each had his style, from the hell-for-leather pursuit of the spectacular find of Schliemann, to Belzoni, who uncovered the Great Temple at Abu Simbel (facing page), and from the single-minded application of Champollion in his quest to decode Egyptian hieroglyphs, to the meticulous, analytical approach to excavation of Pitt Rivers, for whom the everyday was as important as the exotic. Whatever their ways and means, all of these men helped lay the foundations for today's scientific discipline of archaeology, whether by establishing methods, by capturing the public's imagination or simply by inspiring others to follow in their footsteps.

Arthur Evans On the island of Crete, Evans found the remains of Europe's oldest literate civilization, which he named 'Minoan'.

Ephraim George Squier The enigmatic Squier meticulously catalogued the work of the mid-West's so-called Mound Builders.

Max Uhle Known as the father of South American archaeology for his work at Pachácamac and other sites in the Andes.

Giovanni Belzoni

(1778-1823)

After a colourful early career, which included a stint as a strongman in an English circus, this 2m (6ft 7in) giant of a man, Italian by birth, went on to become one of the pioneering figures of Egyptology. Among other achievements, Belzoni uncovered the Great Temple at Abu Simbel.

Born the son of a barber, in Padua in north-eastern Italy, Giovanni Battista Belzoni was peripatetic from the start. At one time he wanted to become a monk, joining a Capuchin monastery, then changed his mind and turned his attention to hydraulic engineering. By his mid-twenties, he was married and living in London, where poverty led him to exploit his exceptional height and strength by working in fairs and

Below Egyptian workers under Belzoni haul the top part of the statue of Ramesses II from the Ramesseum in 1816. The lower section of the seated figure remains in situ.

circuses. Also at this time, he first met his future patron, the painter, traveller and antiquarian Henry Salt.

Arriving in Egypt

Belzoni never gave up his interest in hydraulics, however, and in 1815 he visited Egypt, with the aim of selling a new design of water wheel to the pasha (ruler), Mohammed Ali. When this project failed, Belzoni started to work for Salt, recently appointed British consul-general in Cairo.

His first commission was to retrieve the upper section of a colossal statue of Ramesses II for the British Museum

in London, where it remains today. The Italian's engineering skills came into play as he carefully removed the detached head-and-shoulders portion of the figure from the courtyard of the Ramesseum, on the west bank of the Nile opposite modern Luxor, and had it shipped back to England. He then sailed south to visit Abu Simbel. Back in Luxor, he carried out excavations at the Karnak Temple and discovered the tomb of Ay, Tutankhamen's successor.

In February 1817 Belzoni cleared away the deep blanket of sand under which the Great Temple at Abu Simbel had remained buried. In October he

Above Nineteenth-century travellers pose before the ruins of the Ramesseum. The complex, the mortuary temple of Ramesses II, one of Egypt's longest-reigning pharaohs, lies in western Thebes, opposite modern Luxor.

entrance he had discovered hidden on the north face. He inscribed a message dating his discovery – 2 March 1818 – on the internal wall of the pyramid.

After a journey to the shores of the Red Sea, where he identified the ruins of the Greco-Roman port of Berenice, Belzoni travelled south to the island of Philae, located in the Nile near Aswan, to recover a fallen obelisk on behalf of Englishman William John Bankes. In spite of an altercation with the French Consul, Drovetti, who claimed the column for France, Belzoni succeeded in acquiring it. Bankes erected the obelisk in his garden at Kingston Lacy, Dorset, where it still stands. Belzoni then set out into the Western Desert towards Libya, where he hoped to find the oasis of Jupiter Ammon.

Into print

In 1820 Belzoni published his *Narrative of the Operations and Recent discoveries within the pyramids, temples, tombs and excavations in Egypt and Nubia; and of a journey to the coasts of the Red Sea, in search of the Ancient Berenice; and another in the oasis of Jupiter Ammon*. The work was a bestseller and was followed by a successful exhibition of his finds in the recently completed Egyptian Hall in Piccadilly, London.

In 1822 Belzoni travelled to Russia, where he met Tsar Alexander I. His last adventure was an attempt to reach the fabled city of Timbuktu. But he made it only as far as Benin in modern Nigeria, where he died of dysentery on 3 December 1823, aged 45.

Belzoni operated before the age of scientific archaeology and, judged by its precepts, his methods were open to question. He was more interested in finding monuments than in recording or studying them, and he often caused irreparable damage in the process. He has also been accused of being little more than a 'tomb robber', someone who hunted treasures in order to sell them to European collectors. Even so, his discoveries were groundbreaking and he was an inspiration to future generations of Egyptologists, assuring his place as a pioneer in the field.

made a string of remarkable finds in the Valley of the Kings: the unfinished tomb of Prince Mentuherkhepshef (a son of Ramesses IX), the tomb of 19th Dynasty founder Ramesses I and the beautifully decorated tomb of his son, Seti I, father of Ramesses II.

Belzoni next worked at Giza, where in 1818 he became the first person in modern times to reach the interior of the Pyramid of Khaefre, the second largest of the pyramids at Giza, whose

J.F. Champollion

(1790-1832)

Champollion was the brilliant young scholar who in the early 1820s cracked the code of the Rosetta Stone. In doing so, he made it possible to solve one of the great academic mysteries of the age — how to decipher the lost language of ancient Egypt — and opened up a new era in Egyptology.

Jean-François Champollion was born less than a year after the start of the French Revolution and grew up in the town of Figeac in south-west France. He was a precocious child and enjoyed studying foreign languages, becoming proficient in many, including Italian, English, Latin, Greek, Arabic, Coptic and Chaldean. In 1809, when only 19, he was appointed assistant professor of history at the Lyceum of Grenoble, where he had been a student.

Given his interest in languages, it was natural that Champollion should become involved in the attempt to decipher ancient Egypt's hieroglyphic script. The French discovery, in 1799, of the Rosetta Stone, a stela (inscribed tablet) dating from the Ptolemaic era, offered a realistic chance of doing that, since it bears a decree written in two languages – Egyptian and Greek – but laid out in three texts. The Greek version uses Greek characters, but the Egyptian text is inscribed in both hieroglyphs and demotic script.

Slowly but resolutely, Champollion pieced together the different portions of the puzzle. By late 1821 he had proved that demotic was a late, much simplified version of hieroglyphs. He had also demonstrated that individual hieroglyphs did not necessarily stand for individual words, suggesting that they had a phonetic component – that some, at least, stood for particular sounds or groups of sounds. He knew too that royal names were written in cartouches (flattened ovals). The latter provided an important lead, enabling

Below The Rosetta Stone, discovered in Rosetta, Egypt, in 1799 by French troops, was the primary key to decoding Egyptian script. This is a detail of its hieroglyphic inscription.

Champollion to read 'Ptolemy' on the Rosetta Stone, both 'Ptolemy' and 'Cleopatra' on the obelisk recovered by Belzoni from the island of Philae and 'Alexander' on an inscription from the Karnak Temple. In this way Champollion was able to create an alphabet of 12 hieroglyphs, each one representing a sound, that could be applied to all Greco-Roman names written in Egyptian.

The puzzle completed

This phonetic solution to hieroglyphs worked with non-Egyptian names, but it was far from clear whether it held for Egyptian ones. The breakthrough came on 14 September 1822. While working on texts from the temples at Abu Simbel, which were 1500 years older than the inscriptions on the Rosetta Stone, and thus old enough to contain traditional Egyptian names, Champollion came across a cartouche that ended in a repeated hieroglyph. According to his phonetic alphabet, the symbol represented the sound of the letter 's', so he surmised that the royal name set down in the cartouche ended in a double 's'. Turning to the remaining two hieroglyphs in the cartouche, he postulated that the disc-shaped symbol at the beginning might represent the sun. In Coptic, a form of ancient Egyptian now used only by the Coptic Church, the word for sun is 'ra'. He then deduced that the second symbol in the cartouche stood for 'm' and that the name was Ramesses.

Fame at last

Champollion immediately presented his discoveries to the Academy of Inscriptions in Paris. Two years later he published a more comprehensive work, *A Summary of the Hieroglyphic System of the Ancient Egyptians*, in which he showed that hieroglyphs could represent sounds as well as concepts, depending on the context. The book made him a celebrity and was the foundation upon which all further decoding of hieroglyphs was based.

In 1826 Champollion was named curator of the Egyptian collection of the Louvre Museum in Paris, then in 1828 began a year-long tour of Egypt, his first and only visit to the country. Champollion was created professor of archaeology at the Collège de France in Paris in March 1831 but died from a stroke a year afterwards. His ancient Egyptian grammar and dictionary were published posthumously, in 1836 and 1841 respectively.

Right This cartouche represents the name of Seti I. Cartouches similar to this but containing Greco-Roman names set Champollion on the road to deciphering hieroglyphs.

Sir Arthur Evans

(1851-1941)

On Crete, Arthur Evans discovered the remains of Europe's oldest literate civilization and believed that he had found the palace of the legendary King Minos. His interpretation has been derided as wish-fulfilment, yet Evans' methods mark him as a founder of modern field archaeology.

Arthur Evans first visited the island of Crete in 1894 to look for prehistoric coins and seals (clay tablets). As a boy in Hertfordshire, England, Evans had been fascinated by the inscriptions on ancient coins and artefacts collected by his father, Sir John Evans, who was a noted numismatist (coin specialist) and antiquarian. Sir John was also a successful businessman whose wealth enabled his son to first study modern history at Oxford and afterwards tour the Balkans. In 1876 Arthur Evans became special correspondent in the Balkans for *The Manchester Guardian*, and between then and 1882, when he was expelled from the region on political grounds, he identified the sites of several Roman roads and cities in Bosnia and Macedonia.

Below This fresco from 1700-1400 BC, found at Knossos, depicts bull-vaulting, believed to be a religious ritual among the Minoans.

In 1884 Evans took up a post as a keeper of the Ashmolean Museum in Oxford. He believed that a script, as yet undeciphered, on Aegean Bronze Age coins in the collections belonged to the Mycenaeans. He visited Athens to search for similar inscriptions and learnt that on Crete, peasants often unearthed inscribed seals, coins and gemstones when cultivating their fields.

Travels in Crete

Accompanied by a young student, John Myres (later celebrated for his archaeological excavations on Cyprus), Evans travelled through Crete in 1894-5, searching for sites and inscribed artefacts. The two nurtured the idea that the Greek myths were based on historical fact. The previous year Myres had applied for a licence to dig at the tell (artificial mound) at Kephala (Knossos), where in 1878 the Cretan archaeologist Minos Kalokairinos had uncovered sections of a great building. Evans and Myres were not the only ones interested in digging at Kephala at around this time. Heinrich Schliemann was among the others who applied. All were unsuccessful although in 1895 Evans, with money and all the credentials and contacts of a journalist and antiquarian, was allowed to buy part of the site.

Kephala

Arthur Evans began his excavations at 11 a.m. on Friday, 23 March, 1900. He was assisted by David Hogarth and Duncan MacKenzie, experts in archaeological methods, and also by Theodore Fyfe, a specialist in ancient architecture. MacKenzie kept meticulous records of the excavations in his day books. The chambers and storerooms that the team uncovered and the artefacts they discovered there told them that the site was the palace-city of an early literate civilization. However, Evans's interpretations of the finds at the mound were controversial. Basing his deductions on the Homeric myths and

Above This is the smaller of two cult figurines from *c.*1500 BC discovered close to the central shrine at Knossos. Both figurines hold serpents and may have been snake goddesses.

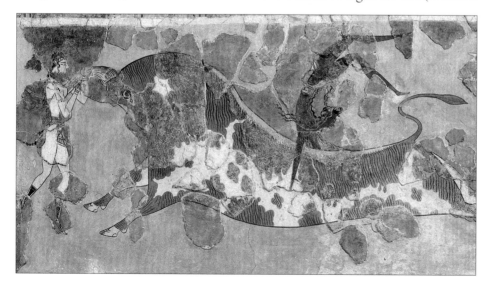

on coins found at the site, which bore images of labyrinths, minotaurs and of Ariadne, daughter of King Minos, Evans declared that he had found the palace of the mythical Cretan king, who had kept the Minotaur (half man, half bull) in a labyrinth.

Some repair of the site's crumbling walls, stairs and foundations proved necessary for safety and for access to some parts of the complex. However, Evans rebuilt walls and reconstructed rooms using reinforced concrete, rebuilt timber structures and painted his 'reconstitutions', as he referred to them, in pink and terracotta; he also decorated rooms with reproduction frescoes. Evans declared one chamber to be the Throne Room of King Minos and restored it in what he considered to be appropriate style. Archaeologists today avoid such 'over-interpretation' and use of modern materials.

Evans excavated most of the palace complex in four years but lived and worked at Knossos for some 30 years, publishing his findings in four volumes between 1921 and 1931. His views on the site were widely accepted at first,

Above Minoan pillars, unlike Greek columns, are wider at the top than the bottom. Evans had many rebuilt and painted to match the plaster he found on some floors and walls.

and in 1911 he received a knighthood. However, his chronology for Minoan civilization clashed with the findings of other archaeologists working in the field and later investigations of the site concluded that the connection with the mythical King Minos was fanciful.

Evans's legacy

Some archaeologists have condemned Evans as a falsifier of history. Yet his achievements outweighed the errors he committed and he was no treasure-seeker. Evans discovered a previously unknown, literate civilization, which dated back beyond the Mycenaeans to the 3rd millennium BC and dominated the Aegean from 1900 to 1300 BC. He remains a towering figure in the development of archaeology, and the names he gave to the site at Kephala that he excavated, 'Knossos', and to the civilization that built it, 'Minoan', continue to be used today.

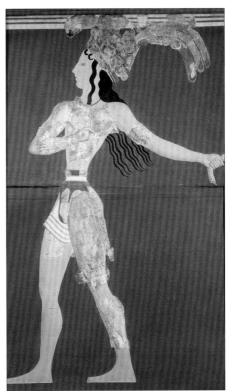

Above This fresco, known as 'the Prince with Lilies' or 'Priest-King', shows a figure wearing a headdress of lilies and peacock feathers. The fragments of this fresco were discovered beneath the Corridor of the Processions in the south section of the complex at Knossos.

21

Henry Layard

(1817-1894)

Layard was responsible, along with Frenchman Paul Emile Botta, for the first serious excavations in Mesopotamia (Iraq) and the rediscovery of the Assyrians. Display of his finds in the British Museum and his descriptions of his digs stimulated public enthusiasm for Near Eastern archaeology.

Born in Paris, Layard was the son of an official in the colonial civil service of Ceylon (Sri Lanka). After receiving an education in Europe and Britain, he entered a solicitor's office in London but left six years later with the aim of taking up a post in the Ceylon Civil Service himself. Travelling eastwards overland, Layard got only as far as the Middle East, which he explored thoroughly, visiting numerous ancient sites, including in Iraq various tells (artificial mounds) hiding the ruins of ancient Mesopotamian cities. The tells and the ruins they held fascinated Layard and he developed a desire to excavate and study them for himself. It was in Iraq that he met Botta, who began excavating in the area of Mosul, in the north of the country, in 1842. That same year Layard's travels took him to Constantinople (Istanbul), the Ottoman capital, where he remained, carrying out unofficial diplomatic tasks for the British envoy, Stratford Canning, until he could fulfil his wish of returning to Iraq to excavate.

Uncovering Assyria

In 1845 Layard secured a gift of £100 from Canning and went back to Iraq to undertake his own excavations. He began at a site called Nimrud, a tell situated near the banks of the Tigris, 30km (19 miles) south-east of Mosul. On the very first day Layard came across the ruins of an Assyrian palace, and a short time afterwards unearthed a second palace.

During two years of digging, Layard uncovered portions of half a dozen palaces decorated with the limestone wall-reliefs characteristic of Assyrian royal buildings, the colossal statues of human-headed winged bulls that guarded palace portals and numerous smaller works of art. Among the latter was the so-called Black Obelisk, which dated from 825 BC and depicted the military exploits of the Assyrian king Shalmaneser III, including the submission of Jehu, king of ancient Israel, to Assyrian dominion. Layard originally believed that he had found the remains of Nineveh, the Assyrian capital from *c.*700 BC until its fall in 612 BC. In fact the ruins were those of Kalhu, the biblical city of Calah, which had been the capital of the empire from the 9th century BC until Sargon II moved it north to Dur-Sharrukin (Khorsabad) in 717 BC.

Layard returned home to England in 1847, where his discoveries initially met with mixed reviews. Many people disparaged the aesthetic qualities of

Left A force of local workers moves an Assyrian winged bull statue at the site of Nimrud in 1849. This engraving is taken from Henry Layard's work *Discoveries in the Ruins of Nineveh and Babylon.*

Assyrian art, and the subject was even raised in Parliamentary committee, where the suitability of Layard's finds for display in the British Museum was discussed. Others, meanwhile, among them Layard's patron Canning, were elated. Layard himself sought popular support: his book *Nineveh and Its Remains* (1848-9) placed emphasis on the adventure of archaeology and the biblical associations of his results.

French competition

In 1846 the Louvre Museum in Paris had opened a display of Assyrian finds recovered by Botta, who three years previously had unearthed Sargon II's capital at Khorsabad. Some eminent British figures were not slow in seeing a challenge. Stratford Canning, for one, expressed in a letter to Prime Minister Robert Peel a belief that Layard's Assyrian finds 'will beat the Louvre hollow'. Persuaded by such appeals, the British Museum provided the then considerable sum of £2000 for the archaeologist to ship his finds back to London and continue his work in Mesopotamia. Layard arranged for the artefacts, including carved wall-reliefs and massive winged bulls, to be transported to Britain via India, where curiosity-seekers opened many crates awaiting passage on the quayside. The British Museum opened its Nineveh Gallery in 1853 to popular acclaim.

Layard used the remaining funds to excavate the tell at Kuyunjik, which lay to the east of the Tigris, opposite modern Mosul. In 1849 he uncovered the palace of Sennacherib and tens of thousands of clay tablets from the library of Assurbanipal. The latter find included Mesopotamian literature, dictionaries and other materials that would open the Mesopotamian world to scholarly study. This time there was no mistake: Layard had discovered the ancient city of Nineveh.

In 1849-50 Layard shifted his focus southwards, where he briefly explored Babylon, near modern Al-Hillah, and other mounds. However, used to the immediate results he had enjoyed with the Assyrian tells and unfamiliar with

the technical demands of excavating mud-brick architecture, Layard found these southern sites disappointing. Nevertheless, Layard again presented his findings to a fascinated public in *Discoveries in the Ruins of Nineveh and Babylon*, published in 1853.

A break with the past

Two years previously Layard had left Iraq and abandoned archaeology. In 1852 he entered British politics as Member of Parliament for Aylesbury, subsequently rising to Under Secretary

Above The ruins of the final Assyrian capital of Nineveh were unearthed at Kuyunjik, near Mosul in northern Iraq. Frenchman Paul Emile Botta was the first to excavate at the site, but the breakthrough was made by Layard.

for foreign affairs and being appointed privy counsellor. He served as an MP until 1869, when he traded politics for diplomacy, becoming ambassador first to Spain and later to the Ottoman court in Constantinople, the position formerly held by Layard's one-time patron Stratford Canning.

Auguste Mariette

(1821-1881)

As first Director of Egyptian Monuments, appointed in 1858, Mariette was the most influential Egyptologist of his generation. His achievements included bringing order to the hitherto largely unregulated excavation of the country's antiquities, and the founding of the Egyptian Museum.

A native of Boulogne-sur-Mer on the north coast of France, Mariette spent a brief period in his late teens working in England, first as a schoolmaster and then as a designer for a ribbon-maker. In 1840 he returned to France to complete his education and then took up a teaching position in Boulogne. His fascination with ancient Egypt was triggered in 1842, when he was asked to put in order the papers of the recently deceased archaeologist and draughtsman Nestor L'Hôte, a relative who had accompanied Champollion on his 1828 expedition to Egypt. After years of private study of the Coptic and Egyptian languages, in 1847 Mariette published a catalogue of the Egyptian collection in the Boulogne Museum. Two years later, he obtained a junior post at the Louvre Museum.

In 1850 Mariette visited Egypt to collect Coptic manuscripts for the Bibliothèque Nationale. However, he

Below *Mariette's first great discovery was the Serapeum. Here is one of the huge granite sarcophagi in which the bulls were buried.*

Above *Ka-aper was a chief lector-priest during the reign of Userkaf (2465-2458 BC). Mariette's workers found the statue near the king's pyramid at Saqqara in 1860.*

found manuscripts in short supply and turned instead to archaeology. His first excavation at Saqqara resulted in the discovery of the Serapeum – the galleries where the sacred bulls of the Apis cult were buried. Mariette went on digging at Saqqara for a further four years before returning to France.

Route to the top

By now an assistant conservator in the Louvre's department of Egyptology, and an archaeologist of some repute,

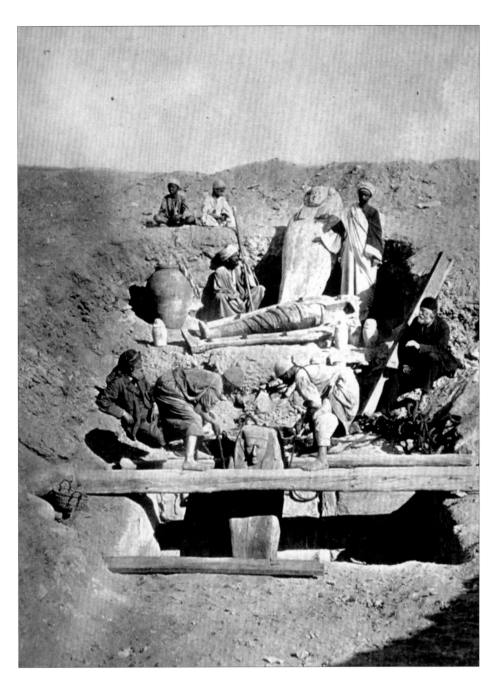

Mariette went back to Egypt in 1857 to help to prepare for a visit by Prince Napoleon, a cousin of the French Emperor Napoleon III. He launched a series of excavations at Giza, Saqqara, Abydos, Thebes and Elephantine, where his workmen busily sought out antiquities, which they then reburied so the prince could 'discover' them. The next year the Ottoman viceroy of Egypt, Said Pasha, appointed Mariette to the newly created post of Director of Egyptian Monuments, giving him effective control of the country's antiquities. From then until the end of his life, Egypt was Mariette's home.

Using his near-absolute powers, the new director restricted the selling and export of Egypt's antiquities. In 1859 Mariette persuaded Said Pasha to set up a museum at Bulaq, near Cairo, where they could be preserved. These collections were the basis for today's Egyptian Museum in Cairo, which was eventually opened on its current site in 1902. Mariette also embarked on a massive countrywide programme of simultaneous excavations, employing a force of almost 3000 workers. His projects included the first digs to take place at the Karnak Temple, situated in modern Luxor, as well as a 20-year excavation in the Nile Delta at Tanis, the biblical city of Zoan and a capital of ancient Egypt. In 1859 Mariette's workers found a virtually intact tomb in the necropolis of Dra Abu'l Naga, on the west bank of the Nile at Thebes (opposite Luxor). The treasure-filled coffin within belonged to Ah-hotep, mother of Ahmose I, founder of the 18th Dynasty, among whose pharaohs were Tutankhamen and Akhenaten. The next year Mariette began clearing the temple at Edfu, situated some 96km (60 miles) south of Luxor. The temple had developed into a village over the centuries, with houses having been built even on the sanctuary roof.

Nevertheless, though he nominally excavated at least 35 sites, Mariette was rarely on the spot to supervise his workforce, and the standard of his digs was not high. Additionally, many of his written records were lost when his house at Bulaq flooded in 1878.

Rank and honour

Mariette published a vast range of books and papers, including *Catalogue of the Boulaq Museum* (1864-76), *The Serapeum of Memphis* (1857) and *Karnak* (1875). He also received numerous honours, among them the Légion d'Honneur in 1852 and acceptance into the Académie des Inscriptions et des Belles-Lettres in 1878; in Egypt he was elevated to the rank of bey and later to that of pasha. In addition to his many accomplishments in Egyptology, he also collaborated on the libretto of Verdi's Egyptian-themed opera, *Aïda*, first performed in 1871 in Cairo.

Mariette died in 1881, having been in poor health for some years, and was interred in a sarcophagus at Bulaq. With the completion of the Egyptian Museum in Cairo in 1902, the coffin was moved to the building's forecourt and remains there, surmounted by a bronze statue of the former Director of Egyptian Monuments, which was unveiled in 1904.

Jacques de Morgan

(1857-1924)

Frenchman de Morgan began his working life as a mining engineer but combined this work with a strong and growing interest in archaeology. He eventually abandoned engineering when he accepted the appointment of Director-General of the Egyptian Antiquities Service.

The son of a mining engineer, Jacques de Morgan was born near the town of Blois in north-western France. His father bequeathed him not only his professional leanings but also his avid interest in prehistory. De Morgan graduated from the School of Mines in 1882 and began a career that took him to many parts of northern Europe and Asia. While managing a copper mine in Russian Armenia, he studied early

Below A photograph taken in the 1950s of the 1897 French excavation site at Susa. The project unearthed some remarkable finds, but the approach used meant that all archaeological context was lost.

metallurgy in the Caucasus. He then headed a scientific mission to Persia (Iran), where he combined geological studies – he was the first person to recognize the presence of petroleum in the south-west of the country – with archaeological inquiry.

Late in 1891 de Morgan returned to France but the following year took up the post of Director-General of the Egyptian Antiquities Service, which he held until 1897. While in Egypt, he founded the Greco-Roman Museum in Alexandria and laid the cornerstone of the Cairo Museum. He also carried out some field work, including a brief exploration of Naqada, a prehistoric

site about 24km (15 miles) north of modern Luxor, and the excavation of several pyramids at Dahshur, where he found a trove of royal jewellery dating from ancient Egypt's Middle Kingdom (*c.*1975-1640 BC).

A move to Persia

In 1897 de Morgan was appointed director of the Délégation en Perse, a permanent mission formed to exploit the archaeological research monopoly that Persia had granted France two years earlier. He decided to focus on the ancient city of Susa in the winters and pass the summers in north-west Iran exploring prehistoric cemeteries. His work in the Caucasus shows he could be a competent prehistorian, but he was not prepared for Susa. Deciding that stratigraphic excavation (layer-by-layer analysis) would not be possible, he treated Susa as a 'strip-mining' exercise. Employing a team of 1200 labourers, he removed huge quantities of earth – according to one estimate, 2.45 million cubic metres (86.5 million cubic feet) in less than a decade. As a result, he recovered some superb pieces of Mesopotamian art, including the Victory Stela of Naram-Sin and the Law Code of Hammurabi, but entirely without archaeological or architectural context.

In 1907 he turned over direction of the Susa dig and in 1912 resigned from the Délégation. Returning to France he devoted the remainder of his life to writing such works as the three-volume *La préhistoire orientale*.

Edouard Piette

(1827-1906)

Edouard Piette was a pioneering prehistorian in 19th-century France, who ruined himself financially with his excavations of Palaeolithic cave sites in the south-west of the country. He also amassed the finest collection of Ice Age portable art objects, including the 'Lady of Brassempouy'.

Piette was a lawyer by profession and worked as a provincial magistrate for most of his life. Born at Aubigny in the Ardennes, in north-eastern France, he developed a strong interest in geology at an early age. While a student of law in Paris, he was able to indulge this passion by attending geology lectures at the Sorbonne and at the School of Mines. From geology, his scope soon spread to archaeology and prehistory, especially in the French Pyrenees.

Cave sites in the Pyrenees

Although he carried out important work on tumuli (burial mounds) and monuments of later prehistory, Piette is especially remembered for his pioneering excavations at much earlier sites, such as the caves at Lortet, Arudy, Gourdan and, in particular, Le Mas-d'Azil – all of which are in or near the Pyrenees. At Le Mas-d'Azil, in the foothills of the central part of the range, he first identified a phase in prehistory between the end of the Ice Age and the start of the Neolithic period. Characterized by flat bone harpoons and small pebbles decorated with red dots and stripes, the culture came to be known as the Azilian.

Like other scholars of the period, Piette did not excavate himself but employed workmen to do it, checking them from time to time. He was, nonetheless, a pioneer in many other ways. Not only was he the first scholar to help fill the 'hiatus' after the Ice Age, but he was also one of the first

to find sites by searching systematically in suitable parts of the landscape. He was remarkably open-minded, willing to explore concepts such as the possibility that Palaeolithic people had already started cultivating plants and had succeeded in at least semi-domesticating horses. Piette was one of the very few prehistorians to believe Sanz de Sautuola's claims that figures of

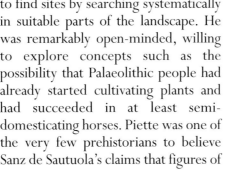

animals in the Altamira cave in northern Spain were painted during the Palaeolithic period. He was also largely responsible for introducing the young Abbé Henri Breuil to the field of prehistory: Piette employed Breuil to produce illustrations of some of his portable art objects.

The beautiful 'Lady'

Piette died in 1906, shortly before the publication of *L'Art Pendant l'Age du Renne* (1907), a magnificent volume devoted to his collection of Ice Age portable art. Even though his research and excavations had left him ruined financially, Piette bequeathed his art collection to the French nation. As well as numerous fine pieces that he had found himself, it also contained items he had acquired from others. Among its best-known pieces is the 'Lady of Brassempouy', a tiny but exquisite carving of a female head, fashioned from a mammoth tusk. Dating from about 21,000 BC, it was found in 1894 in the Grotte du Pape, a cave at Brassempouy in the foothills of the Pyrenees. The statuette can be seen at the National Museum of Antiquities at Saint-Germain-en-Laye near Paris.

Left The 'Lady of Brassempouy', also known as the 'Lady with the Hood', is a statuette standing 3.6cm (1½in) high. It is one of the earliest known examples of a sculpture of the human face – a generalized representation rather than the portrait of an individual.

Augustus Pitt Rivers

(1827-1900)

Nearly 40 years in the British army equipped Pitt Rivers with a military precision, which he brought to the field of archaeology. He established new standards in excavations, insisting on keeping meticulous records of exactly where artefacts were found and the prompt publication of results.

Archaeological excavations during the 19th century were largely unscientific affairs. Diggers often paid little attention to recording the positions of artefacts in the ground, and haphazard methods of excavation prevented accurate logging of the soil layers and the collection of other key information. Furthermore, published documentation was very scarce. It took a retired

Below Pitt Rivers (standing on the top of the mound) supervises the excavation of Wor Barrow on his estate in 1893-4. This long barrow was a Neolithic burial site.

British army general, known to us by his inherited name of Pitt Rivers, to begin to place archaeological field research on a professional footing.

A military career

Pitt Rivers was born Augustus Henry Lane Fox in Hope Hall, Yorkshire, the son of a British military officer. In 1841 he entered the Royal Military Academy at Sandhurst and embarked on his own army career, receiving a commission in the Grenadier Guards in 1845. He was a soldier for almost 40 years, serving in England, Canada,

Ireland, the Crimea and Malta. Lane Fox retired in 1882 with the rank of lieutenant general.

During his military service, Lane Fox began to collect artefacts from the places in which he was stationed. He started by acquiring weapons and then extended his collecting to a broader range of objects, both practical and decorative. His interest went beyond simple acquisition; he was concerned with charting the development down through the ages of practical objects, among them the rifle, a field of study he described as 'typology'.

Left Pitt Rivers was an avid collector throughout his adult life. The items shown here were all found by the 'father of scientific archaeology' and are a jar from London, a Bronze Age axe (below left) and a Neolithic flint axe from Farnham, Dorset.

As his army career went on, Lane Fox also began to excavate archaeological sites and to make detailed notes about his work. Beginning in Ireland in the early 1860s, when he was in his 30s, he investigated sites of many different periods in Brittany, southern England, Wales and even Denmark. In general, Lane Fox worked alone or with a few chosen companions and, from time to time, with hired workers.

In 1880, in his early 50s, Lane Fox inherited an estate of 3500 ha (8650 acres) as well as a large annual income of about £20,000 under the will of his great uncle, Henry Pitt, the second Lord Rivers. The terms of the will required Lane Fox to assume the name of Pitt Rivers; they also enabled him to retire comfortably. His estate spread out over a large expanse of chalk downland in the south of England. Called Cranbourne Chase, it lies where the counties of Hampshire, Dorset and Wiltshire meet. In medieval times, the area had been a royal hunting ground and, until the 19th century, farming there was strictly limited, which meant that any archaeological sites on the estate, such as barrows (burial mounds), had survived largely untouched.

Excavating the Chase

Recognizing the archaeological riches of his land and the neighbouring parts of Cranbourne Chase, Pitt Rivers devoted the rest of his life to their meticulous excavation. He worked on dozens of Bronze Age barrows, as well as investigating several Bronze Age, Iron Age, Roman and Romano-British enclosures. To help him, he had a staff of draughtsmen, surveyors, foremen, excavators and clerks – all labouring under the retired general's demanding and eccentric personality. Pitt Rivers's techniques were ahead of their time, setting standards for documentation and publication that established the foundations upon which archaeology developed in the twentieth century. The results of this work appeared in four imposing volumes, *Excavations in Cranbourne Chase*, published between 1887 and 1898.

Safe pair of hands

When the appointment of Inspector of Monuments was introduced in 1882, Pitt Rivers became the first to hold it, and approached the task of cataloguing and protecting Britain's archaeological sites with customary meticulousness. Despite the fact that his own archaeological research was overshadowed by spectacular finds made elsewhere during his lifetime, such as those of Schliemann at Troy and Mycenae, which had not benefited from such a painstaking approach, Pitt Rivers's contribution to archaeological method came to be appreciated in the decades after his death. A particular disciple was Sir Mortimer Wheeler, himself a military man, who hailed the excavation principles used by Pitt Rivers as the inspiration for his own field work. Pitt Rivers died on 4 May 1900, at the age of 73.

The Pitt Rivers Museum

In 1884, sixteen years before his death, Pitt Rivers gave a collection of about 20,000 archaeological and ethnographic artefacts to the University of Oxford. Today, the Pitt Rivers Museum is one of the world's most remarkable museums, organized by artefact function rather than period or region. This means that all artefacts with a particular purpose can be seen together. The museum's collections have now expanded to include more than 250,000 objects.

Above The fascinating collections at the Pitt Rivers Museum in Oxford give the visitor an insight into how different cultures overcame similar problems.

Above Like the items at the top of the page, this Anglo-Saxon pot, found by Pitt Rivers, is part of a collection that was acquired by the Salisbury and South Wiltshire Museum in 1975.

Henry Rawlinson

(1810-1895)

Soldier, politician and Orientalist, Henry Creswicke Rawlinson was also a noted linguist, whose work from the 1830s to the 1850s on the inscriptions at Behistun helped to decode the cuneiform scripts and make possible the study of the writings of the ancient Mesopotamian world.

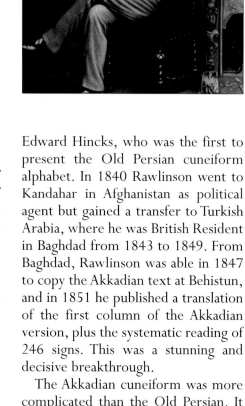

Born in the north Oxfordshire village of Chadlington, Rawlinson joined the East India Company as an officer cadet in 1827. Five years later he was posted to Persia (Iran) to help reorganize the Shah's army. During his two years in Persia, he acquired and developed the fascination with cuneiform scripts that would last the rest of his life.

Until the 1830s comparatively little progress had been made in decoding cuneiform scripts, partly for lack of a key like Egypt's Rosetta Stone, a text in several languages, one of which could already be read. Rawlinson and a number of other scholars eventually created that key with their work on the long cuneiform texts that the Persian king Darius I (reigned 521-486 BC) had had inscribed on his tomb near Persepolis and on a cliff at Behistun in western Iran. This text was written in three tongues: Elamite (the language of Susa), Akkadian (the language of Babylon and the Assyrians) and Old Persian. Rawlinson began copying the Behistun inscription in 1835 but had completed only the Old Persian and Elamite versions of the text when tensions between Britain and Persia obliged him to leave.

Another in the field

Rawlinson was not the only scholar attempting to decipher the cuneiform scripts, but he undertook much of his early work in isolation. In 1838 he published the still incomplete results of his work on the Old Persian text from Behistun, unaware of the more successful efforts of the Irish cleric Edward Hincks, who was the first to present the Old Persian cuneiform alphabet. In 1840 Rawlinson went to Kandahar in Afghanistan as political agent but gained a transfer to Turkish Arabia, where he was British Resident in Baghdad from 1843 to 1849. From Baghdad, Rawlinson was able in 1847 to copy the Akkadian text at Behistun, and in 1851 he published a translation of the first column of the Akkadian version, plus the systematic reading of 246 signs. This was a stunning and decisive breakthrough.

The Akkadian cuneiform was more complicated than the Old Persian. It was a syllabic script, with numerous logograms (signs representing whole words). Sceptics doubted the claims of Rawlinson and others that they had decoded it. In 1857 the Royal Asiatic Society put these doubts to rest. The society placed a newly discovered text before four scholars, among them Rawlinson and Hincks, who returned basically similar translations.

Though known chiefly as a linguist, Rawlinson also undertook some field archaeology. In 1851, having given a collection of Near Eastern antiquities to the British Museum, he received funding from the museum to continue Henry Layard's explorations in Iraq. Retiring from the East India Company in 1855, Rawlinson served as a crown director of the company. He also held a number of diplomatic and cultural posts, including a trusteeship of the British Museum, and was an MP in the 1850s and 1860s.

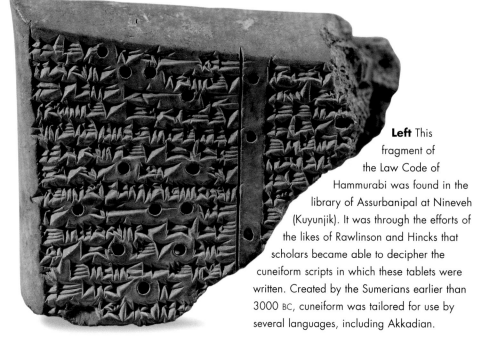

Left This fragment of the Law Code of Hammurabi was found in the library of Assurbanipal at Nineveh (Kuyunjik). It was through the efforts of the likes of Rawlinson and Hincks that scholars became able to decipher the cuneiform scripts in which these tablets were written. Created by the Sumerians earlier than 3000 BC, cuneiform was tailored for use by several languages, including Akkadian.

Sanz de Sautuola

(1831-1888)

Don Marcelino Sanz de Sautuola will forever be linked with the cave of Altamira in Cantabria, northern Spain, whose huge coloured wall and ceiling decorations dating from the Ice Age led him to realize that Palaeolithic people had produced great works of art.

Born in the coastal city of Santander, the capital of the region of Cantabria in northern Spain, Sanz de Sautuola trained as a lawyer. Nevertheless, as a prominent landowner, he did not need to work and was able to devote his time to his numerous interests, among them geology, botany and prehistory.

The marvellous find

In 1876 Sanz de Sautuola paid a visit to a hill called Altamira, which lay on land owned by his family. He had been informed of the existence of a cave by local farmer Modesto Cubillas, who while out hunting eight years earlier had followed his dog into an opening in the hillside, only to discover a series of chambers and passages. During his 1876 visit Sanz de Sautuola noticed some black painted signs on a wall but paid them little attention. In 1879 he returned to do some excavating, and while he was digging in the cave floor for prehistoric tools and portable art of the kind he had not long ago seen displayed at a Paris exhibition, his five-year-old daughter Maria was playing in the cavern. Suddenly, she spotted a number of coloured paintings of animals on the ceiling.

Her father was utterly dumbstruck. He found that the figures seemed to have been created with a fatty paste and noticed the similarity in style between these huge depictions (the red deer is 2.2m/7ft 3in long) and the smaller portable figures he had seen in Paris. He therefore deduced that both types of art were of a similar age, but when he attempted to convince the academic establishment, his ideas met with widespread rejection. Indeed, so well preserved were the paintings that he was even accused of forgery. In 1902 academia recanted and declared that Sanz de Sautuola had been right. Sadly, the news came too late for the Spaniard, who died in 1888, a sad and disillusioned man.

Below The Altamira paintings date from c.14,000-12,000 BC. The animals depicted include bison, horses and deer.

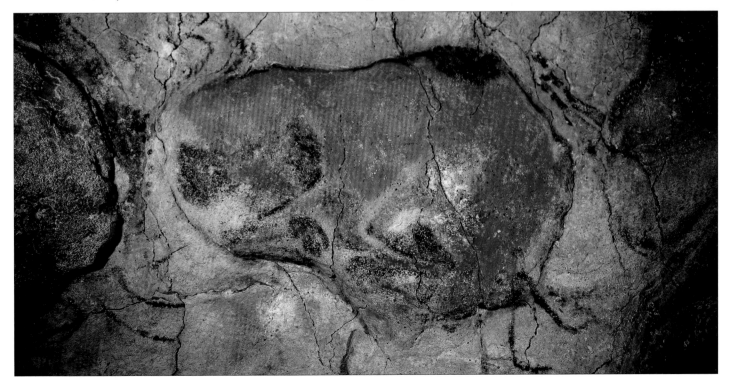

Heinrich Schliemann

(1822-1890)

Self-made businessman and self-taught archaeologist, Schliemann defied the opinions of experts and proved that places described by Homer had existed. By 1873 he had unearthed the site of Troy, and in 1876 he brought to light the Bronze Age civilization of Mycenae.

Schliemann was born into the large family of a poor Protestant minister in the Duchy of Mecklenberg-Schwerin in northern Germany. He mantained that his father imbued in him a love of Homer, which seeded his desire to find the ruins of Troy. This claim may have been wishful thinking, because records show that after the death of Schliemann's mother, his father sent him away, aged 11, to a fee-paying school in a neighbouring duchy. Only months later, though, he had to leave, his father having been accused of embezzling church funds. He then attended a vocational school until, at 14, he was apprenticed to a grocer.

At the age of 19, Schliemann signed on as a cabin boy to work his passage to the Americas but was shipwrecked and washed up in Holland. He was taken on by a commodities company and later by an import/export firm, where he displayed acute judgement and a flair for languages. He was sent to St Petersburg as an agent, then in 1851 sailed for California, where he set up in banking, buying and reselling gold dust from prospectors. In 1852 he returned to Russia, cornered the market in indigo, then moved into munitions when the Crimean War began. By his early forties, having made his fortune three times over, he had retired from business.

Troy and Mycenae

Free of the need to work, Schliemann travelled widely and, in 1868, while on a visit to Ottoman Turkey, he met Frank Calvert, a British archaeologist and consular official. Some historians surmise that Schliemann's obsession with proving the historical existence of Troy, then thought to have existed only in legend, may have emerged at this point. For 20 years Calvert had believed that a tell (artificial mound) at Hissarlik in Turkey was the site of Troy but could not raise the funds to excavate it. Schliemann became his financial partner and, after writing a thesis in support of Calvert's ideas, took over his excavations. He began

Below Schliemann's second wife, Sophia, wears the 'Jewels of Helen', part of the cache known as 'Priam's Treasure', found in the 1870s at Level II of the excavation at Troy.

digging in 1871 and soon found that several cities lay beneath the mound at progressively lower levels. Reasoning that Homeric Troy must be the city at the bottom, Schliemann dug through the ruins of later cities – destroying much archaeological evidence as he went. Later Wilhelm Dörpfeld would divide the site at Hissarlik into nine levels, with Level I, the oldest, at the bottom. In the event, Schliemann got down to Level II, and believed he had uncovered Homeric Troy.

Priam's Treasure

By 1873 Schliemann had unearthed not only the remains of a fortified city but also a spectacular treasure of gold and jewellery. This he believed to be the treasure of King Priam, ruler of Troy during the war against Greece, immortalized in Homer's epic *Iliad*. However, controversy overshadowed his discovery of the treasure, since Schliemann, possibly with Calvert's cooperation, smuggled it out of the country. Schliemann published an account of his excavations in 1874. It was met with a mixture of acclaim and scepticism: archaeologists disparaged both his destructive methods and his fanciful theories. Indeed, Level II at Hissarlik was later dated to about 2500-2300 BC, a thousand years too early for the Troy of the *Iliad*, which has been placed at Level VI/VII.

Schliemann, meanwhile, had a new project. He determined to prove the claim of Pausanias, a geographer of the 2nd century AD, that Agamemnon, who led the Greek attack on Troy, was buried at the hilltop site of Mycenae. He selected a site just inside the gate of the citadel and in August 1876, under the supervision of the Greek Archaeological Society, began digging. Within a month he had uncovered the first of several tombs of Bronze Age chieftains in what is now labelled 'Grave Circle A'. Five wore gold face masks and each had been buried with spectacular weapons, ornaments and vessels of precious metals. Schliemann announced that he had discovered the tombs of Agamemnon, Cassandra and Eurymedon, and the finest of the five masks became known as 'the face of Agamemnon'. Once again, however, these finds were later found to be too old, this time by 300 years.

Troy and Mycenae were not the whole sum of Schliemann's projects. In 1868 he excavated on Ithaca, the legendary island home of Odysseus in the Ionian Sea, and in 1884 he dug at

Tiryns, the Mycenaean hill fort whose ruins Pausanius had visited. Yet Schliemann went back time and again to reopen his site at Troy: in 1878 when he found two more small caches of treasure; again in 1882; and finally in 1888, two years before his death in Naples from an ear infection.

Schliemann's reputation suffered as a result of his damaging excavation methods, dubious site interpretations, lawsuits resulting from his theft of ancient grave goods, and the untruths in his autobiographical writings. He has even been accused of forging some of the treasures he claimed to have found and has often been dismissed as a treasure-seeker. Yet archaeologists today grant his claim to have 'opened up a new world for archaeology' and pay tribute to his determination, energy and dedication – he funded all his excavations – in furthering and publicizing archaeology.

Above This gold chalice with rosette decoration was recovered from Tomb IV of Grave Circle A at Mycenae in Greece and has been dated to the 16th century BC.

Below This photograph from the turn of the 20th century shows sightseers examining Grave Circle A, uncovered by Schliemann in 1876 amid the ruins of Mycenae.

Ephraim Squier

(1821-1888)

Employed variously as journalist, political official and diplomat, Squier is one of the most enigmatic figures in the history of American archaeology. His major work was to catalogue and classify for posterity the prehistoric earthen mounds of the mid-West, many of which are now lost.

Born in Bethlehem, New York, Squier was the son of a Methodist minister. After flirting with civil engineering, education and the law, he became a journalist, editing various publications in New York State, Connecticut and Ohio. He then entered the political world as clerk to the latter state's House of Representatives. While living in the mid-West, Squier became one of the best-known antiquaries in America for his work on the 'Mound Builders'.

The mid-Western states are famous for the many earthen mounds that dot the landscape. These mounds reach back to the prehistoric period, some as far back as the 4th millennium BC,

and had a variety of functions: some were burial sites, for instance, while others were religious in nature. The site of the ancient city of Cahokia in Illinois, inhabited from about AD 700-1400, has mounds of many shapes, the largest of which is believed to have supported the chief's residence; Great Serpent Mound in Ohio is, as its name suggests, in the shape of a snake.

Enter Ephraim Squier

Squier's contribution to the discussion over the origins of these earthworks was the publication in 1848 of *Ancient Monuments of the Mississippi Valley*, a landmark in American scientific research whose byline he shared with

local antiquarian E.H. Davis, although he was responsible for most of the writing. This volume was unique in its comprehensiveness and its accuracy in describing and drawing the mounds, for its meticulous classification of the different categories of mounds and the detailed descriptions of the artefacts and their art styles. Squier felt that the mounds had been built by a lost race of Mound Builders – not the ancestors of contemporary Native Americans as some had postulated. Indeed, it was the prevailing view at the time that the forerunners of the Native Americans would have been incapable of such feats of engineering. The book made him a household name. Furthermore, since so many of the sites he described have since disappeared as a result of development, the volume is invaluable to modern archaeologists.

In 1848 Squier's support for newly elected president Zachary Taylor led to his being appointed US chargé d'affaires in Central America. While he was there, he published works on the region's monuments as well as on its peoples. Squier was able to extend his study of ancient monuments to South America when President Lincoln sent him to Peru as US commissioner in 1862. He returned to New York six years later and in 1873 was divorced. During his life he suffered periodic bouts of mental illness until his death in 1888.

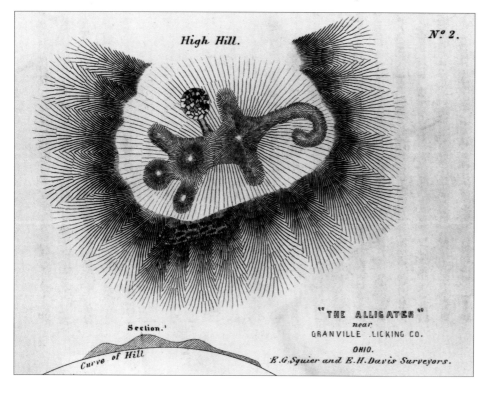

Left The Alligator in central Ohio is one of a number of mounds in the shape of an animal.

Thomsen and Worsaae

(1788-1865 and 1821-1885)

Long before the age of scientific archaeology, Christian Jurgensen Thomsen, curator of the Danish National Museum, and his one-time assistant Jens Jacob Asmussen Worsaae instigated and developed the Three-Age System, still the framework for organizing Eurasian prehistory.

Thomsen was born in Copenhagen, Denmark, following his father into the family wholesale business. When his parents died, he sold up and devoted himself to his antiquarian interests. In 1816, despite his lack of training, he was entrusted with the curatorship of the nation's Collection of Northern Antiquities, later to develop into the Danish National Museum.

His appointment occurred because by the start of the 19th century, it was clear to scholars throughout most of

Below This burial site north of Alborg, Denmark, dates back as far as the Germanic Iron Age (AD 400-800), which was the final phase of the Iron Age in Northern Europe.

Europe that ancient objects lay in the soil. Collections of artefacts began to develop as the activities of farming and industry disturbed many sites. With a view to conserving its wealth of material, Denmark set up a Royal Committee for the Preservation and Collection of National Antiquities, which in turn appointed Thomsen.

Based in the loft of Trinitatis Church in Copenhagen, Thomsen sought to bring order to the chaotic collections and figure out a logical way to display them. He chose to classify the cutting tools according to the material used to make them: stone, bronze and iron. This way of working was not new, but Thomsen extended the classification

Above This cremation urn lid, from Bronze Age Denmark, is thought to depict the marriage of the god and goddess of fertility.

to the other materials that were found along with the tools. Certain types of pottery, for example, were associated only with stone implements, while glass beads were found only with iron tools. In this way Thomsen was able to impose order on the collections and propose a chronological scheme: the Stone Age, succeeded by the Bronze Age, followed by the Iron Age. Today we call this the 'Three-Age System'.

One step further

Worsaae, born in Vejle, Denmark, was an assistant to Thomsen from 1838 to 1843 and his successor as the National Museum's curator. Worsaae extended the Three-Age System from museum displays into the field, using layer-by-layer excavation to demonstrate its validity. Some have called Worsaae the 'first professional archaeologist' for his analytical approach to excavation and the study of finds. As a result of his work Thomsen's Three-Age System was adopted throughout Europe.

The Three-Age System still survives as a convenient organizing principle of Eurasian prehistory, and the Stone and Iron Age categories are also applied in Africa. While it is not considered to be an inevitable progression of cultural and technological development, and many of the most interesting times straddle the ages, it still provides a set of basic chronological markers.

Max Uhle

(1856-1944)

It is impossible to study the ancient civilizations of the Andes without coming across the work of Max Uhle. He brought scientific methods to South American archaeology and formed the basis for our understanding of the relationships of the region's ancient peoples.

Uhle was born in the city of Dresden in eastern Germany. Archaeology did not exist as a discipline when he was growing up and studying, and in 1880 he received his Ph.D. at the University of Leipzig in linguistics; his thesis was on Chinese grammar. Uhle then found work in a Dresden museum, where he came into contact with archaeological objects from around the world. In particular he got the chance to study a range of pieces from the Andes, which were flowing into Germany at that time along with people fleeing the 1879-1884 War of the Pacific between Chile, Bolivia and Peru. Meanwhile, a geologist friend, Alphons Stübel, provided him with data from the ruined city of Tiwanaku (Tiahuanaco) in Bolivia, including photographs and moulds, as well as measurements of architectural features.

After studying the Americas from afar and publishing on Tiwanaku and other aspects of the archaeology of the region, Uhle eventually visited South America in the early 1890s. It was the beginning of a prolific career as a field archaeologist during which he became one of the most important figures in the study of the ancient civilizations of the Americas. Uhle's work was critical both to establishing a number of the main stylistic sequences of Andean archaeology, including those of Nasca

Below Uhle was instrumental in showing that Tiwanaku, Bolivia was a pre-Inca site. This is the ruins' Kalasasaya mound.

and Tiwanaku, and to our knowledge of the archaeological sequence of Andean South America.

First studies

Uhle's early archaeological projects included explorations in Argentina, Bolivia and Chile. His research at Tiwanaku helped establish it as one of the most important pre-Inca cities in the region, and also convinced the Bolivian government to protect what is now one of their most important tourist destinations. It was his analysis of the styles and content of the images on the stonework at Tiwanaku, based on the material brought back by his geologist friend Stübel, that showed that the site predated the Inca. Uhle's identification of similar styles in pottery and other artefacts found at Pachácamac and other sites in coastal Peru laid the groundwork for the timeline of Andean archaeology in use today, although that has been greatly refined in the past century.

Another of Uhle's analyses that has withstood the test of time is his 1917 classification of the mummies of the ancient Chinchorro people, a small-scale society of fishers and hunters of the coastal Atacama desert. Uhle came across the mummies during a visit to northern Chile and he arranged them into three types – simple, complex, simple but clay-covered – a system which is still in use. Since chronometric dating techniques were not available to Uhle in those days, he had no idea how old the mummies were. Later work showed that they are the world's oldest artificially prepared mummies, predating those of ancient Egypt by around 2000 years.

However, Uhle's best-known work was on the site of Pachácamac, now an important tourist destination around 40km (25 miles) south of Lima, Peru. A vast settlement built of mud brick but with some stone architecture, it housed one of the most sacred shrines of the Andes under the Inca. Uhle's excavations at Pachácamac included painstaking analysis and documentation of the soil layers, in which he was able to identify several different styles of pottery. He argued that the variations in style represented different periods

Left Among the artefacts given up by Tiwanaku is this incense burner in the form of a puma, for use in religious ceremonies.

Above These human remains were unearthed in 2005 in an Inca cemetery in Pachácamac, a sacred site first excavated by Uhle in 1896.

of occupation. This work was not only a rich source of data but also produced fabulous and important archaeological collections. Furthermore, it laid the groundwork for the ongoing study of Pachácamac and the chronological and geographical relationships of different archaeological cultures.

Widely considered to be the 'father of South American archaeology', Uhle nevertheless published little. His few works include *The Ruins of Tiahuanaco in the Highlands of Ancient Peru* (with Stübel, 1891) and *Pachácamac: Report of the William Pepper, M.D., LL.D., Peruvian Expedition of 1896* (1903).

PIONEERS OF ARCHAEOLOGY

The early 20th century saw the emergence of a new breed of archaeologists, the first true professionals. Their methods were fast becoming more rigorous and careful than those of their predecessors, and they laid the foundations for the scientific and painstaking approach of our own times. Many of the scholars of the period – Carter, Petrie, Wheeler, Woolley – are among the greatest names in the history of the subject; some of archaeology's most famous discoveries, such as Machu Picchu, the tomb of Tutankhamen, the burials of Ur and the Indus city of Mohenjo-Daro (facing page), are owed to their skill and luck. The first great women archaeologists also came to the fore – Dorothy Garrod and Gertrude Caton-Thompson, for example. The arsenal of techniques available for studying the past also expanded dramatically, with the arrival of aerial photography, pollen analysis and eventually radiocarbon dating.

Henri Breuil During his lifetime, this French archaeologist was considered the foremost authority on Palaeolithic cave art.

Gertrude Caton-Thompson Her excavations at Great Zimbabwe were to challenge western notions of African culture.

Max Mallowan The husband of Agatha Christie. He made important contributions to Mesopotamian archaeology.

Hiram Bingham

(1875-1956)

One of the best-known names in Andean archaeology, Hiram Bingham brought Machu Picchu to the attention of the world. Today, the once lost city of the Inca, perching on the eastern slopes of the Andes, is the most visited site in South America.

Hiram Bingham III was born and raised in Hawaii, the son and grandson of missionaries. He attended Yale University as an undergraduate and then returned for a time to Hawaii. He began graduate studies at the University of California before moving to Harvard, where he studied History and Political Science, obtaining a Ph.D. in 1905. Bingham returned to Yale as an adjunct professor in 1907.

In 1899 Bingham had married Alfreda Mitchell, an heiress and granddaughter of Charles L. Tiffany, founder of the New York jewellery and luxury goods store. His wife's wealth would be important in allowing him to pursue his research interests in South America.

Bingham first travelled to South America in 1906, visiting historical sites in Venezuela and Colombia, and then Argentina and Peru. He attended the first Pan-American Scientific Congress in Chile in 1908, later visiting Cuzco, Peru, the ancient capital of the Inca. He became interested in the early colonial Inca and particularly in finding the lost Inca city of Vilcabamba, where Inca royalty had held out against the Spanish Conquistadors for several years.

A spectacular discovery

Bingham set out for South America again in 1911. With the help of local historians he studied colonial documents and began exploring archaeological ruins along the Urubamba Valley (now known as the Sacred Valley of the Inca) outside Cuzco. On 24 July 1911 he was led by a local guide through the jungle and up a steep path to a spectacular set of Inca ruins located in a spot known as Machu Picchu (Old Mountain Peak). Believing he had found the ruins of Vilcabamba, Bingham announced the discovery of the site and received funding from the National Geographic Society for additional research.

Bingham assembled a team of scholars and scientists to assist him in a multidisciplinary study of the important site. On two subsequent expeditions he cleared, documented and excavated the site. Although his excavation methods were limited, he produced a great deal of data and important collections that continue to be studied. A portion of the collections were taken to the Peabody Museum at Yale, where they remain today. Extensive analyses were done by Bingham and his colleagues and the project received a great deal of publicity. The National Geographic Society devoted the entire issue of their April 1913 magazine to Bingham's discovery. His story of trekking through the wilderness to discover a lost Inca city captured the public's

Left Located near the Main Plaza at Machu Picchu is the sacred Intihuatana, or 'hitching post of the Sun', which was used in Inca religious festivals. It is unique as the Spanish destroyed all other such stone structures as evidence of idolatry.

Above A panoramic view of Machu Picchu, with Mount Huayna Picchu towering in the background. The Inca builders constructed their remarkable buildings from stones cut to fit tightly together without mortar.

imagination. In one account he describes his first view of the site, 'We rounded a knoll and suddenly faced tier upon tier of Inca terraces rising like giant stairs. Each one, hundreds of feet long, was banked by massive stone walls up to ten feet high.'

Bingham abandoned archaeology after the Machu Picchu project, serving in the US military during World War I before entering into politics. He was elected as a member of the US Senate in 1924.

Royal estate

Although it was Bingham who put Machu Picchu on the map, most of his ideas have since been superseded by new information. We now know that Machu Picchu, far from being the last outpost of Inca royalty, had actually been abandoned by the time the Spanish arrived in Peru in 1532. Spanish colonial documents studied by the American archaeologist John Rowe and his students indicate that the site had in fact been built as a royal estate for the Inca ruler Pachacuti (AD 1438-71).

Machu Picchu was inhabited for most of the year by a relatively small group of retainers, with the palaces and other spectacular buildings reserved for seasonal use by the ruler and his entourage. The archaeological materials that Bingham recovered consist largely of everyday items used by those who lived at the site year-round, and not the fabulous luxury goods of the Inca elite. The materials found in the burials indicate that Machu Picchu's retainers came from throughout the Inca Empire, from the coast to the rainforest. Why the city was eventually abandoned, however, remains a mystery.

The site today

Bingham's theories about Machu Picchu may not have endured, but his legacy has, both in the US and in Peru. Archaeological exploration has continued at the site since Bingham's day and in 1983 it was listed as a World Heritage Site by UNESCO.

A recent exhibition entitled *Machu Picchu: Unveiling the mystery of the Inca*, organized by Yale University, toured the United States to great acclaim, sparking renewed interest and increased US tourism to Peru. The Peruvian government cooperated with Yale in the development of the exhibition, but it also requested that Yale return the Machu Picchu collections permanently to Peru.

Henri Breuil

(1877-1961)

Henri Edouard Prosper Breuil was one of the towering figures in the study of Old World prehistory during the first half of the 20th century, and was the pioneer of the study of Ice Age cave art. His views on Palaeolithic art were considered definitive by a whole generation of archaeologists.

Although the French archaeologist Henri Breuil trained as a priest in his youth, and remained one until his death, it was only a title – he was allowed to devote his whole existence to studying prehistory; he undertook virtually no religious duties, and made almost no contribution to the reconciliation of prehistory's findings with religious teachings.

Awakening

The son of a lawyer, Breuil was born and grew up in northern France, a place that infused him with an intense love of nature, especially of insects, and entomology remained a lifelong interest. An important early influence was his relative, the well-known geologist and archaeologist Geoffroy d'Ault du Mesnil, who showed Henri his collection of fossils and took him to the ancient sites of the Somme region. Here he met Louis Capitan, who introduced him to the study of prehistoric tools. Breuil also had the supreme good fortune, as a young man

with a talent for drawing animals, to make the acquaintance of Edouard Piette and Emile Cartailhac, two of France's greatest prehistorians at the turn of the century, when they needed help with the study and illustration of Palaeolithic portable and cave art.

Breuil was to go on to become the world's leading authority on Palaeolithic art until his death. He discovered many decorated caves or galleries himself, and copied their art – by his own reckoning he spent about 700 days of his life underground.

Although now seen as excessively subjective and incomplete, his tracings are nevertheless recognized as remarkable for their time. For some caves they constitute our only record of figures that have since faded or disappeared. Breuil concentrated not only on Palaeolithic art, but also on the megalithic art of France and (during World War I) the Iberian peninsula. In World War II he began a long campaign of copying rock art in parts of southern Africa.

Breuil's greatest contributions to tool typology were made in France, where he set out the first detailed description of the characteristic tools of each French Palaeolithic period, dividing the Magdalenian into six phases on the basis of changing tool types. This scheme was both durable and influential, but has now been replaced by a simpler and more flexible

Early/Middle/Upper Magdalenian. In the same way, Breuil conceived of two cycles in the development of Palaeolithic art, the 'Aurignaco-Perigordian' followed by the 'Solutreo-Magdalenian' – two essentially similar but independent cycles, each progressing from simple to complex forms in engraving, sculpture and painting. This system, however, was inconsistent and unsatisfactory, and was eventually replaced by the four 'styles' of André Leroi-Gourhan, themselves now in the course of abandonment.

Breuil saw Palaeolithic art primarily in terms of hunting magic, and he generally considered decorated caves to be accumulations of single figures, unlike Leroi-Gourhan who saw them as carefully planned compositions.

An irascible and egotistical man, Breuil nevertheless had a lasting influence on numerous devoted friends and pupils. So ingrained was his image as the 'Pope of Prehistory' that he was often thought virtually infallible. It is only in recent years that it has become possible in France openly to criticize and re-examine his work like that of any other scholar. His huge legacy of publications and tracings has been found to contain many errors, but equally an abundance of insights that are now supported by new finds.

Left A drawing of a bison from the cave of Altamira, in Spain. Breuil copied and published hundreds of examples of rock carvings and paintings from Europe and Africa.

Howard Carter

(1874-1939)

The discovery of the tomb of Tutankhamen in Egypt's Valley of the Kings in the 1920s is one of the great events in archaeology. The story behind this magnificent find by the English archaeologist Howard Carter continues to fire the imagination.

Howard Carter was born in London on 9 May 1874. Art was a major influence in his youth. His father, Samuel John Carter, was an artist known for his paintings of animal scenes. The young Howard's educational interests, however, led him down the route of history and archaeology. At the age of only 17, he started his Egyptological career, working as assistant to Percy Newberry in the rock-cut tombs of Beni Hasan and el-Bersha.

Early career

After a brief spell with Flinders Petrie at Amarna, Carter worked at the Delta site of Mendes. He then worked with Edouard Naville at the Deir el-Bahari mortuary temple, Thebes, until in 1899 he was offered a permanent position with the Egyptian Antiquities Service.

After five happy years working in Luxor, Carter was transferred to Saqqara. Here he became involved in a diplomatic incident. A party of drunken Frenchmen had attempted to force their way into the antiquities holdings, and Carter had allowed his workmen to defend themselves. Owing to the subsequent row, in which Carter sided with his local workers rather than with the Europeans, he resigned in October

1905 to become an artist and antiquities dealer. He would soon return to archaeology, however.

In 1909 Carter came under the patronage of Lord Carnarvon, who had made a visit to Egypt in 1905 and had been inspired to pursue some archaeological work there. Rather than permit Carnarvon himself to work unsupported, however, the Antiquities Service appointed Carter as the expert.

Three years' work in the Theban necropolis was followed by a brief excavation at Xois and a mission to Tell el-Balamun. The war years were spent working for the War Office in

Cairo, although Carter continued to undertake a series of small-scale digs at various sites.

Carter was convinced that the 18th Dynasty king Tutankhamen still lay in the Egyptian Valley of the Kings. However, as Theodore Davis had been granted sole permission to excavate in the Valley, Carter could only watch and wait. When, in 1914, Davis gave up his concession, the war prevented any new field work.

Royal tomb

In 1917 Carter began to clear the Valley. It was slow and expensive work, and Lord Carnarvon started to

Right A wall painting depicts Tutankhamen, riding on a chariot and firing arrows at the Nubian enemy. The vultures act as protective guardians over the king.

Above A throne found in the tomb of Tutankhamen, made from ebony and ivory with gilt features on the sides.

doubt the existence of the tomb. Eventually, it was agreed that there would be one last season. On 1 November 1922 workmen started to clear rubbish lying beneath the tomb of Ramesses VI. Three days later they discovered 16 steps leading to a blocked doorway. Carter rushed to the telegraph office to call his patron.

The drama of such moments was captured in Carter's journals, which he maintained throughout his work in the Valley. The following extract was written on Sunday, November 5: 'Though I was satisfied that I was on the verge of perhaps a magnificent find ... I was much puzzled by the smallness of the opening in comparison with those of other royal tombs in the valley. Its design was certainly of the XVIIIth Dyn. Could it be the tomb of a noble, buried there by royal consent? Or was it a royal cache? As far as my investigations had gone there was absolutely nothing to tell me. Had I known that by digging a few inches deeper I would have exposed seal impressions showing

Tut.ankh.Amen's insignia distinctly I would have fervently worked on and set my mind at rest ...'

Three weeks later work resumed. Soon it was possible to read the name of the tomb owner: 'Tutankhamen'. The doorway was dismantled, and the entrance corridor cleared.

By 26 November Carter had entered the antechamber, a storeroom packed with grave goods. A second chamber in the western wall, the 'annex', held more grave goods, while the northern wall included the sealed entrance to the burial chamber. It was to take the team seven long weeks to empty the antechamber. Each object had to be numbered, photographed, planned and drawn before it could be moved. On 17 February 1923 the wall sealing the burial chamber was demolished and an enormous gilt shrine was revealed. Inside was another gold shrine, then another, and another.

Later that month, however, Lord Carnarvon was bitten on the cheek by a mosquito. He sliced the scab off the bite while shaving, and started to feel unwell. Blood poisoning set in, and pneumonia followed. Lord Carnarvon died in Cairo on 5 April 1923.

Sarcophagus

On 3 January 1924, the doors of the innermost shrine were opened, revealing the sarcophagus. On 12 February, the cracked lid was hoisted

Below Howard Carter (left) stands holding a crowbar, having opened the doorway to the chamber of Tutankhamen's tomb. Arthur Mace of the Metropolitan Museum is on the right.

Above Wall paintings around Tutankhamen's sarcophagus. The Burial Chamber was the only part of the complex to contain wall paintings.

off the quartzite base. The next day the wives of the archaeologists were to be allowed a viewing of the coffin. The government objected, however. Carter was furious. Work stopped, and did not resume until early 1925.

Tutankhamen had been buried in three coffins – the outer pair made of gold-covered wood, and the inner coffin of solid gold. A gold mask had been placed over the mummy. Resin-based unguents had been poured over the dead king and they had hardened, gluing the king into his coffin. The golden mask, therefore, had to be removed using hot knives.

Carter spent a decade recording and preserving the tomb. Yet before he could complete the publication of his greatest work, he died in London on 2 March 1939.

King's burial

Tutankhamen's burial followed the funerary orthodoxy of ancient Egypt. Body fluids were purged, internal organs were removed and placed in canopic jars and the body was treated with the preservative natrum, the complete process lasting a required 70 days. The body was then wrapped in 13 layers of treated linen, into which were inserted 143 assorted amulets and charms. Tutankhamen's preparation was completed with a magnificent solid-gold death mask covering the head and shoulders. Objects found around the body included items of jewellery and flowers.

Right One of the two wooden and painted sentry statues posted in the antechamber at the sides of the walled door that led into the king's burial chamber.

G. Caton-Thompson

(1888-1985)

Gertrude Caton-Thompson is a towering figure in the history of African archaeology. Her work at Great Zimbabwe would cause an ideological storm in western academia, upsetting many of the racially motivated preconceptions about Africa prevalent at the time.

Born in London in 1888, Gertrude Caton-Thompson enjoyed a privileged upbringing and education. From Newnham College, Cambridge, she proceeded to the British School of Archaeology in Egypt, training under the eminent Egyptologist, Sir Flinders Petrie. With Elinor Gardner, she initiated the first archaeological survey of the northern Faiyum and served as a field director for the Royal Anthropological Institute. After further work on predynastic sites in Egypt, Caton-Thompson undertook work at the site of Great Zimbabwe, in modern Zimbabwe.

Great Zimbabwe

The extensive ruins in Africa had first been excavated by Theodore Bent in 1891, and then by R.N. Hall as part of the imperialist programme of Cecil John Rhodes. Hall, whose abilities as

an excavator were questioned even in his own time, proposed that Great Zimbabwe was the site of the legendary goldfields of Ophir. He argued that Great Zimbabwe had been made by a highly civilized society that (almost by definition) could not be indigenous to Africa.

The British Association for the Advancement of Science sent David Randall-McIver to investigate. He concluded that the site was medieval in date and African in origin. When Caton-Thompson took over the excavations in 1929, she was able to demonstrate that Randall-McIver's ideas about Great Zimbabwe were valid. Working with two female assistants, she conclusively established the site's African origin.

Her findings challenged colonial prejudices about African inferiority and caused furore in an ongoing

controversy about the intellectual capacity of African peoples and their place in colonial societies. Caton-Thompson, resolute in her findings and her scientific detachment, declared that she was quite 'unconcerned with speculations'.

Legacy

Caton-Thompson is remembered for her intrepid life and formidable personality as well as for her archaeological researches, which continued apace after her Zimbabwean work. In the early 1930s she conducted important excavations at the Egyptian site of Kharga Oasis, later working also in south-west Asia. In later life she was vice-president of the Royal Anthropological Institute, president of the British Prehistoric Society, held offices at the University of London and was a Fellow of Newnham College.

Her autobiography, *Mixed Memoirs*, was published in 1983 when she was in her mid-nineties. In it she describes herself as 'not easily alarmed'. Others have described her as 'fearless', 'fastidious' and possessed of 'extraordinary energy and powers of leadership'. She once listed her favourite recreation as 'idleness'. However, there is little evidence of her indulging in it. Gertrude Caton-Thompson retired in 1957 and died in Worcestershire in 1985.

Left The Great Enclosure, which was built in several stages, is the largest and most impressive structure at Great Zimbabwe.

Li Chi

(1896-1979)

Li Chi was one of the pioneers of modern Chinese archaeology. His familiarity with western methods of research gave him a fresh perspective on China's archaeological finds, and had a major impact on the quality of his field work, most famously at Anyang.

Regarded as the father of modern Chinese archaeology, Li Chi was born on 12 July 1896 in Zhongxiang, Hebei province. In the west he is best known for his excavation of the city of Anyang, Henan province, and his research on the so-called 'oracle bones'.

Although he had a Chinese education, Li Chi belonged to the first generation of Chinese archaeologists to be trained by leading scholars in universities and colleges in western Europe and the United States and, as such, was open to new methods of archaeological investigation. Li Chi studied anthropology and received a Ph.D. from Harvard in 1923.

In China Li Chi began working on Neolithic materials and soon became involved with the Academia Sinica's Institute of History and Philology, becoming its first director in 1928.

New research

At the beginning of the 20th century, field archaeology had been brought to China as a new western discipline. The Swedish geologist J.G. Andersson (1874-1960) discovered the first Neolithic site in China – the cave of Peking Man. Li Chi was the first Chinese archaeologist to apply western techniques on the first scientific excavation of Xiyincun, Anyang, carrying out field excavations in situ. A major focus of this new generation of Chinese archaeologists was to search for the origins of Chinese civilization and also to stop the looting of Chinese relics.

Old bones

In 1899 hundreds of bones inscribed with Chinese characters came to light in today's city of Anyang. They had been dug up by peasants and were being ground into medicine. It is said that in that year an official under the last of the Chinese dynasties, the Qing (1644-1911), fell ill and was prescribed 'dragon bones'. These bones, both tortoise shells and cattle shoulder blades, dated from about 3000 years earlier.

In 1928 the Academia Sinica decided to undertake excavations in Anyang at a site called Yin, the city that proved to be the last capital of the historical Shang Dynasty (1700-1027 BC) and the most important Bronze Age site in East Asia.

Between 1928 and 1937 a total of 15 seasons of excavations were carried out in Anyang under Li Chi's leadership. By 1937 archaeologists had excavated more than 100,000 objects, including thousands more inscribed bones, which they recognized as tools of divination. The ancient texts inscribed on the bones provide invaluable information about rulers, battles, folk religion and religious rites.

Excavations were halted by the outbreak of the Sino-Japanese war. Li Chi and his fellow research colleagues, together with their collection, were evacuated to western China. Publications and research continued and finally, in 1948, the Academia Sinica moved to Taiwan. Li Chi continued the work there and also trained young archaeologists, such as Kwang-Chih Chang (1931-2001), who finally brought the archaeology of China to the attention of the western world. In 1950 Li Chi became the head of anthropology and archaeology at the National University in Taipei and began directing publication of his remaining Anyang materials. He published a number of books, including *The Beginnings of Chinese Civilization* (1957) and *Anyang* (1977).

Li Chi died on 1 August 1979 in Taipei, Taiwan.

Above A food vessel cast in bronze with relief designs found at Anyang and dating from c.1300-1000 BC shows a high-quality of workmanship.

Dorothy Garrod

(1892-1968)

An important figure in prehistoric studies, Dorothy Garrod conducted important excavations at the Palaeolithic caves of Mount Carmel in Israel, where she was able to identify the longest stratigraphic record in the region, spanning about 600,000 years of human activity.

The archaeologist and prehistorian Dorothy A.E. Garrod was the first woman to be appointed a professor at the University of Cambridge, holding the Disney Chair of Archaeology from 1939 to 1952. Garrod was the only daughter in a distinguished medical family, and the loss of her three brothers in World War I inspired her determination to achieve a life worthy of the family tradition, though in a different field. She was taught at Oxford by the prehistorian R.R. Marett and subsequently in France by Abbé Henri Breuil, who encouraged her research for her first book on the Upper Palaeolithic in Britain. Thereafter her work centred mainly on the Palaeolithic, with notable success.

Garrod owed her first major excavation (in 1926) to Breuil, who had identified the Devil's Tower site in Gibraltar. There she found a Middle Palaeolithic flint industry and the skull fragments of a Neanderthal child.

Rising reputation

The excavation and the publication of her findings established Garrod's place in Palaeolithic studies. Her lasting reputation was determined largely in Palestine during the years 1928-37, first by her excavation of Shukbah Cave in the Wadi en-Natuf. There she found human remains associated with a previously unknown Epipalaeolithic culture, which she named 'Natufian', whose people were apparently taking early steps towards agriculture. In a deeper level she recognized traces of Neanderthal occupation.

After a brief period in southern Kurdistan (where she identified further evidence of Middle and Upper Palaeolithic occupation), she returned to Palestine to begin the major work of her career in archaeology at the

Left Human remains at a Mount Carmel cave site. Garrod's excavations at Mount Carmel in the 1930s helped expand the anthropological picture of the Middle East.

Mount Carmel caves. In el Wad Cave she again found the Natufian culture, though in a later and richer phase than at Shukbah, with decorated burials and more complex lithic (stone) and bone industries.

Tabun Cave

In Tabun Cave, deepest of the group, the uppermost level corresponded to the lowest in el Wad, with a further seven levels descending to a pre-handaxe lithic industry. Garrod's skill in typological analysis enabled her to identify a cultural succession in the caves spanning some 600,000 years of human occupation. At different periods in history, Tabun and the nearby Skhul Cave 2 (which was excavated by her American colleague T.D. McCown) were occupied by two Palaeolithic human populations – Neanderthal and Anatomically Modern People – now known to have genetic differences.

Academic advance

Garrod's final report on the Mount Carmel excavation (*The Stone Age of Mount Carmel, vol.1*, 1937) established a new standard for its time, earning her a D.Sc. from Oxford University. When the Disney Chair at Cambridge became vacant, Garrod didn't think she stood much chance. She told a friend at the time, 'I shan't get it, but I thought I'd give the electors a run for their money'. Her election on the eve of World War II was an important landmark in higher education for women. In 1942 she was recruited to the RAF Medmenham Unit for Photographic Interpretation (staffed by several archaeological colleagues) for the duration of the war.

Returning to Cambridge, she worked to raise the status of archaeology as an academic subject in the university; it became part of the full Tripos and degree scheme in 1948.

Final work

Long vacations were devoted to excavation with French colleagues at the French sites of Fontéchevade and Angles-sur-l'Anglin. In 1952, four

years after women were admitted as full members of the university, she retired from Cambridge and settled permanently in France. In 1958 (aged 66) she resumed work in the Levant.

Garrod devoted this final phase of her working life to the eastern Mediterranean, where ancient caves and beaches preserved evidence that related Quaternary sea levels to the Ice Ages of Europe. Thus, when no absolute dating methods existed, their

Above As much as in Garrod's time, the Mount Carmel site is an enormous challenge to any archaeologist. The range is 26km (16 miles) long and reaches 7.2km (5 miles) wide.

respective prehistoric sequences could be correlated. However, the prolonged and difficult excavation, which ran from 1958 to 1963, was to take its toll on her health. She was awarded a CBE in 1965 three years before her death in Cambridge.

William Grimes

(1905-1988)

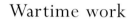

William Grimes devoted much of his career to the archaeology of both his native Wales and the city of London. His expertise in handling fragile sites saw him busily employed around the bomb-damaged capital during and following World War II. He is famous for his work on the London Mithraeum.

Born in Pembrokeshire, Wales, Grimes studied classics at the University of Wales in Cardiff and was employed in the National Museum of Wales. This brought him into contact with the prehistoric and Roman antiquities of Wales and his subsequent career reflects this dual interest. One of his first projects was the publication of material from the legionary workshops at Holt in north Wales, which had served the fortress at Deva (Chester). He worked on a number of prehistoric sites in Wales in the 1930s and in 1939 published a catalogue of prehistoric antiquities in the National Museum.

Grimes had developed an expertise in working on waterlogged sites that had preserved organic material. In 1938 he went to work as an archaeologist for the Ordnance Survey, which was responsible for mapping in the United Kingdom. It was in this capacity that he was invited to work with O.G.S. Crawford at the Sutton Hoo ship burial in Suffolk in 1939. Contemporary reports acknowledge his skill in extracting a range of delicate finds from the ground.

Wartime work

During World War II, Grimes was responsible for excavating many archaeological sites before their development as military locations, such as airfields. One of the more famous excavations conducted at this time was the Iron Age temple on the site of what is now Heathrow airport to the west of London.

In 1945 he was appointed director of the London Museum and was responsible for a number of rescue excavations in the city, which had been devastated by enemy bombing. In 1954 he famously excavated a Roman Mithraeum on a bomb site off Walbrook in central London. He succeeded in salvaging many of its finds, including marble statuary.

Grimes was appointed the director of the Institute of Archaeology in London in 1956 and subsequently served on many national bodies, where his archaeological expertise was much in demand.

Left Excavations at the Roman temple to the god Mithras in London. This photograph was taken on the site's public open day.

David Hogarth

(1862-1927)

Born in Lincolnshire into a clergy family, David George Hogarth went on to have a distinguished archaeological career. He conducted excavations at many locations in southern Europe and the Middle East, including Cyprus, Crete, Ephesus, Melos, Egypt and Syria.

As a young man Hogarth studied classics at Oxford and was the first student from that university to be admitted to the newly opened British School at Athens. One of his interests was in Greek inscriptions, which were seen as an important supplement to classical literary and historical texts. While at Athens he studied the inscriptions of Thessaloniki, then part of the Ottoman empire.

Ottoman Journey

In the late spring of 1887, Hogarth joined the archaeologist and biblical scholar William Mitchell Ramsay for a journey across Anatolia from Smyrna (Izmir) on the Aegean coast to Cilicia in the south-east. This was to be the first of a series of such travels in the Ottoman empire, and it included a survey of the upper Euphrates Valley. Hogarth's introduction to the world of archaeological excavation came on the island of Cyprus as part of the British project to record some of the classical sites there.

Hogarth's archaeological expertise took him to Egypt, initially to work on the Greek and Latin inscriptions found by Flinders Petrie. One of the projects in Egypt was a survey of Graeco-Roman Alexandria. In the mid-1890s he worked on a survey of the Faiyum in search of papyri that, it was hoped, would provide new examples of classical literature.

In 1897 Hogarth was appointed director of the British School at Athens. During this period there was

continuing work at the Bronze Age site of Phylakopi on Melos, and in 1899 Hogarth returned to the western Nile delta to work at the Greek trading station of Naukratis. With the removal of Crete from the control of the Ottoman empire, Hogarth turned his archaeological attention to the island, working on a number of sites including Knossos and Kato Zakro.

Hogarth next directed the British Museum excavations at Ephesus and in 1908 he returned to the Euphrates Valley to initiate work at Carchemish, where one of the excavators was T.E. Lawrence ('of Arabia'); the two men

Above Hogarth conducted an excavation of the Temple of Artemis at Ephesus between 1904 and 1905, publishing *The Archaic Artemisia of Ephesus* in 1908.

worked together during World War I when Hogarth ran the Arab Bureau in Cairo. In 1908 Hogarth was appointed Keeper of the Ashmolean Museum in Oxford. After war service in the eastern Mediterranean as part of the military intelligence community, Hogarth returned to Oxford where he developed his interest in the Hittites, publishing *Kings of the Hittites* in 1926. He remained keeper of the Ashmolean until his death in 1927.

Alfred Kidder

(1885-1963)

Alfred Vincent Kidder is still rightly regarded as one of the most important and influential American archaeologists, his reputation built on both his technical innovations in excavation and his contribution to theory, especially in the area of chronology building.

Alfred Kidder grew up in New England and originally wanted to become a physician. However, after entering Harvard he found himself uninspired by medical training and after taking a short course in anthropology became consumed by the subject, developing a particular interest in archaeology.

After working on sites in the American Southwest, mainly in Arizona and Utah, he changed his major and in 1914 received a Ph.D. in anthropology (concentrating on ceramics); he was only the sixth person in the United States to receive a doctorate that concentrated on this sub-discipline.

Chronologies

At the time American archaeology was still desperately trying to organize the burgeoning amount of data from excavations into some coherent system. Even in the Southwest, the technique of tree-ring dating was still in its infancy, and the most pressing concern there, as elsewhere on the continent, was to establish baseline chronologies. Kidder was well aware of

this when, in 1915, he initiated excavations at the Pecos Ruins in northern New Mexico, which at the time was the largest archaeological undertaking in the United States. This large complex prehistoric ruin was perfect for the application of stratigraphic excavations, whereby different levels in a variety of sites in a region could be identified by

Below The interior of a kiva (a dug-out used for religious ceremonies) at the Pecos ruins. Kidder was director of excavations at Pecos from 1915 to 1929.

Above An exterior view of a kiva at Pecos with the ruins of a mission in the background. Kidder's work helped the development of a cultural chronology of the American Southwest.

diagnosing their material culture. The temporal sequence could then be checked through excavation at other sites and then applied on a region-wide basis, so that a relative chronology between the sites could be established.

The sheer quantity of material coming out of Pecos, as well as from other archaeological excavations in the Southwest, led Kidder to convene the first Pecos Conference in 1927. The result was the so-called 'Pecos Classification', by which South-western prehistory was organized into a series of stages that quickly became time periods, each one recognizable by particular pottery styles and architectural forms. The selection of a relatively small number of temporally diagnostic artefacts per period is reminiscent of the geological process of identifying type fossils unique to a particular stratum. It is also similar to the 'chest-of-drawers' archaeology used for European prehistory. The Pecos Classification, with some modification, is still the primary time-space framework for the northern part of the American Southwest.

Theoretical attack

In 1929 Kidder took up a prestigious position with the Carnegie Institution in Washington, being appointed the director of the Division of Historical Research. Beginning in the 1930s, Kidder switched his practical interests to Central America and conducted excavations at Mayan sites such as Chichén Itzá, among others. Kidder employed a team of inter-disciplinary scholars to try to portray as holistic a picture of the past as possible.

In 1950 Kidder retired from the Peabody Museum and Carnegie Institution, although he remained active in the field of archaeology up until his death in 1963. However, towards the end of his career Kidder became the target of an attack by one of archaeology's first 'angry young men', Walter Taylor. He argued that Kidder and his generation had held archaeology back for concentrating too much, in Taylor's view, on the construction of cultural history rather than investigating the processes by which cultures changed. In this, Taylor's critique presaged the revolution in archaeology of the 1960s called the 'New Archaeology', a revolution that explicitly advocated the scientific method to answer why and how cultures change through time and space. Kidder and others of his generation were, in Taylor's view, guilty of concentrating too much on the artefacts of the past, rather than trying to learn about the people who made and used them.

Despite this criticism, which stung Kidder personally, his place in the pantheon of American archaeologists is assured. The Society for American Archaeology, for instance, calls its most prestigious award after him.

Below An 800-year-old painted pottery bowl made by Anasazi Indians at Pecos, where Kidder excavated a large collection of pottery fragments.

Winifred Lamb

(1894-1963)

The classical archaeologist Winifred Lamb carried out pioneering excavations in Greece, the Aegean islands and Anatolia. She rose to become the honorary keeper of Greek Antiquities at the Fitzwilliam Museum, Cambridge.

Winifred Lamb was born in London, the only child of a colliery owner and Liberal Member of Parliament. She read classics at Newnham College, Cambridge. Upon completing her studies in 1917 she joined the Naval Intelligence Department (Room 40) at the Admiralty in London, where one of her colleagues was the Oxford archaeologist Sir John Beazley. It may have been at his prompting that she purchased Greek pottery from the Hope sale at Christies in 1917, which included part of the 18th-century collection formed by Sir William Hamilton. Lamb's first published article appeared in the *Journal of Hellenic Studies* in 1918.

Recognition

In 1919 Lamb was invited to become the honorary keeper of Greek and Roman Antiquities at the Fitzwilliam Museum, Cambridge. For nearly 40 years she fulfilled this role against a background of active field work in Greece and Turkey.

She was one of the first people to be admitted to the British School at Athens after World War I. One of her responsibilities was to work on the excavation of the Bronze Age palace at Mycenae under the direction of Alan Wace. Her interests in Greek prehistory are reflected by her creation of a prehistoric gallery back at the Fitzwilliam Museum.

Lamb became involved in pioneering excavations in Macedonia and she was keen to show a link between the Balkans and north-west Anatolia. She also worked with the British School's resumed excavations at the historical site of Sparta, where she published some of the small bronzes. Lamb had a strong interest in this category of antiquities and published one of the defining studies of Greek and Roman bronze statues.

The death of her father in 1925 gave Lamb the financial means to direct her own excavations and through the late 1920s and '30s she worked on a series of sites on the island of Lesbos, most notably Thermi. From Lesbos she looked to Anatolia and was one of the first women to excavate in the new republic of Turkey at the site of Kusura.

Lamb was badly injured in London during World War II when a German V2 rocket hit her lodgings, killing her housemates. Although this restricted her activities, she continued to travel in Turkey and was a moving force behind the creation of the British Institute of Archaeology in Ankara in 1948. She retired in 1958 and died of a stroke on 16 September 1963.

Left The theatre at Sparta, one of Winifred Lamb's excavation sites during the 1920s. She conducted her work at Sparta under the auspices of the British School at Athens, where she was admitted in 1920 and was in attendance there into the early 1930s. In 1931 she was given the title Honorary Student by the School.

Sir Max Mallowan

(1904-1978)

Better known to the wider world as the husband of the mystery writer Agatha Christie, Max Mallowan made lasting contributions to Mesopotamian archaeology. His work established the basic outline of the prehistoric and early historic cultures of northern Iraq and Syria.

Max Edgar Lucien Mallowan was born in London on 6 May 1904. The seeds of his interest in archaeology were planted at New College, Oxford, where he read classics. Following his graduation, Mallowan began an archaeological career at Ur, where he worked as an assistant to Leonard Woolley from 1925 to 1930.

Aged 26, he met Agatha Christie at Ur when she visited in 1930 and the two were married in Edinburgh six months later. Woolley, however, banned spouses from the field, and so Mallowan left Ur and worked with R. Campbell Thompson at Nineveh in 1931 and 1932.

At Nineveh Mallowan developed a stratigraphic sequence for that long-occupied site; the sequence survives today in the name Ninevite 5, in reference to an early 3rd-millennium BC pottery style.

Major projects

Mallowan launched his first independent project in 1933, at Arpachiyah in northern Iraq. He would spend the best part of a year at the site, and during his excavations there he exposed remains of Halaf (6th millennium BC) and of Ubaid (5th millennium BC) occupations. Arpachiyah remains an important reference site for the Halaf culture, known for its elaborately painted pottery and circular *tholos* houses.

Mallowan then moved his field work to Syria during the remainder of the 1930s. At Chagar Bazar he found a

Below A Middle Eastern sculpture from the 3rd millennium BC depicts a bull's body with a human head. Mallowan found many such zoomorphic images during his work in Iraq and Syria. Tragically, many of the Nimrud ivories discovered under Mallowan's direction were looted or damaged in Baghdad during the fighting of 2003.

cultural sequence beginning with Halaf materials and continuing into the 2nd millennium BC. At Tell Brak he uncovered the Uruk-period Eye Temple (*c.* 3500-3100 BC), so named for the many small stone idols with prominent eyes found there, and a palace belonging to the Akkadian king Naram Sin (2213-2176 BC). In the Balikh Valley he undertook a survey and soundings at several sites.

Knighthood

In 1949, having been recently named director of the British School of Archaeology, Baghdad (a position he kept until 1961), Mallowan resumed the long-interrupted excavations at

Nimrud, which he continued until 1957. The project focused on the domestic quarters and administrative wing of the North-west Palace, and also explored the remains of Fort Shalmaneser, along with other palaces, temples and private houses near the city wall. The most spectacular result was the discovery of the Nimrud ivories.

Mallowan garnered many academic positions during his career, including president of the British Institute of Persian Studies between 1961 and 1978, and received a knighthood in 1968. He wrote his autobiography *Mallowan's Memoirs* in 1977, a year before his death.

Sir John Marshall

(1876-1958)

John Marshall's defining work was at Taxila in India, to which he committed over 20 years of research and investigation. Marshall also directed excavations at Mohenjo-Daro, work that would alter the historical understanding of the Indian subcontinent.

John Hubert Marshall was born on 19 March 1876 in Chester. Having attended Dulwich College as a young man, he then proceeded to King's College, Cambridge, where he undertook a Classical Tripos between 1898 and 1900.

Early work

Marshall gainied invaluable experience of excavation and archaeological exploration at the British School in Athens, where many of Britain's foremost archaeologists would cut their teeth. In 1902 he was appointed Director-General of Archaeology in India, a post that had been in abeyance for more than a decade. India's long and varied history had left a wealth of art and architecture whose preservation had been sadly neglected, and little of its rich prehistory had been investigated. Marshall devised and initiated appropriate conservation measures for known monuments and began a programme of excavations.

Among his main foci were the Early Historic cities and Buddhist monuments located by Sir Alexander Cunningham, who had retired as director-general in 1885 after decades of exploring sites known from early Buddhist literature.

Marshall's principal excavation, begun in 1913 and continued until 1936, was at Taxila, a long-lived

Above Here is the famous 'Priest King' of Mohenjo-Daro, discovered by Marshall during his work there in the 1920s. Note the ornamentation around the forehead and the broad trefoil sash.

trading, political and cultural centre, but he and his officers also investigated other Early Historic cities, including the site of Pataliputra. Equally important was the clearance, survey, excavation and restoration of Buddhist monasteries and stupas (relic mounds). Between 1912 and 1919 Marshall also worked at Sanchi, where the Mauryan emperor Ashoka had built a stupa to house relics of the Buddha. This had been enlarged and several others were constructed by later kings, along with monasteries. Marshall concentrated

Left Mohenjo-Daro has produced some of the finest archaeological finds in the Indian sub-continent, and at one time had an estimated 35,000 occupants.

on the Great Stupa, revealing its magnificent gateways, lavishly decorated with reliefs depicting scenes from the Buddha's life, as well as figures from folk tradition.

A few prehistoric Indian sites were known, but the Early Historic cities that emerged in the mid-1st millennium BC were thought to have been the first flowering of Indian civilization. This picture was changed dramatically in 1922, when investigations by Archaeological Survey officers at Harappa and Mohenjo-Daro in the Indus valley unexpectedly revealed the remains of two great cities with distinctive and previously unknown material that was clearly considerably older than the Early Historic period.

Marshall publicly announced their discovery in 1924; Mesopotamian scholars were immediately able to demonstrate that the Indus Civilization, as it was now called, had been contemporary with Sumer, the first civilization in the Near East.

Mohenjo-Daro

Marshall took personal control at Mohenjo-Daro for the major excavation season of 1925-6, assisted by senior staff and with more than a thousand labourers.

The excavations revealed a huge and well-planned city with brick drains and many public wells. Often the houses had bathrooms and private wells. The city was divided into two parts – the residential Lower Town, and a higher Citadel Mound, soon identified as the locus of important public buildings. These included the Great Bath, a large rectangular tank of baked brick made watertight with bitumen, probably for ritual bathing.

One part of the Lower Town yielded a quantity of jewellery, including a fine necklace of extremely long

carnelian beads. Etched carnelian beads were found widely within the city, as were pottery vessels decorated with fishscale, geometric and animal designs. There were many steatite seals also bearing animal designs, particularly the unicorn, along with a few signs in what was now identified as the Indus script. In one building was discovered a rare piece of sculpture, depicting the head and upper torso of a bearded man wearing a garment decorated with trefoils – the now-famous 'Priest-king'.

After one season Marshall returned to his work at Taxila, but excavations continued at Mohenjo-Daro until 1931. Outstanding finds included the lively bronze statuette, known as the 'dancing-girl', and the so-called 'Proto-Shiva' seal, which bears a design showing a three-faced horned deity surrounded by wild animals.

Marshall officially retired as director-general in 1928, but continued to work until 1934 when he returned to England. There he

Above A steatite seal from Mohenjo-Daro, depicting an elephant and assorted monograms and dating from around 2500 BC.

worked on the mammoth report on his excavations at Taxila, which finally emerged in 1951.

The list of publications he left at the time of his death on 17 August 1958 included *The Monuments of Sanchi* (reprinted 1983), a large three-volume work which he co-authored with Alfred Foucher.

Right The Great Stupa at Sanchi (the dome rising in the background) was the focus of one of Marshall's great studies. An elegantly carved gateway (torana) depicts scenes of Buddhist worship.

Pierre Montet

(1885-1966)

Pierre Montet is most closely associated with the one-time royal capital, Tanis, in the northern Nile Delta. Here, just before and after World War II, he discovered a series of magnificent burials dating from the 21st and 22nd Dynasties in the 11th-8th centuries BC.

Born at Villefranche-sur-Saône in the Beaujolais region of central France, Montet first studied Egyptology at the University of Lyon, where he was taught by Victor Lore, a former head of the Egyptian Antiquities Service. He then moved to the French Institute of Eastern Archaeology in Cairo until the outbreak of World War I.

Royal tombs

From 1921 to 1924 Montet excavated at the Lebanese site of Byblos, where he discovered a temple and a series of tombs belonging to local rulers. This early work sparked a lifelong interest in the connections between Egypt and her eastern neighbours. In 1929 he

began work in the Nile Delta at Tanis, the Egyptian capital during the 21st and 22nd Dynasties. It was also the favoured burial place of the monarchs of these dynasties, who abandoned the royal necropolis in the Valley of the Kings in favour of the better-guarded precincts of the temples there. The French archaeologist Auguste Mariette carried out excavations at the great Amen temple of Tanis in 1859, discovering a series of 12th-Dynasty royal sculptures; now Montet cleared the temple area, uncovering yet more royal statuary.

His greatest finds, however, came from a temple dedicated to the goddess Mut (known elsewhere in the

eastern Mediterranean as Anta or Astarte), where in February 1939 he discovered a multi-chambered royal tomb (labelled Tomb I) lying beneath ruined Ptolemaic buildings. Buried there were King Osorkon II and his son Prince Hornakht.

In a neighbouring tomb (Tomb III), which he entered in March 1939, he found the disturbed burial chamber of Psusennes I and the mummies of Sheshonq II and Siamun, along with the undisturbed chambers of Psusennes II and Amenemope (who had usurped a chamber originally prepared for Queen Mutnodjmet).

The outbreak of World War II brought the work at Tanis to a halt, but as soon as peace returned Montet was back. In February 1946 he discovered the burial chamber of General Wendjebauendjedet, also in Tomb III. Today, the contents of these magnificent burials are displayed in Cairo Museum.

Montet was Professor of Egyptology at the University of Strasbourg (1919-48), then at the Collège de France, Paris. He published many books and articles, including *La Nécropole Royale de Tanis* (1958), *Everyday Life in the Days of Ramesses the Great* (1958) and *Eternal Egypt* (1964). He also founded the journal *Kêmi*. He died in Paris on 19 June 1966.

Left An overview of the arrowhead fortification wall at Byblos. Systematic excavations of the ancient Phoenician city did not begin until the 1920s.

André Parrot

(1901-1980)

André Parrot helped shape our cultural and historical understanding of the Middle East. His archaeological career stretched from the 1920s to the 1970s, and he is best known for his 40-year directorship of the excavations at Mari in Syria.

Parrot was born on 15 February 1901, the son of a minister, Charles Parrot. Like his father, Parrot seemed destined for a religious career, studying Protestant theology at the Sorbonne. However, a series of art history courses at the École du Louvre, then a year of antiquity sciences at the École Biblique et Archéologique Française in Jerusalem, expanded his interests to include archaeology, particularly that of the Near East.

Between 1926 and 1933 Parrot undertook numerous excavations, first at Nerab in northern Syria then Baalbek in the Lebanon, before moving to the Mesopotamian sites of Telloh (originally Girsu, capital of Lagash state) and Tell Senkere (Larsa). He directed excavations at Telloh and Tell Senkere from 1961 to 1967.

Life achievement

In 1933 Parrot began excavations at Tell Hariri in Syria, formerly ancient Mari. He was director of work there until 1972, during which time the site yielded constant riches, including over 20,000 cuneiform clay tablets and the Old Babylonian palace of Zimri-Lim (1782-1759 BC). Parrot commented that 'each time a vertical probe was commenced in order to trace the site's history down to virgin

soil, such important discoveries were made that horizontal digging had to be resumed'.

Parrot's work in the Middle East ran alongside professional advancement in France. He became the Inspecteur Géneral des Musées in France in 1965, and the Louvre's director between 1968 and 1972. He held numerous other institutional and honorary academic posts. Parrot was also a prolific author, his works including *Sumer* (1960), *Assur* (1961) and *L'aventure archéologique* (1979). Many of his writings explored the relationship

Above A haunting figure from the Mari Temple of Ishtar, created from alabaster, gypsum and lapis lazuli.

between biblical scripture and archaeology, Parrot believing that the latter threw a 'powerful light … upon the religion and beliefs of a people in search of supernatural forces'.

Right Parrot remains the central figure behind the excavations at Mari, to which he dedicated much of his working life. He probed its history back to its foundations in around 2900 BC.

Sir Flinders Petrie

(1853-1942)

The British Egyptologist Flinders Petrie transformed both our knowledge of ancient Egypt and the techniques of field archaeology. In particular, he developed sequence dating, a method of reconstructing the histories of ancient cultures on the basis of their pottery and other remains.

Surveying was in the blood for Flinders Petrie. His father was an engineer and surveyor, and his grandfather was the navigator Matthew Flinders, who first charted large parts of the coast of Australia. Flinders Petrie was still only in his late teens when he started recording the prehistoric monuments of southern England. Later, with his father's assistance, he made the most accurate survey of Stonehenge at that time.

The Great Pyramid

In 1880, aged 26, he made his first trip to Egypt to survey the Great Pyramid at Giza. At the time, many believed that the pyramid had been built using a divinely inspired 'pyramid inch' as the basic unit of measurement – some even thought this was related to the cubit used to build Noah's Ark and the Tabernacle of Moses. Petrie wanted to find out the truth. Employing just one workman,

he spent two seasons on the survey and structural examination. The end result, so accurate that Petrie's survey is still used today, showed that the 'pyramid inch' theory was false.

In 1883 he started working for the newly founded Egypt Exploration Fund, with excavations at Tanis (modern San el-Hagar) in the Nile

Below A view of the Great Pyramid, one of the Seven Wonders of the Ancient World.

Delta. This was followed by a season at the Greek trading centre Naucratis (el Nibeira). Later, with the support of two wealthy private backers – the Manchester businessman Jesse Haworth and the collector Martyn Kennard – he moved to Hawara in the Faiyum region, south-west of Cairo. Here, on the north side of the Middle Kingdom pyramid of Amenemhat III, he found a large Roman cemetery, which yielded a series of mummies with beautifully painted wood-panel faces. Next, he moved to Illahun (Lahun), also in the Faiyum region, where he excavated some 1800 rooms in a village that had been built for pyramid construction workers.

After a brief interlude working in Palestine, Petrie returned to Egypt, working first at the pyramid cemetery of Meidum, then at Akhetaten (modern Amarna). In Akhetaten he was denied access to the royal tombs, so he excavated in the central city instead, uncovering a beautiful painted gypsum pavement in the Great Palace.

Devising sequence dating

In April 1892 Petrie was appointed Professor of Egyptology at University College, London. From then on, he taught for half the year and spent the winter months in Egypt.

At Koptos (ancient Gebtu, modern Quft), Petrie discovered a series of statues, including three prehistoric colossal sculptures representing the fertility god Min. At Tûkh, close to the southern town of Nagada, he investigated a curious cemetery housing many hundreds of prehistoric graves – the remains of the peoples who had lived in the Nile valley before Egypt became one unified country. There were no texts with these graves, and so Petrie had to devise a new way of dating them, which came to be called sequence dating. This involved identifying the different types of pottery associated with the different burials, and using these to arrange the burials into successive chronological phases.

Excavations at Luxor, Qurna, Deshasha and Dendera followed. Petrie then moved to Abydos, where he was principally interested in the tombs of the 1st and 2nd Dynasty kings. He re-investigated 13 royal tombs, which allowed him to join his prehistoric Nagada grave sequence to the beginning of Egyptian history. He continued his field work at Giza, where he discovered 2nd Dynasty tombs which confirmed that Giza had been used as a cemetery long before Khufu built his Great Pyramid. In a cemetery at another site, Tarkhan, he found amazing quantities of textiles.

Then, in 1914, the Egyptian government imposed a change in archaeological protocol. All future excavations were to be under strict state control.

Above The Sphinx at Memphis excavated by Petrie in 1912. The Sphinx, 8m (26ft) long, is carved from a single piece of alabaster.

The old practice of dividing finds on a more or less 50:50 basis between the excavator and the Egyptian state was abolished; from this point on, all discoveries would automatically remain in Egypt unless the authorities chose to make an exception. These new regulations caused problems for Egyptologists like Petrie, whose private backers expected to receive some material reward for their funding. As a result, Petrie left Egypt after World War I to work in Palestine instead. He retired from University College, London, in 1933 and died in Jerusalem on 29 July 1942, at the age of 89.

Julio C. Tello

(1880-1947)

The Peruvian Julio C. Tello was one of those rare archaeologists whose work shaped the way an entire nation perceived itself. He expanded Peru's understanding of its pre-Columbian past, and also invested much of his time and effort training future generations of archaeologists.

Julio C. Tello is considered the Father of Peruvian Archaeology by most Peruvians. His work was central to establishing the importance of the early civilizations of Peru among academics, the public and, significantly, among Peru's political class. His work synthesizing and summarizing the sequence of ancient civilizations of the Andes, as well as at specific sites such as the famous Chavín de Huantar, inspired a generation of young archaeologists.

Tello was to become the first academically trained Peruvian archaeologist. His career included service as the director of the National Museum, as a professor at Peru's most important universities and even in the Peruvian congress. He established major museum collections, trained dozens of Peruvian archaeologists and promulgated laws to protect Peru's archaeological sites and resources. He also helped establish Peru's pre-Columbian past as an important part of her history.

Below The ruins of a wall at the site of Chavín de Huantar, Peru.

Right A carved stone nail head (Cabezas Clavas) at Chavín de Huantar.

Early promise

Tello was born and raised in the highlands of Huarochiri, outside Lima. He went to Peru's capital to study, working for the famous Peruvian intellectual Ricardo Palma and becoming interested in archaeology. He studied medicine, graduating from San Marcos University with a thesis on syphilis in ancient Peru in 1908. He then earned a scholarship to Harvard, where he did his post-graduate studies. During this time he worked with the famous physical anthropologist Ales Hrdlicka. Upon his return from the United States, Tello focused his work largely on pre-Inca civilizations in Peru. His work at Chavín de Huantar and other sites was extremely influential.

Scientific archaeology was in its infancy at the beginning of Tello's career, and many scholars at the time believed that civilization had emerged in only a few places, then spreading, or diffusing, to far-reaching areas. Peru was viewed, by the German scholar Max Uhle among others, as part of a larger American civilization that had its roots in Central America rather than locally. Tello disputed this idea, and much of his work was focused on establishing the local origins of Andean civilization. His work at Chavín de Huantar was particularly important.

Challenging ideas

Radiocarbon dating and other chronometric methods had yet to be invented, and stylistic analysis and stratigraphy were the main methods of assigning relative dates to, and establishing the relationships in time and space among, archaeological cultures and materials. Tello argued that Chavín greatly pre-dated Inca and other later Andean civilizations, and that it formed the original, or matrix, civilization of the Andes. More recent work has demonstrated that the origins of Peruvian civilization

pre-date even Chavín. The Chavín were, however, one of the first groups whose style spread widely across the Andean region. The influence of the Chavín style can be seen in architecture, pottery and other objects made throughout a wide area of Peru about 2500 years ago.

Archaeologists now believe that Chavín de Huantar was a major political and religious centre with trading relationships that extended from Peru's desert coast to the jungle. Tello published widely, writing books and newspaper articles during his lifetime, and he left reams of unpublished notes (some have been published posthumously).

While many of his ideas have been updated or modified by more recent studies, new techniques and more detailed analysis, Tello's influence is still felt today in several ways. First, Tello was correct in his assertions that Peruvian civilization developed locally, and we now know that the cultural sequence of the Andes extends back well over 12,000 years. Second, Chavín de Huantar was, as Tello believed, one of the most important early sites in the Andes, although it was neither the first nor the only early centre of civilization. Finally, Tello and some of his contemporaries shifted the perspective of Peru's intellectual and

political communities concerning the nature of Peruvian history and the importance of the pre-Columbian past and the indigenous civilizations. Peru's ancient civilizations and local traditions are now viewed by many educated Peruvians as a significant part of their country's past, and as something to be claimed as heritage by all Peruvians.

Below A relief sculpture covers the ruins of a monolith at Chavín de Huantar, Peru. Tello's work revealed much about the sophistication of early Andean culture.

Alan Bayard Wace

(1879-1957)

One of Britain's foremost archaeologists working in Greece and the Mediterranean in the first half of the 20th century. He was director of the British School at Athens from 1914 to 1923 and held positions at the Victoria and Albert Museum in London and Cambridge University.

Alan John Bayard Wace was born on 13 July 1879, the son of a Cambridge mathematics fellow. The young Wace later studied classics at the same university as his father. At Pembroke College he developed a strong interest in the sculpture of the Hellenistic period and on graduation went to Greece to continue his research at the British School in Athens. His interest in sculpture brought with it an invitation from Henry Stuart-Jones, director of the British School at Rome, to contribute to the study of sculpture in the civic collections there, and Wace worked as a librarian in the school from 1905. Thus, Wace

would spend part of each year in the Italian capital working on museum collections, and the other part in Greece undertaking field work.

In Greece, Wace participated in the British School's excavation and survey in and around Sparta. However, he had a long-standing interest in Greek prehistory and was soon involved in a major survey of Thessaly in central Greece, hunting for prehistoric mounds; sites at Theotokou and Zerélia were excavated.

In 1914 Wace became director of the British School at Athens. Although working in part for naval intelligence, he also undertook excavations with

Carl Blegen of the American School at Korakou. Their close friendship underpinned the post-war excavations at Zygouries and the British work at Mycenae. Blegen and Wace challenged the view of the supremacy of Crete held by Sir Arthur Evans and instead promoted the influence of the mainland Mycenaean Greeks.

Major positions

Wace, who was a recognized expert in Greek island embroideries, returned to London to work as a curator of textiles at the Victoria and Albert Museum. In 1934 he was appointed to the Laurence chair of Classical Archaeology at Cambridge.

He then returned to excavate at Mycenae in 1939, but World War II intervened. Following the Allied evacuation of Greece, he ended up in Egypt. Here he served as the chair of Classics and Archaeology in the Farouk I University at Alexandria. This post allowed him to return to his earlier Hellenistic interests and he worked on some of the Ptolemaic sites. Returning to Mycenae in 1950, he was responsible for discovering Linear B tablets in the city. His writings include *Mycenae: an Archaeological History and Guide* (1949).

Left Wace was as passionate about his academic instruction as about his field work. Here he lectures a group of students about a statue of Leonidas, the king of Sparta, where he conducted excavations with the British School at Athens.

Sir Mortimer Wheeler

(1890-1976)

Sir Mortimer Wheeler was not only a renowned archaeologist in his own right, he was also passionate about the development of new generations of researchers and helped create programmes and institutions that trained dozens of future archaeologists.

Robert Eric Mortimer Wheeler was born in Glasgow, Scotland, the son of a journalist. He studied classics as a student at University College London, where he was introduced to archaeology by Ernest Gardner, a former director of the British School at Athens. He graduated in 1910 and continued his studies by working on Roman pottery from the German frontier. Wheeler later joined the Royal Commission on Historical Monuments in 1913, but this job was interrupted by war service in the Royal Artillery; he was awarded the Military Cross in 1918.

Roman forts

Wheeler was appointed as the Keeper of Archaeology at the National Museum of Wales; he was later promoted to director (1924). During this period he excavated a number of Roman forts across Wales, including Caernarfon (Segontium), Y Gaer near Brecon and the amphitheatre at the legionary fortress at Caerleon (Isca) in south-east Wales.

As excavations were underway at Caerleon, Wheeler moved to the London Museum as keeper. Over the next decade he worked with his wife, Tessa, to create an institute to train future archaeologists. The Institute of Archaeology was opened as part of the University of London in 1937; sadly Tessa died of a heart attack the year before it opened. Together 'the Wheelers', as they were affectionately known, had excavated at a series of Romano-British sites, notably Lydney Park in the Forest of Dean, Gloucestershire, and the major city of Verulamium near St Albans.

War past and present

Wheeler's interests then turned to the Iron Age societies that faced Rome during the invasion of Britain in the 1st century AD. He conducted a major excavation at the Iron Age hillfort at Maiden Castle in Dorset. Just outside one of the gates he found the corpse of one of the defenders who had been killed by a piece of Roman artillery; the bolt from the ballista was still sticking in the spine. On the eve of World War II he excavated Iron Age hillforts in northern France, shedding light on the settlements described by Julius Caesar.

Wheeler returned to military service and served in North Africa and then in the invasion of Sicily. Before he could get involved in the Italian campaign, however, he was transferred to the Archaeological Survey of India. After partition, Wheeler returned to London as professor of the archaeology of the Roman provinces; however, he maintained links with Pakistan, acting as adviser to the new archaeological service and ran a training excavation at Mohenjo-Daro. In Britain, Wheeler returned to his earlier interests in Iron Age and Roman archaeology by excavating the major Iron Age site at Stanwick in Yorkshire.

He was dedicated to supporting British archaeology around the world through the development of the British Academy and the creation of foreign institutes of archaeology. Wheeler was knighted in 1952 and after numerous appearances on radio and TV was named British TV Personality of the Year in 1954.

Below Maiden Castle is the largest hillfort in Europe, covering an area of 19ha (47 acres).

Sir Leonard Woolley

(1880-1960)

Leonard Woolley received international acclaim in the 1920s with the discovery of the 'Royal Cemetery' at Ur in southern Mesopotamia. While spectacular, the Royal Cemetery was but one of many important finds at Ur, and Woolley undertook several major projects during his career.

Leonard Woolley, born in Upper Clapton in England, was the son of a clergyman. At first he intended to take up his father's calling, but on leaving New College, Oxford, he accepted the advice of the warden and pursued a developing interest in archaeology.

Woolley served his apprenticeship on excavations in Egypt, Italy and England, and then at Carchemish in Syria, where he headed up the excavations beginning in 1912. T.E. Lawrence was another member of the Carchemish project, and the two also collaborated on a survey of Wadi Arabah south of the Dead Sea.

After World War I (part of which he spent as a prisoner-of-war), Woolley undertook a final season at Carchemish and another at Tell el-Amarna in Egypt, before heading the excavations at Ur from 1922 until 1934. He initiated his third major project in 1937 at Tell Atchana and the nearby Mediterranean port of al-Mina in north-west Syria, a project that was to run for seven seasons until 1949.

Carchemish and Ur

Carchemish, on the banks of the Euphrates river just south of the current Turkish-Syrian border, is an immense mound with a very long history of occupation. Woolley's excavations

Above From Ur, the god Ningirsu depicted as a lion-headed eagle.

uncovered remains of a local Neo-Hittite (9th-8th century BC) capital, including palaces, temples and fortifications. At the time, the Neo-Hittite kingdoms were particularly enigmatic (indeed, the kingdoms remain inadequately studied), and Woolley's excavations provided good information about Neo-Hittite architecture, art and general culture.

Ur, in the deep south of Mesopotamia, was first settled in the 5th millennium BC and was occupied more or less continuously until around 200 BC. During his 12 seasons at Ur, Woolley excavated remains from every period of this long history. The most prominent results include: traces of the earliest village at Ur, covered by an alluvial silt that Woolley equated with Noah's flood; the ziggurat of the Ur III period (c.2112-2004 BC) when Ur was the capital of a strong regional kingdom; and residential districts belonging to the same period and to the Old Babylonian period (c.1800 BC). Because Near Eastern archaeologists traditionally focus on public monuments, the residential districts provide all too rare evidence for ordinary life in ancient Mesopotamia.

Left A detail from the 'Standard of Ur' found by Woolley and dating from c.2500 BC. It was found in a grave in the Royal Cemetery.

Right The staircase of the monumental
stepped ziggurat at Ur, which Woolley
excavated in 1923.

Right The staircase of the monumental
stepped ziggurat at Ur, which Woolley
excavated in 1923.

Royal cemetery

Of Woolley's results, the Royal
Cemetery attracted by far the most
attention. For roughly 500 years the
residents of Ur buried thousands of
their dead in a cemetery near the main
temple of the city. Of the several
thousand tombs that Woolley
excavated there, most were simple
interments accompanied by few
grave-goods. But some tombs
(Woolley identified a total of 16
tombs used for royal burials) were
elaborate chambers entered through
ramps, containing thousands of
objects, plus the bodies of retainers
sacrificed to accompany their masters
in death.

Among the objects placed in the
tomb are some of the most famous
pieces of ancient Sumerian art ever
found: the golden royal helmet of
King Meskalamdug; the 'Standard
of Ur', a plaque showing scenes of
warfare and ritual rendered in nacre
and lapis lazuli inlay originally on a
wooden frame; lyres and 'ram in
a thicket' statues ornamented with
gold, silver, lapis and nacre; and
intricate headdresses of gold
and silver. Even the more 'ordinary'
objects could be luxurious, such as
weapons made of gold or silver,
containers made of expensive stone or
metal, toiletry kits of precious metals,
and a variety of other jewellery. These
extravagantly rich royal tombs date to
around 2600 BC.

A forgotten kingdom

After the splendours of Ur, Tell
Atchana is something of an anti-
climax, but even so the site gave
Woolley important results. His
excavations uncovered palaces and
temples from the Middle and Late
Bronze Ages (c.2000-1200 BC).
Archives of cuneiform tablets, plus a
long inscription on the statue of a
king, identify Tell Atchana as ancient
Alalakh, and these texts remain today

among the most important available
sources for north-west Syria during
these periods. The concurrent
excavations at al-Mina found
structures, perhaps warehouses, dated
to the 8th-4th centuries BC. The Greek
pottery and other objects associated
with these structures remain a central
reference in discussions about Greek
commerce in the east.

Woolley was also a prolific writer.
During his lifetime he published over
25 books, many of which
expressed his love of archaeology
as much as the findings
of his work. His work includes
Spadework: Adventures in Archaeology
(1953) and *Excavations at Ur: A Record of
12 Years' Work* (1954). Woolley was
knighted for his services to
archaeology in 1935.

Right Ornate jewellery and hair ornaments
found in burial pits by Woolley at Ur.

67

MODERN
ARCHAEOLOGISTS

With a few exceptions such as Mary Leakey, it is probably fair to say that few of the archaeologists of the mid- to late-20th century became household names. The increasingly scientific and academic nature of the subject has generally brought relative anonymity, except for those who feature on television. Nevertheless, the quality of the work carried out has constantly improved in tandem with the battery of new techniques available for dating, analysis, excavation and survey. The great archaeologists of the 20th century, including Ignacio Bernal, Rhys Jones, Kathleen Kenyon, Michael Ventris and others featured here, have dramatically deepened our understanding of human civilization. The scope of subject areas and locations has been incredibly diverse, ranging from the decipherment of Linear B to excavations at the ancient Zapotec capital of Monte Albán (facing page), and from new interpretations of Palaeolithic art to pioneering studies in Aboriginal Australia.

Meave Leakey Continuing the Leakey family tradition, her work has helped to redefine our understanding of human evolution.

Maria Reiche Her life's work was devoted to the Nasca lines etched into the face of the Peruvian desert.

Spyridon Marinatos He excavated an ancient city preserved under volcanic rock on the island of Thera (Santorini).

Manolis Andronikos

(1919-1992)

The discovery of rich royal tombs from the 4th century BC at Vergina in Greece – which Andronikos identified with the Macedonian king Philip II, father of Alexander the Great – marked the pinnacle of a long, prestigious career in archaeology.

Above A small ivory head of a bearded man, which Andronikos identified with Philip II, was excavated from Tomb II.

Manolis Andronikos was born in Prousa (the Turkish city of Brusa) on 23 October 1919, the son of Greek parents who had settled in Salonica (or Thessaloniki) after World War I.

At the age of 17 he joined the excavations of the Macedonian royal palace at Vergina, which were being undertaken by K.A. Rhomaios. These uncovered an impressive series of sumptuous dining rooms that gave views over the great western plain of Macedonia. Andronikos's career was interrupted by the German occupation of Greece during World War II. After serving with the Greek forces in the Middle East, he later resumed his studies at the Aristotelian University of Thessaloniki, receiving his doctorate in 1952. From there he went to Oxford where he worked with Sir John Beazley, whose expertise lay in the field of Greek, and especially Athenian, figure-decorated pottery.

Vergina

From Oxford Andronikos returned to Thessaloniki, first as a lecturer and then as professor of archaeology. He next worked on a series of excavations in Macedonia, eventually returning to the royal palace at Vergina in 1962, where his interest in archaeology had begun. He also turned his attention to the Iron Age burials around Vergina, and in particular to the Great Mound that lay at the heart of an extensive mound cemetery around the modern town. Excavations were initiated in 1976 and Andronikos uncovered two burials, one of which remained intact.

Tomb II was particularly rich, with a series of silver drinking vessels and jugs, an ivory-inlaid couch, elaborate armour and a stone sarcophagus, which held a solid gold burial chest, or larnax. The British scholar Nicholas Hammond had proposed that Vergina was the site of the ancient Macedonian capital of Aegae, which led Andronikos to conclude that he had opened the grave of one of the members of the Macedonian royal family. He also believed that the plate and pottery from the tomb should be dated to the third quarter of the 4th century BC. On this evidence he concluded that this must be the burial of Philip II of Macedonia, who had been assassinated in the theatre at Aegae.

The cremated remains found in the larnax in Tomb II were those of a middle-aged man. A team of professional forensic archaeologists from the University of Manchester have attempted a reconstruction based on known images of Philip II.

Left The site of the Macedonian Royal Palace at Vergina. In 1993 an underground building was constructed to enclose and protect the royal tombs. The treasures found in the tombs have been on display since 1997.

Above The Rhomaios Tomb at Vergina is broadly contemporary with other royal burials found by Andronikos at the site.

Tomb III contained a beautiful silver hydria (a Greek water jar) decorated with a gold wreath. This had been used as the container for the cremated remains of an individual who was aged about 14. A likely candidate is Alexander IV, who was murdered around the year 309 BC.

Disputed finds

Scholars have now started to question the date of Tomb II and therefore the identification with Philip II. The Attic black-glossed 'saltcellars' may be as late as the early 3rd century BC, and the barrel-vaulted style of the tomb may have been introduced to Macedonia after the eastern conquests of Philip's son, Alexander the Great. The Lion Hunt frieze that decorated

the front of Tomb II also seems more in keeping with the iconography of Alexander and his successors.

Recent re-examination of all the skeletal evidence from the tomb has suggested that the body had been cremated some time after the person had died, which makes it unlikely to be that of Philip II. Moreover, questions have been raised about the identification of damage to one of the

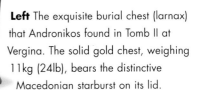

eyes that had convinced many that this was indeed Philip, who was known to have been blinded in one eye by an arrow injury. It has now been proposed that Philip II was, in fact, buried in (the robbed) Tomb I adjacent to a hero shrine that is likely to have been associated with a religious cult linked to Philip II.

Andronikos continued his work at Vergina, and subsequently revealed many more royal tombs. He wrote up his findings in *The Royal Graves at Vergina* (1978) and *Vergina: The Royal Tombs and the Ancient City* (1984). He received the Order of the Phoenix from the Greek government, Greece's highest civilian honour, just prior to his death on 30 March 1992.

Left The exquisite burial chest (larnax) that Andronikos found in Tomb II at Vergina. The solid gold chest, weighing 11kg (24lb), bears the distinctive Macedonian starburst on its lid.

Ignacio Bernal
(1910-1992)

*One of the giants of Mexican archaeology, Ignacio Bernal devoted his
long and distinguished career to unravelling the archaeological history
of the Oaxaca valley of southern Mexico, and in particular the Zapotec
capital of Monte Albán.*

Although he was born into a
distinguished family of historians,
Bernal did not turn to archaeology
until he was in his early thirties, when
he began working with the great
archaeologist Alfonso Caso at Monte
Albán. Thus began a close
collaboration with Caso and a lifelong commitment to the archaeology
of Oaxaca. Very little was known
about the Zapotecs prior to Caso and
Bernal's work, but based on their
extensive archaeological explorations,
and those of subsequent scholars,
Oaxaca is now among the best-known
regions of Mesoamerica.

Bernal received his Ph.D. in 1950
from the National Autonomous
University of Mexico (UNAM) and
enjoyed a diverse career that included
both administrative posts directing the
National Institute of Anthropology and
History (1968-71) and the National
Museum of Anthropology (1962-68
and 1970-77). He served as a cultural
attaché in Paris, and as president of the
Society for American Archaeology
(1968-69). In addition to his active
service, he was a charismatic instructor
both at the UNAM (1948-76) and at
Mexico City College (1951-59).

Monte Albán

Bernal worked at Monte Albán from
1942 to 1944 and again between 1946
and 1953. His initial research

Above The oldest carved stones at the site are
the so-called *danzantes* (dancers), depicting
the contorted figures of slain captives.
These slabs were displayed on façades
and bear some of the earliest hieroglyphs
known in Mesoamerica.

considered the Formative era of
Monte Albán (500 BC to AD 200),
while his dissertation was based on the
late Classic period (AD 500-800),
spanning the rise and decline of the
great city.

He also branched out from Monte
Albán to explore other areas both
within the valley of Oaxaca and in the
mountainous Mixteca region to the
west. His projects at Coixtlahuaca and
Tamazulápan were among the first
scientific investigations of the
Mixtecs, a cultural group of great
interest to his colleague Caso.

Bernal also led a long-term project
at Yagul (1954-62), where a
Postclassic palace complex revealed
the final phase of pre-Hispanic
Oaxaca. The interaction of Mixtec
peoples in the Zapotec region of
Oaxaca was documented in colonial
histories, and Bernal sought to apply
archaeological rigour to test the
chronicles. Between 1966 and 1972,

Below A spectacular view across the ruins at
Monte Albán. By AD 300 the population of the
city numbered around 50,000.

Bernal returned to his interest in Formative Oaxaca, directing an extensive project at the site of Dainzu, contemporary with the founding of Monte Albán, where carved stones depict the pre-Columbian ballgame.

Lifetime's work

Bernal's prolific publication record was documented on his 80th birthday, when it tallied 267 books and articles. Notable contributions include a book on the funerary urns of Oaxaca (with A. Caso), *Mexico Before Cortes* (1975; originally published in Spanish in 1959), an exhaustive bibliography of Mesoamerican archaeology and ethnography with 30,000 entries, a comprehensive volume on the ceramics of Monte Albán (with A. Caso and J. Acosta), which is popularly referred to as the 'blue bible', and *A History of Mexican Archaeology* published in 1980.

As is demonstrated by the tremendous scope of Bernal's publications, as well as his active service to Mexican archaeology and to

training archaeology students, Bernal was passionate about his craft and tirelessly committed to sharing his passion with academic and popular audiences alike. France awarded him the Légion d'Honneur in 1964 and Britain the Royal Order of Victoria in 1975. Similar honours were also

Above The ballcourt at Monte Albán. There are no stone rings and the court is shaped like a capital 'I'. Some experts think that the sloping walls were used in the game, not for spectators.

bestowed on him by countries including Germany, Italy, Belgium, Denmark and the Netherlands.

Monte Albán

The capital of the Zapotec empire between 500 BC and AD 800, Monte Albán (which means 'white mountain' in Spanish) was arguably the first urban centre in Mesoamerica. Located on a series of ridges, the city looms 300m (1000ft) above the valley of Oaxaca. Its acropolis was artificially modified into an enormous plaza surrounded by pyramids and civic-ceremonial buildings. Hieroglyphic texts, many of which remain undeciphered, represent the earliest known writing system in the Americas, and low-relief carvings embedded in the architectural façades depict sacrificial victims and imperial conquest.

While much of the initial reconstruction was directed by Caso and Bernal, research has continued through intensive survey of the 2000+ residential terraces, excavations of elite and commoner residences, and archaeo-astronomical interpretations of the enigmatic Building J. Together with the settlement-pattern surveys of the valley surrounding the city and investigations at many of the subordinate sites in the region, Oaxaca is one of the best-known regions for interpreting pre-Columbian Mesoamerica.

Alfonso Caso

(1896-1970)

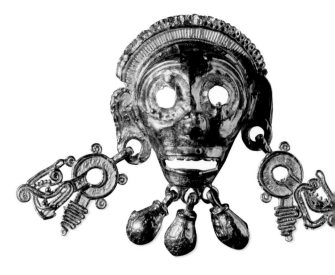

The Mexican archaeologist Alfonso Caso made important contributions to pre-Columbian studies in Mexico. His most celebrated discovery was Tomb VII at Monte Albán, which presented components of both Zapotec and Mixtec cultures.

Born in Mexico City in 1896, Alfonso Caso was one of the foremost Mexican archaeologists of the 20th century. He shaped the direction of the Mexican archaeological and anthropological institutions, while also making numerous major contributions to the interpretation of the pre-Columbian cultures of Mesoamerica. Caso's early training was as a lawyer, but early on his imagination was captured by the ancient cultures of his country and he began studying at the School of Advanced Studies under renowned scholars, such as Eduard Seler, Hermann Beyer and Manuel Gamio. He was later awarded an honorary doctorate from the National Autonomous University of Mexico.

Over the course of his career, Caso founded many of the cornerstones of Mexican archaeology, including the *Revista Mexicana de Estudios Antropológicos* (*Mexican Journal of Anthropological Studies*), the National Institute of Anthropology and History, the National School of Anthropology and History and the National Indigenous Institute. Particularly in the second half of his career, he was deeply committed to the development of the discipline of anthropological archaeology.

Above A gold bead, beautifully carved in the shape of a mask, shows the sophistication of pre-Columbian metalworking.

Below An impressive view across the Grand Plaza at Monte Albán. Building J, in the foreground, may have been an observatory.

Oaxaca

Caso is best known for his archaeological investigations in central Mexico, particularly in the state of Oaxaca. His long-term excavation at Monte Albán, the capital of the Zapotec civilization, added important breadth to a pre-Columbian history dominated at the time by Maya and Aztec cultures.

In addition to clearing and restoring numerous monumental structures on the ceremonial acropolis, Caso and his team also explored 180 tombs in elite residential compounds. The most famous of these was Tomb VII, where over 500 elaborately worked precious objects of gold, silver, jade, turquoise, alabaster and shell were found in association with a shrine to an earth/fertility goddess. Prominent among the grave offerings were carved weaving battens, inscribed with texts using the Mixtec hieroglyphic writing. Spurred on by these discoveries, Caso gained further

Above An ornate gold pendant excavated from Tomb VII at Monte Albán. This and other treasures from the tomb are now kept in the Oaxaca regional museum.

renown by making significant strides in the practical decipherment of this complex writing system.

Above A section of a pre-Columbian codex, named the Codex Zouche-Nuttall and now in the British Library in London. It is one of three codices that record the genealogies, alliances and conquests of several 11th- and 12th-century rulers of a small Mixtec city-state in Oaxaca.

Legacy

The inter-relationship of archaeology and epigraphy was a trademark focus of Caso, who also published works on Aztec and Tarrascan calendar systems. His several books on the Aztecs, notably *People of the Sun* (1958), remain among the most important treatments of the subject. His other publications include *Thirteen Masterpieces of Mexican Archaeology* (1938).

A true 'Renaissance-style' scholar, Caso's interests were diverse and his approach to research rigorous. In recognition of his profound influence on Mexican archaeology, he was buried in 1970 in the Rotunda of Illustrious Men in Mexico City.

Rhys Jones

(1941-2001)

Welsh-born archaeologist Rhys Jones was a true pioneer of modern Australian archaeology. Through his extensive field work he was able to reshape the chronology of Australia's prehistory and advance our knowledge of the Aboriginal culture.

Rhys Jones belongs to a group of several young archaeologists, many of them Cambridge-trained, who took up positions in Australia as part of the expansion of universities there in the 1960s. This period saw an explosion of knowledge in Australian archaeology as archaeologists tackled questions such as the age of human settlement, the impact of people on the environment and the role of ethnography in interpreting the past. The relatively new technique of radiocarbon dating dramatically extended the beginnings of Aboriginal occupation of Australia from 10,000 to 40,000 years ago in just over a decade of research. Rhys Jones's contribution to answering these questions cannot be overstated. He was also an excellent teacher and an eloquent communicator.

Jones was born into a Welsh-speaking family in north Wales, attended grammar school in Cardiff and went on to read Natural Sciences and Archaeology at Cambridge University. He took up a Teaching Fellowship at the University of Sydney

Below Jones's observations of modern Aboriginal life helped to inform his interpretations of their prehistory.

Left A rock formation in Kakadu National Park, Arnhem Land.

in 1963, where he completed a Ph.D. Jones then moved to the Research School of Pacific Studies at the Australian National University in 1969, where he would spend the remainder of his career.

Tasmania and Arnhem Land

Jones's first field research in Australia focused on Tasmania, where his excavations at the Rocky Cape site confirmed that occupation there predated the separation of Tasmania from the mainland due to rising sea levels. He also conducted a study, via their records, of the early French explorers' encounters with Tasmanian hunter-gatherers. Jones's fascination with the Tasmanian story and the tragedy of their encounter with European society led to a collaboration with Tom Hayden on the film *The Last Tasmanian*.

In the 1980s Jones also played a key role in the discovery of an Ice Age occupation in south-west Tasmania and successfully campaigned to save these important sites from being drowned by the damming of the Franklin River for hydroelectric power.

In Arnhem Land (Northern Territory) he worked with his long-term partner and fellow archaeologist Betty Meehan, documenting the lives of the Anbarra people of the Blyth River area. From them he gained an insight into Aboriginal life and culture. The use of ethnography as a source of models for interpreting the historical past strongly informed his work.

Much of Rhys Jones's work focused on broad questions of chronology and also on the impact of human colonization on the Australian environment. He promoted the development of new dating methods based on luminescence, resulting in claims for the age of Australian human colonization as far back as 60,000 years and establishing the age of rock art through dating the sediments trapped in mud wasps' nests.

Firestick farming

Jones studied the issues of Aboriginal transformation of the natural environment through the use of fire, and developed the concept of 'firestick farming'. He first coined the term in 1969 after he observed how the Aborigines used controlled burnings to clear land for hunting and to change the local plant species. Firestick farming symbolized a change in attitude to Aboriginal people, and hunter-gatherers in general, as active managers of their environment, rather than random wanderers at the mercy of nature.

He had a flair for the dramatic, once famously announcing his land claim over Stonehenge as a Welshman and thus an indigenous person and true descendant of the builders of the sacred

Above A young Aboriginal woman deliberately sets fire to grasses as a precaution against more dangerous fires during the dry season in Arnhem Land.

British place. He believed passionately in the importance of Australian archaeology, both in terms of its contribution to the broader human story and the potential it held for the development of important theories in the study of hunter-gatherer societies. He made full use of the media and film to project his knowledge of Aboriginal studies and succeeded in putting Australian archaeology firmly on the international stage.

He died on 19 September 2001 at the age of 60 and was buried at Bungendore cemetery wearing his well-worn bushman's hat.

Kathleen Kenyon

(1906-1978)

An eminent British archaeologist of the ancient Near East whose excavations at Jericho during the 1950s made landmark discoveries, especially for early Neolithic periods. She also excavated at Samaria and Jerusalem, and published influential studies of Levantine archaeology.

Kathleen Kenyon was born in London on 5 January 1906, the daughter of Frederic Kenyon, a biblical scholar of high reputation, director of the British Museum and president of the British Academy. This background clearly influenced her choice of future career. She read history at Somerville College, Oxford, where she became the first woman president of the Oxford University Archaeological Society.

She gained her first archaeological experience in 1929 when she worked as a photographer on Gertrude Caton-Thompson's famous expedition to Great Zimbabwe in Africa.

During the 1930s Kenyon devoted much of her time to Roman Britain: she was a regular participant in the excavations carried out by Mortimer and Tessa Wheeler at Verulamium (St Albans), and she conducted her own

excavations at Jewry Wall (Leicester). Kenyon also assisted the Wheelers in establishing, in 1934, the famed Institute of Archaeology at the University of London. Mortimer Wheeler was at this time developing and applying his method of careful stratigraphic excavation (exploring a site in strata), and Kenyon's association with him deeply influenced her own approach to archaeological excavation.

During World War II Kenyon served as a divisional commander of the Red Cross, in Hammersmith, London, and also as the acting director of the Institute of Archaeology. When she resumed archaeological field work after the war, Kenyon initially pursued her Roman interests, with work in Britain and in Libya. But she soon launched the work in the Near East that would make her famous.

Apprenticeship at Samaria

Kenyon had received initial experience in the field of Near Eastern archaeology in the early 1930s, when she assisted in the excavations headed by John Crowfoot at Samaria, the capital of the biblical kingdom of Israel. The site had been heavily destroyed at the end of the 8th

Left Kenyon's work at Jericho took her back to the very beginnings of human civilization. The Pre-Pottery Neolithic stone tower dates to c.8000 BC. The tower, built of solid stone and standing 9m (30ft) high, was entered through an internal staircase.

century BC and then reoccupied through Roman times – its stratigraphy was very challenging. Kenyon's contribution to that project was a stratigraphic section through the site that extended from the Iron Age II (c.1000-600 BC) through the Roman periods.

Ancient Jericho

After the war Kenyon returned to the Near East where she was involved in the reopening of the British School of Archaeology in Jerusalem. Such is Kenyon's place in the life of this centre of learning that in July 2003 the British School was officially renamed the Kenyon Institute.

In 1952 Kenyon launched excavations at Jericho (Tell al-Sultan), which she continued until 1958. Jericho, a mound in a spring-fed oasis west of the Jordan river, had been the object of excavations by John Garstang during the 1930s. Kenyon's thorough excavations produced results that far exceeded those of the earlier work, making landmark contributions to regional and even world archaeology.

She exposed a Pre-Pottery Neolithic (roughly 8300-6200 BC) settlement protected by a massive stone wall and tower – a very early example of the coordination of community labour. The plastered skulls and plaster statues at the site were part of a mortuary cult characteristic of the period.

The subsequent Pottery Neolithic period (c.5800-4500 BC) levels contained pit houses, as well as pottery that helped elucidate this still poorly known period. The Early Bronze Age (mid-3rd millennium BC) town had been surrounded by a wall with towers, while the Middle Bronze Age (c.2000-1550 BC) town had been enclosed by earthen ramparts. Cemeteries situated around the mound contained collective burials in caves, the mortuary assemblages of which helped to refine significantly the chronology of Bronze Age material culture.

A Jerusalem finale

After Jericho Kenyon shifted her attention to Jerusalem, where she carried out the first modern excavation in the 'City of David' just south of Temple Mount. Begun in 1961 and brought to a close by the 1967 Six-Day War, the Jerusalem excavations must be counted as less successful than those at Jericho. Kenyon did find remains of the Iron Age II (1000-600 BC) capital of Judah, including traces of the town wall and of houses constructed on terraces up the hill slope, and also remains of later periods of occupation. However, these results are largely superseded by the work of Israeli archaeologists, who have been conducting many further excavations since 1967.

An influential figure

Kenyon's contribution to Near Eastern archaeology was not limited to the technical publication of results that are a necessary conclusion to any field project. She also wrote important overviews of Levantine archaeology, such as *Archaeology of the Holy Land* (1960), which helped shape a framework and questions that are still pertinent today. In addition, she encouraged several generations of budding archaeologists with her *Beginning in Archaeology* (1952), in which she explained the techniques and goals of archaeological field work. Other publications include: *Jerusalem - Excavating 3000 Years of History* (1967) and *Royal Cities of the Old Testament* (1971). In 1962 she was appointed Principal of St Hugh's College, Oxford and on her retirement in 1973 was made a Dame of the British Empire. Kathleen Kenyon died on 24 August 1978, in Wrexham, Wales.

Below A statue, fitted with remarkable shell eyes, from Jericho, dated to the 7th millennium BC. Kenyon also discovered plaster models made by sculpting the plaster over human skulls (these proved difficult to excavate).

The Leakey Family

(1903-present)

The Leakey family has had a huge impact not only on archaeology, but also on the general understanding of how the human species has evolved. Several generations of Leakeys have conducted research in Africa, exploring finds related to early human and proto-human life.

Louis and Mary Leakey formed a legendary partnership in the history of African archaeology and in the founding of the modern science of palaeoanthropology. The Leakey name is synonymous with human origins research in East Africa, though the couple's contributions also shaped many adjacent fields of academic study, such as primatology.

African investigation

Kenyan-born Louis Leakey (1903-1972) studied archaeology and anthropology at Cambridge University, graduating in 1926. Suspecting that Africa was the cradle of human evolution, he returned to East Africa and began seeking hominid fossils. He later met Mary Douglas (1913-1996), an English archaeologist and illustrator, whom he married in 1937. In early work, Louis Leakey explored the existing idea that Africa had experienced intermittent wet periods (known as pluvials) that corresponded to the European Ice Ages. In this model, culture and change were explained by correlating archaeological industries and sequences and palaeoclimatic episodes.

The popularity of the pluvial hypothesis waned, and Louis devoted himself to palaeoanthropological studies. There were few early

breakthroughs, but in 1948 the couple made a notable find near Lake Victoria of an 18-20 million-year-old Miocene primate named *Proconsul africanus*. It is not ancestral to humans, but its discovery heralded remarkable future finds, assisted by what became known as 'Leakey's luck'.

Olduvai Gorge

Work in Olduvai Gorge, in northern Tanzania, focused world attention on the Leakeys' quest for human origins. Olduvai is a ravine 48km (30 miles) long and 91m (300ft) deep. Partly an ancient lake basin, it is made up of a

series of beds, representing a build-up of layers of lava, volcanic ash and water-borne sediments. The hominid fossil-bearing beds had accumulated over approximately 2 million years.

Assuming that different artefact cultures might be associated with different early human species, the Leakeys set out to find the fossil remains of the makers of the stone-tool industries found in Olduvai Gorge. Correlating hominid species and artefacts recalls the idea of the 'pluvial hypothesis', in which cultural materials were linked to climatic episodes. Mary Leakey meticulously

Right Meave Leakey (b.1942) has continued the family tradition of African research. Her work in the Turkana Basin in Kenya produced some of the oldest surviving hominid remains.

classified the Olduvai artefactual industries as the Oldowan, Developed Oldowan and Early Acheulean.

The Olduvai Gorge work bore fruit in 1959 when Mary discovered a hominid cranium in Bed II. They named it *Zinjanthropus boisei* (in honour of Charles Boise, whose funding had enabled the work). *Zinjanthropus*, now known as *Australopithecus boisei*, was a robust (heavily built) species of australopithecine (a species of extinct hominid). It is now known that it lived in different East African locations between 2.3 and 1.2 million years ago.

At the time of the discovery, scientists believed that humans had most likely evolved in Asia, and at a much later date. The australopithecines are now regarded by most palaeoanthropologists to have been in the direct line of human ancestry. However, neither Louis, Mary nor their son Richard, also an eminent palaeoanthropologist, endorsed this interpretation. The excitement generated by the discovery of 'Zinj' attracted funding from the National Geographic Society, which allowed the Leakeys to continue and deepen their important research.

In 1960 their searches revealed a mandible and other bones that came to be named *Homo habilis* ('handy man'). The Leakeys believed this was the first tool-making hominid and probably a direct human ancestor. It may have given rise to *Homo erectus* fossils, another species found at Olduvai. (Early African specimens are also named *H. ergaster*.)

In time, Richard Leakey's team at Koobi Fora and Lake Turkana would reveal many more *H. ergaster* specimens, as well as individuals of a species named *Homo rudolfensis*, contemporary with *H. habilis*. Anatomical studies aside, the existence at Olduvai of in situ (undisturbed) materials, including 'home bases' and butchery locations, has been proposed but also contested. Such sites offer opportunities for investigating early human behaviour and society.

Fossil footprints

In later years Mary remained in East Africa with her beloved dalmatians while Louis travelled the world, giving lectures and raising essential funding. Louis died in 1972. Mary continued working in East Africa and in 1976-77 made a unique and important find. A volcanic eruption approximately 3.6 million years ago,

Left An anthropologist examines Laetoli footprints during a 1995 excavation. The hominid prints discovered at Laetoli were accompanied by dozens of animal prints.

Above The Olduvai gorge has produced a wide range of rich archaeological finds, ranging from 2.3 million to 15,000 years old.

at Laetoli in northern Tanzania, had rained ash over two, and probably three, sets of footprints – perhaps 70 prints in all. Initially stamped in soft ground, they were preserved by the hardening ash. Scientific examination suggested a pattern of movement and weight-transference characteristic of a creature walking upright. Mary believed they were made by early *Homo*, but most now attribute them to *Australopithecus afarensis* – the same species as the famous 'Lucy' – from Ethiopia. The significance of the Laetoli footprints lies in the light the find may shed on human evolution. Formerly it had been thought that the hominids before *Homo* had not been bipedal and that tool use may have preceded upright walking techniques.

The Leakey legacy

Though best known for their East African discoveries, and their many books and monographs, the Leakeys' influence went further. Studies by the primatologists Jane Goodall, Dian Fossey and Birute Galdikas-Brindamour of chimpanzees, gorillas and orang-utans, respectively, were made possible by Louis Leakey's support. Mary Leakey is also remembered for recording Tanzanian rock art, dating to the more recent African past. She diligently worked on, almost until her death in 1996 at the age of 83.

The Leakeys' studies have helped many researchers to rethink existing ideas about a single line of human descent. Instead, it seems that some of the hominid species had evolved in parallel with each other. Most of all, their work truly established the importance of Africa as the place where our species evolved.

The work of the Leakey family in the field of human evolution is perpetuated by the Leakey Foundation and by scores of independent and associated international researchers. They include Richard Leakey's wife, Meave, whose work has brought new species of hominid to light and, most recently, their daughter Louise.

Below The skull of *Australopithecus boisei*, discovered at the Olduvai Gorge, Tanzania.

André Leroi-Gourhan

(1911-1986)

Leroi-Gourhan's abiding interest was in the Palaeolithic period, particularly in the study of cave art. He saw a sophistication in the distribution of art around a cave not previously observed, and he produced one of the defining books on the interpretion of this primitive art form.

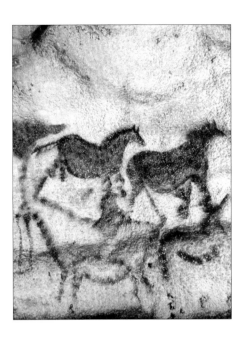

Above Leroi-Gourhan interpreted Palaeolithic art as structured and composed, rather than as a random collection of images.

André Leroi-Gourhan was a French archaeologist who made enormously important contributions to the excavation of Palaeolithic sites as well as to the study of Ice Age art. Born in Paris in 1911, he spent his early student years learning Russian and Chinese, after which he turned to ethnology and archaeology. He was involved in setting up Paris's Musée de l'Homme, of which he was a sub-director, and he was later professor at the Collège de France (1969-82).

Leroi-Gourhan carried out many major excavations, first in the caves of Arcy-sur-Cure – where he discovered the first known examples of ornaments made by Neanderthals – and subsequently at the late Ice Age open-air site of Pincevent near Paris, a camp of reindeer hunters. Here he pioneered techniques of horizontal excavation, the minute study and moulding of occupation floors, and ethnological reconstruction of the life of stone-age people.

Interpreting cave art

Leroi-Gourhan's huge book *Préhistoire de l'Art Occidental* (1965) embodied his revolutionary approach to Palaeolithic art. Previously, cave art had been seen as simple accumulations of figures (most notably by the Abbé Breuil) and interpreted through simplistic use of supposed analogies to modern cultures. Leroi-Gourhan, together with Annette Laming, strove to avoid such analogies, and saw the figures as purposefully arranged within each cave. He found that horses and bison dominated the art numerically, and tended to cluster in the central parts of the caves. He believed that horses were male symbols, and bison female, even when the bisons were clearly bulls.

Leroi-Gourhan was also the first to tackle the enigmatic 'signs' in Palaeolithic art, deciding that, like the animal figures, they constituted a dual system for exploring and explaining the world, which might perhaps be interpreted in the sexual terms of vulvar signs and phallic signs.

Subsequent work inevitably modified or cast doubt on much of this approach, but it nevertheless remains the single greatest contribution to the interpretation of Palaeolithic art.

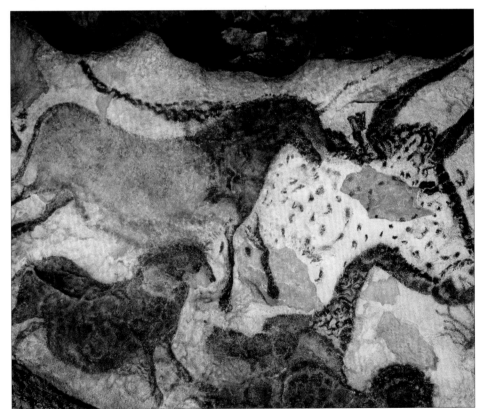

Left A detail from one of the reproduction cave paintings at Lascaux II, a facsimile site opened in France in 1983.

Spyridon Marinatos
(1901-1974)

*A Greek archaeologist with an international reputation, Marinatos
excavated several famous sites of the Aegean. One of his greatest finds was
the remains of an ancient Minoan city entombed beneath volcanic rock on
Thera, wiped out by a cataclysmic volcanic eruption around 1500 BC.*

Spyridon Marinatos was born on the Greek island of Kefalonia on 4 November 1901, a time when the earlier discovery of Mycenae and Knossos had heightened world interest in archaeology. At the age of 19, while still an undergraduate reading archaeology at Athens University, he was appointed an inspector of antiquities.

In 1929, after postgraduate study in Germany at Berlin and Halle, he became director of the Archaeological Museum of Heraklion, Crete. Here his excavations at the Villa of the Lilies (so called because fragments of frescoes found there depicted red and white lilies), and other buildings in the nearby settlement of Amnissos, gave him a valuable first-hand experience of Minoan archaeology.

The Thera volcano

Like other Minoan sites on Crete, Amnissos had been struck by an earthquake, then rebuilt, and was later mysteriously abandoned after a fire. Pumice found in a seafront building is said to have led Marinatos to think of the Cyclades island of Thera – modern Santorini – situated 100km (62 miles) to the north of Crete, which had been torn apart by a massive volcanic eruption. In 1939 Marinatios published in the journal *Antiquity* his theory that this eruption had actually taken place around 1500 BC, and had caused such devastation that it had brought about the demise of the flourishing Minoan civilization.

Marinatos proposed excavating on Santorini where, during the late 1800s, artefacts had been exposed by minor earthquakes and during quarrying. French, German and Greek archaeologists had dug around the village of Akrotiri, exposing the remains of ancient buildings. However, the outbreak of World War II and then the Greek Civil War made work impossible and Marinatos busied himself with other projects. In 1946 he travelled abroad in search of antiquities stolen by occupying forces, and during the 1950s he excavated the Minoan settlement and palace complex at Vathypetro, Crete, where he found a wine and olive press and a potter's kiln. Intending to turn Vathypetro into a museum, Marinatos had the remains reconstructed, for which he was criticized by his peers, since this made further excavation and interpretation difficult.

Left A view of the ancient city of Akrotiri, Thera, as it has emerged from the volcanic rock. Despite its great age, the site has been impressively preserved, with many staircases still standing alongside numerous pithoi (storage jars) and the framework of a sophisticated drainage system.

Excavating Akrotiri

Geologists had been sceptical about Marinatos's 1939 theories, arguing that earthquakes occurring on Santorini were never as powerful as he claimed. In the 1960s, however, American scientists from Columbia University found thick ash deposits in ooze that was dredged up from the Mediterranean. The ash was found to be from the Thera volcano and it covered so vast an area that the eruption that produced it must have been of the magnitude of the 1883 eruption of Krakatoa, Indonesia. Interest revived and in 1967 the Greek Archaeological Society licensed Marinatos, then General Inspector of Antiquities, to excavate on Santorini near the village of Akrotiri.

Marinatos's team chose a point on the southern tip of the island, where the tephra (solidified ash) was thinnest, and at about 30m (98ft) they uncovered streets, squares, multi-storey dwellings and workshops of the most important Minoan port outside Crete. The earliest pipes and water closets ever discovered showed that the port was inhabited by an advanced civilization that used cold water and hot (from thermal springs). Jars in ancient storerooms contained traces of olive oil and other food – but there were no skeletons, indicating that people had prior warning of the eruption and had fled.

Some of the dwellings excavated at Akrotiri displayed delicate, well-preserved Minoan frescoes. One depicts saffron-gatherers presenting their harvest of stamens to a seated figure, perhaps a goddess. In another two youths are shown boxing.

From 1968 Marinatos published annual reports of his findings at Akrotiri. His team uncovered just a corner of Akrotiri, however, and excavations continue to this day. Geologists have also recovered evidence that suggests that the Thera

eruption may have been many times the magnitude of Krakatoa, creating a dust cloud so great that it blocked out the sun for a prolonged period.

Marinatos also made other highly significant excavations that yielded important archaeological finds. In 1966 he unsuccessfully searched the seafloor for the fabled drowned city of Helike, but in the early 1970s he located the site of the Battle of Thermopylae and excavated the ancient burial mound constructed after the Battle of Marathon.

Marinatos was killed in an accident at Akrotiri in October 1974 when an ancient wall collapsed on him. At the site a fitting memorial marks his immeasurable contribution to the archaeology of the Aegean.

Right One of the most beautiful frescoes at Akrotiri is this young fisherman holding his catch on a string.

Harald Pager

(1923-1985)

Harald Pager was one of the most accomplished and dedicated rock art researchers of our time. His name is synonymous with Ndedema Gorge in southern Africa where he uncovered and meticulously recorded thousands of cave paintings.

Born and brought up in a small town in Czechoslovakia, Harald Pager settled in Austria after World War II, where he trained as an industrial designer and artist at an art college in Graz.

He emigrated to South Africa in 1956 where he worked as a commercial artist before embarking upon the recording of rock art made by the San (Bushmen), a Stone Age hunter-gatherer people.

Ndedema Gorge

In 1971 Pager's work was published in a large volume entitled *Ndedema*. This work is perhaps the most significant book on rock art ever produced. It documented five years' work with his wife Shirley-Ann, who always assisted him, locating and recording the rock paintings of one richly painted valley – Ndedema (now known as Didima) – in the Drakensberg Moutains, KwaZulu-Natal, South Africa. The couple found 17 sites in the 5.5-km (3.4-mile) long valley and meticulously recorded each of the almost 4000 individual images painted on the walls of the rock shelters.

The work was a milestone in South African rock-art research. Only in the 1950s had A.R. Willcox effectively and systematically first used colour photography in recording. Previously, recorders had relied on freehand drawings, watercolour copies and, later, monochrome photographs.

Only photography, with its total faithfulness to detail, reproduced the all-important details of the rock face, and only colour reproductions conveyed the palette on which the images rely for their visual impact. Pager, who was both visually and scientifically trained, recognized that colour photography was problematic in recording less well-preserved images. To accommodate this, he developed an innovative technique that entailed first photographing the paintings in black and white. The couple then returned to the site and painted onto the photographs with oil paints, which were carefully colour-matched.

Professor Raymond Dart's enthusiastic foreword to *Ndedema* hailed the book as the 'first and only' publication to be directly modelled on archaeological and scientific principles. Pager's precision recording included plotting every mark and compiling quantitative data, not only on subject matter but also on composition, perspective, technique and postures. The quantitative data are

Left Harald Pager at work copying a panel of three tall hunters and eland (Africa's largest antelope) at Botha's Shelter, Ndedema Gorge. The pigments used in the cave paintings were mainly black, white and orange, although there is great depth in this palette.

integrated into a detailed discussion of the archaeology of the Drakensberg San peoples and the environment of the region. Colour plates and line drawings of true virtuoso quality complete the tour de force.

Before relocating to Namibia, Pager published another important book on South African rock art, *Stone Age Myth and Magic*, comprising an extended discussion of the significance of the paintings.

Pager and rock art

Today, some researchers question the value of science for understanding art and culture. However, though in *Ndedema* Pager chose to suspend the question of aesthetics, his appreciation of visuality underpinned his approach. The shamanistic model, which subsequently emerged, reverted to analysing the art almost exclusively in terms of subject matter. That model has been widely criticized, for example by art historians, better equipped than anthropologists to appreciate Pager's close attention to the visual characteristics of the rock paintings.

Pager's visual acuity, and his vast and empathetic familiarity with the materials, enhanced his insights into San rock-art traditions. He was, for example, sceptical of the claim that the imagery derived from the hallucinations of 'shamans', noting that the shamanistic explanation was insufficiently tied to the paintings themselves and their visual attributes.

Namibian rock art

In 1978 Pager embarked on another, perhaps even more, ambitious recording programme, this time in the Brandberg Mountains, Namibia. There, together with two Namibian field assistants, he recorded nearly 900 sites containing over 40,000 figures. Five volumes have been published so far, covering the Amis Gorge, Hungorob Gorge, the Southern Gorges, Umuab and Karuab Gorges, Naib Gorge and the Northwest. Regrettably, the economics of publishing demanded reliance on line drawings rather than colour reproductions, but Pager's efforts have nevertheless resulted in a truly monumental record of the colour and vibrancy of Namibian art.

Harald Pager died prematurely in 1985. Though remembered for his recording, his legacy lies also in the domains of conservation and in raising awareness of African rock arts.

Right A crowded panel from Sebaaini Shelter, Ndedema Gorge. Many paintings are superimposed on other older paintings. There were 1146 paintings in all at the site when Harald Pager was there to copy them.

Tatiana Proskouriakoff

(1909-1985)

Proskouriakoff was one of the 20th century's pioneering researchers into Maya peoples and cultures. Training as an architectural artist enabled her to bring ruins to life in her published work, while her new interpretation of Maya hieroglyphics changed the way inscriptions are studied.

Above A Mayan stela (carved stone slab) from Piedras Negras. Many of the stone carvings depicted either rulers or local deities.

Born in Tomsk, Siberia, on 23 January 1909, Tatiana Proskouriakoff moved to the United States in 1916 where her chemist father was posted to oversee munitions production for the Russian war effort. She received a Bachelor of Science in Architecture from Pennsylvania State University in 1930. Lack of work as an architect during the Depression led her to take a job as illustrator at the university museum.

First expedition

Her work at the museum attracted the attention of archaeologist Linton Satterthwaite, who invited her to join his 1936 expedition to the site of Piedras Negras, Guatemala. So began her illustrious career as ethnologist and archaeologist. During her time at Piedras Negras, Proskouriakoff would create some of the best-known archaeological reconstructive drawings from sites all over the Maya world.

While studying the hieroglyphic inscriptions on monuments at Piedras Negras, Proskouriakoff noticed a repetitive pattern of dates and signs which she identified as a succession of seven rulers spanning 200 years. From this she demonstrated that Maya texts spoke of rites of passage and the major accomplishments of rulers, rather than – as had previously been believed – purely astronomical and calendrical knowledge. This work, on which current knowledge of epigraphy (study of inscriptions) is based, won Proskouriakoff the Alfred V. Kidder Medal (which she herself had designed) in 1962.

Over the course of her career, Proskouriakoff published numerous pioneering works, including *An Album of Maya Architecture* (1946), *A Study of Classic Maya Sculpture* (1950), *Portraits of Women in Maya Art* (1961) and *Jades from the Cenote of Sacrifice, Chichén Itzá, Yucatan* (1974). In addition to the Kidder Medal, she was awarded Pennsylvania State Woman of the Year (1971), honorary degrees from Tulane University and Pennsylvania State University, and the prestigious Order of the Quetzal from the people of Guatemala (1984). Her friends and family remember her as a disciplined scholar and free-spirited individual, who was not afraid to follow her ideas and contradict those of her colleagues. She died on 30 August 1985.

Left Maya hieroglyphs on a stela from Tikal, Guatemala. The complex writing system is made up of hundreds of unique signs, or glyphs, in the form of humans, animals, supernaturals, objects and abstract designs.

Maria Reiche

(1903-1998)

For over 50 years the German-born Maria Reiche devoted her life to exploring the Nasca lines in Peru. Her work revealed some of the secrets of the lines, while also helping to preserve this amazing archaeological phenomenon for future generations.

No major archaeological site is perhaps more closely linked with a single name and personality than the Nasca (Nazca) lines of Peru. These huge lines form designs etched into the desert between the Nasca and Ingenio river valleys, several hours' drive south of Lima. They would almost certainly have been destroyed long ago had it not been for the work of Maria Reiche.

Reiche was born in Dresden, Germany, in 1903. Her father, a judge, died in World War I, and her mother, who had studied in England as well as Berlin, taught and did other work to support the family. Reiche spoke and read several languages, and she studied mathematics at Hamburg and Dresden and became a teacher. In 1932 she left Germany to accept a position as governess to a family in Cuzco, Peru, later moving to Lima where she made a living teaching and working as a translator at San Marcos University. It was through her academic connections there that she was eventually drawn to Nasca.

Desert lines

The Nasca lines had been virtually unknown until commercial air traffic began in Peru during the 1920s. Pilots for Faucett, the first company to run flights between Lima and the southern city of Arequipa, noticed huge lines, triangles and other markings on the desert pampa to the north of the town of Nasca.

The Peruvian archaeologist Toribio Mejía Xesspe conducted the first formal study of the lines in 1927, publishing an article in which he suggested that the lines were ancient ceremonial pathways. In 1941 the American historian Paul Kosok, who had come to Peru to study ancient irrigation canal systems and the origins of Andean civilization, became interested in the Nasca lines. He observed that some of the lines

Left This glyph of a dog is one of the most complex of the Nasca figures.

Above An aerial photograph of the outline of a hummingbird. Like other Nasca lines, it can be recognized as a coherent figure only from the air.

marked the winter solstice from a central location and theorized that the lines might have been used to make astronomical and calendrical observations. Kosok had hired Reiche to make translations for him, and he inspired her to begin researching the Nasca lines in her own right.

The Nasca lines consist of a huge complex of gigantic figures etched into the surface of the desert across nearly 40km (25 miles) of the south coast of Peru. Most of the lines form geometric designs, including loops, triangles and other forms, but some 30 or so of the designs on the Nasca plain itself are figures, mostly animals.

The many lines were made by removing rocks and sand that had been blackened by centuries of exposure to the elements (forming the surface known as 'desert varnish'), leaving lighter coloured lines on the surface of the plain. The designs, and the pottery associated with the lines, indicate that they were made by the ancient Nasca, a civilization known for its spectacular polychrome pottery and masterful use of underground water resources for irrigation of the desert. The Nasca culture thrived during what is known as the Early Intermediate Period, beginning roughly 2000 years ago and lasting for approximately 600 or 700 years.

Left The Nasca monkey with its huge spiral tail was first recognized by Maria Reiche in 1946. Such is the scale of the artworks, that they probably took several hundred years to complete.

A life's work

Reiche's work on the Nasca lines began after the end of World War II, when she was allowed to move freely in Peru after a period of severe restrictions on German citizens ended. She spent virtually all of her remaining years living there, mostly in primitive conditions, studying the lines and working for their preservation. Although she received some funding, and occasional support (particularly in the area of aerial photography) from the Peruvian military, plus the attention of scholars and intellectuals inside and outside of Peru, she worked largly alone. She battled to save the lines from destruction due to increasing traffic from the Panamerican highway and other development. Peru's National Cultural Institute declared the lines an intangible zone in 1970, laying an important foundation for their protection. It was Maria Reiche, however, who hired and paid the guards that protected the lines.

Regarded for many years as a somewhat eccentric foreigner by the local people, Reiche eventually became a revered member of the community as tourism, based largely on the fame of the lines, began to take off in the 1970s. She spent the latter years of her life installed in the relative luxury of the Tourist Hotel in Nasca, becoming one of its major attractions herself. By the 1980s she was suffering from glaucoma and Parkinson's disease, but she continued to give daily lectures to visitors and to advocate her theory that the lines had been made by Nasca astronomers to mark major calendrical events.

Maria Reiche believed strongly in her own theories of the Nasca lines, paying little attention to the work of other scholars, and she saved the lines and carefully documented them. Scientific studies of the lines have demonstrated that some do mark major calendrical events, such as the summer and winter solstice, but many do not. Current theories about their significance focus on Andean cosmology and posit that some may have served to guide pilgrimages, ceremonial processions and other rituals. The lines have drawn the interest of scientists and pseudo-scientists for the past 50 years. Although many scholars disagree with Reiche's theories about the purpose of the lines, they all acknowledge that without her they would not be there today for us to study.

Above The Nasca lines, including this impressive parrot, were declared a UNESCO World Heritage Site in 1995.

Below The surface of the Nasca desert (one of the driest in the world) consists of rock, not sand, hence the Nasca lines have been preserved.

John Howland Rowe

(1918-2004)

His total dedication to accurate research and his vast knowledge of the history of South America made John Rowe a world authority on Andean culture and history. His seminal 1946 paper on the Inca at the time of the Spanish Conquest remains an international standard reference.

John Howland Rowe is one of the most important figures in the development of Andean archaeology as an academic discipline in the United States. His work is likely to have a deep and lasting importance over archaeological debate for years to come. While many American archaeologists focused on field work and techniques of analysis in archaeology, and worked in multiple areas applying basically similar approaches to different regions, Rowe emphasized a different approach – deep expertise in a single region. Furthermore, instead of applying one academic approach to multiple regions or sites, he applied approaches from multiple disciplines – including archaeology, history and linguistics – to the study of the Andean past, and especially to the history of the Inca. Unsurpassed in his knowledge of the Inca for more than a generation, his

Below The carved rock 'Inca throne', one of the key features of the Inca temple (or fortress) overlooking Cuzco at Sacsayhuaman, Peru.

interpretations of Inca history and archaeology formed the basis for virtually all research on the Inca in the late 20th century.

Beginnings

Rowe stated that he had been interested in archaeology from the time he was three years old. He was born on 10 June 1918, in Sorrento, Maine. His father, Louis Earl Rowe, had spent a single field season in Egypt, an experience that left him with a lifelong interest in the ancient past which he passed on to his son.

John Rowe studied classical archaeology at Brown University before moving to Harvard to study anthropology, receiving his master's degree in 1941. From there he went to Peru, where he conducted research and taught in Cuzco before serving with the US Combat Engineers in Europe between 1944 and 1946. He later returned to Harvard, where he received his Ph.D. in Latin American History and Anthropology in 1947. Rowe was hired by the University of California at Berkeley in 1948 and he spent the rest of his career there, teaching and building the anthropology library at one of the premier anthropology departments in the United States.

Rowe's scholarship was greatly influenced by his background in classical studies. The study of classical archaeology required proficiency in ancient languages, as well as in history, art styles and archaeology. Rowe's linguistic abilities and training enabled him to master Spanish easily and then to learn Quechua, the language of the Inca that was still widely spoken in Cuzco and other areas of Peru. He was also able to read and understand Spanish colonial records of many kinds. His application of art historical techniques of stylistic analysis led to a rigorous approach to definition and classification of the iconographic and artistic styles of archaeological cultures of the Andes, an approach that he passed on to his students.

Study method

Rowe believed in studying data in great detail. He read colonial documents thoroughly and assessed their relevance and also the accuracy of their information based on his knowledge of Inca history and archaeology. His reliance on historical evidence, and particularly on those sources that he viewed as reliable, led him to discredit many other previously well-regarded sources, or at least portions of what they said.

His most influential body of work is his description of Inca civilization before the Spanish conquest, as well as his interpretations of the impact of the Spanish on the indigenous culture during the early colonial era. His most widely read paper is called 'Inca Culture at the Time of the Spanish Conquest', published in the multivolume *Handbook of South American Indians* in 1946. In this and related works, Rowe synthesized his knowledge and interpretations of Inca civilization and provided a picture of Inca society that scholars, tour guides and interested lay persons could grasp.

A lasting contribution

Rowe left an important legacy to archaeology in the students he trained both in the United States and Peru, the scholarly organization he founded, with its academic journal dedicated to Andean studies, and the anthropology library he founded at the University of California. His scholarly papers and editorial productions number more than 300 from 1940 to 2005, with a large proportion in Spanish.

His emphasis on detailed knowledge and deep understanding of the available data set high standards that have helped Andean archaeology to grow as a discipline. His interpretations of the Inca remain important, even as the details of the Inca civilization are clarified and modified by new research. Rowe retired in 1988, but continued research work until his death in Berkeley in 2004.

Below A figurine depicting one of the 'chosen women' (often called 'Virgins of the Sun'), who were concubines of the Inca emperor and given to seal political marriage alliances between Inca and other societies.

Sir J. Eric Thompson

(1898-1975)

The English archaeologist John Eric Sidney Thompson is widely regarded as the pre-eminent scholar of the pre-Columbian Maya civilization of the first half of the 20th century. He made a lasting contribution to the decipherment of Maya.

Above A detail of a carving at the ruined Maya city of Coba. Thompson published a detailed description of the site in 1932.

Thompson was born in London on 31 December 1898. He was sent to Winchester College in 1912, but at the outbreak of World War I he joined the army under the assumed name Neil Winslow, giving false information about his age. An injury ended his army career with the Coldstream Guards in 1918. After working as a gaucho in Argentina, he went on to study anthropology at Cambridge University.

Researching the Maya

In 1926 Thompson went to Chichén Itzá, Mexico, to work with the celebrated Mayanist Sylvanus Morley of the Carnegie Institution. During his time with the Institution, Thompson was sent to numerous sites around the Maya world. Most notable were his travels through the British Honduras (Belize). His work there involved some of the first excavations of smaller sites beyond elite ceremonial centres, focusing on the lives of 'common' Maya. During this time he also gathered information from many modern Maya people, recognizing the continuity of certain beliefs and practices that dated all the way back to pre-Hispanic times.

Thompson was also sent to the Maya site of Coba in Mexico, and his report of the large ruined city and its many hieroglyphic inscriptions prompted Sylvanus Morley to carry out a more thorough investigation of the remote site.

Thompson's work produced a correlation between the Maya calendar and the Gregorian calendar that remains in use to this day. During the 1940s he also conducted considerable work on the decipherment of Maya hieroglyphics, developing a numerical cataloguing system for the glyphs that survives in the modern discipline.

Thompson was a prolific writer and was passionate about transferring his knowledge to the wider world. His incredible corpus of respected publications includes *The Civilisation of the Mayas* (1927), *Ethnology of the Mayas of Southern and Central British Honduras* (1930), *Maya Hieroglyphic Writing: Introduction* (1950), *A Catalogue of Maya Hieroglyphs* (1962), *Maya History and Religion* (1970), and also an amusing autobiography entitled *Maya Archaeologist* (1963).

Thompson received many honours in recognition of his work and was knighted in 1975, shortly before his death in Cambridge that year.

Left An aerial view of the ruins at Coba. Thompson made his first visit through the jungle by mule while on his honeymoon.

Michael Ventris

(1922-1956)

By the time he was 30, Michael Ventris had deciphered Europe's oldest written language, which had been found half a century before in engravings on clay tablets at Knossos. He proved what experts had refused to consider: that Linear B writing was an archaic form of ancient Greek.

Michael Ventris was a 14-year-old schoolboy when he attended a lecture and exhibition on Minoan civilization given in London by the 86-year-old archaeologist Sir Arthur Evans. On display were tablets engraved with a script which, Ventris was told, no one could decipher. When excavating Knossos, the Minoan palace-complex on Crete, in 1901, Evans had excavated more than 3,000 tablets and had identified their faint engravings as writing. Evans distinguished a hieroglyphic script and two scripts composed of glyphs and other symbols, which he named 'Linear A' and 'Linear B'. Certain that they were examples of Minoan writing, Evans devoted the next several decades to their decipherment but to no avail.

Ventris, who had learned Polish from his mother, French and German during his childhood in Switzerland, and studied Latin and Greek at his English prep school, resolved to decode the hieroglyphics of Linear B. At 18 he published his first conclusions – that Linear B was the script of the Etruscans – in the *American Journal of Archaeology*, which aroused academic interest.

Background

Rather than read classics at university, however, Ventris trained as an architect, enrolling at the Architectural Association School of Architecture in 1940. In 1943, with World War II at its height, he joined the RAF and flew as a navigator but continued his professional training after the war. He also worked diligently on deciphering the elusive Linear B in his spare time.

Leaps in the dark

An American philologist Alice Kober had already prepared some of the groundwork for the decipherment of Linear B by working out a grid expressing the relationships between vowels and consonants in the script. After Kober's death in 1950, Ventris built on her work. Inspired guesses speeded his progress. For example, he assumed that the most common symbol was the vowel 'a'; that certain symbols followed by glyphs were women's names and others men's; and that commonly occurring symbols on the tablets found on Crete, but not on others excavated on the Greek mainland, were town names.

As he deciphered more of the hieroglyphics, Ventris noticed a connection between Linear B and the ancient Greek language. A link with Greek had been firmly rejected for 50 years, but in 1952 Ventris publicized this idea in a BBC talk. Afterwards, he received an offer of assistance from John Chadwick, a recognized specialist in archaic Greek.

The two men deciphered the tablets more completely and in 1953 they jointly published their conclusions: Linear B, they announced, was a written form of the ancient Greek used by the first Greeks – the Mycenaeans – and was used from around 1450 BC. The discovery met first with scepticism, then with acclaim. Yet for Ventris it marked the end of his obsession with Linear B.

Having solved the problem, his interest waned. He returned briefly to architecture but, dissatisfied with his achievements, soon abandoned it. Always a loner, he had little to fall back on: his marriage had failed; his children had become strangers. On 6 September 1956, he died in a car accident at the age of just 34.

Below A clay tablet from the Mycenaean Palace at Pylos, in Greece. The Linear B tablets revealed financial records and lists of livestock and agricultural produce, tableware, textiles and furniture.

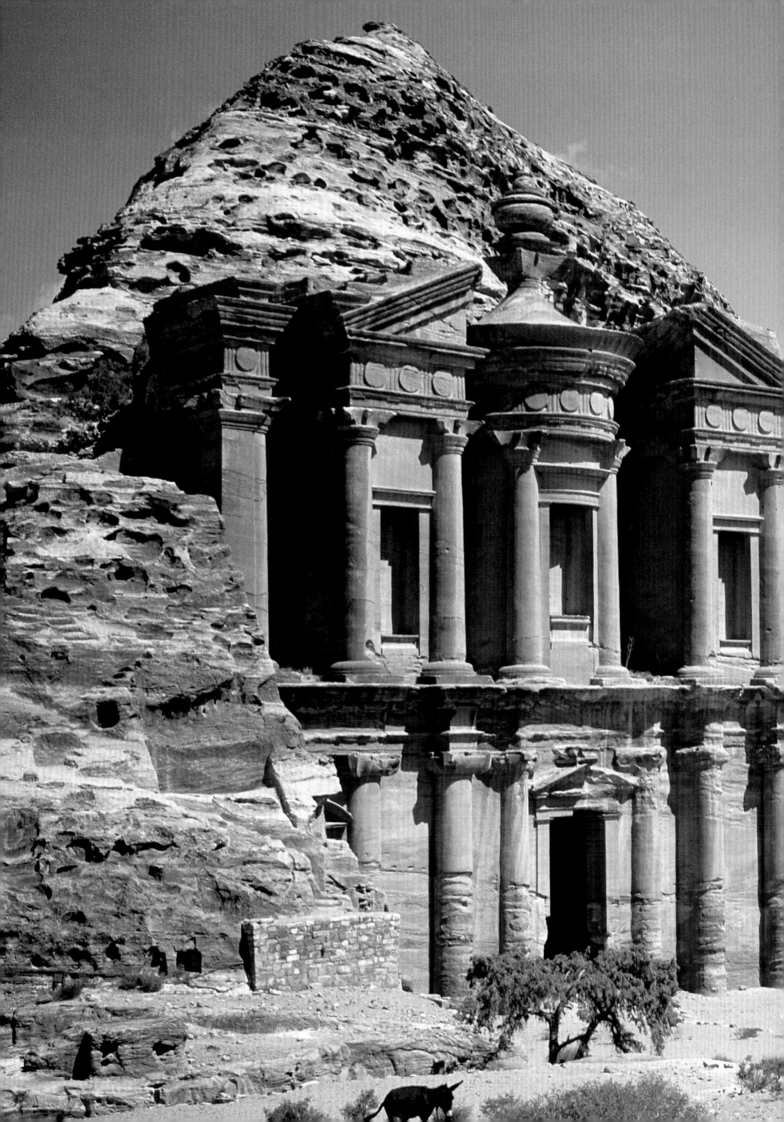

ARCHAEOLOGICAL SITES

'Match me such marvel save in Eastern clime,
A rose-red city half as old as time.'

J.W. BURGON (1845)

The beautiful rock-hewn tomb façades of Petra, a desert city rediscovered in 1812, stand as an enduring testament to the skill and vision of our ancestors. Other equally impressive sites from across the ages and continents are explored in the following chapters.

Saqqara This vast necropolis contains an array of monuments, including mastaba tombs and pyramids.

Giza The royal pyramid complex includes the Great Pyramid of Khufu, one of the Wonders of the Ancient World.

Karnak From the New Kingdom, this complex was the most important religious establishment in the Egyptian empire.

Zawiyet Umm el-Rakham

Giza
Saqqara
Amarna
Abydos
Karnak/Thebes
Valley of the Kings
Abu Simbel

Saharan rock art

S a h a r a
D e s e r t

Red Sea

Nile

Lake Nasser

Meroe

Lake Tana

Blue Nile
White Nile

Lalibela

A F R I C A

Ife
Benin

South Atlantic Ocean

Lake Victoria

Indian Ocean

Great Zimbabwe
Mapungubwe

MADAGASCAR

Sterkfontein, Swartkrans, and Kromdraai

Ife and Benin Ancient cities in what is present-day southern Nigeria have yielded a remarkable series of sculptures.

Blombos Cave

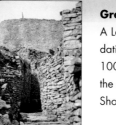

Great Zimbabwe A Late Iron Age site dating back around 1000 years. Once the capital of a vast Shona empire.

Lalibela A site in Ethiopia noted for its impressive churches, some of which are cut from solid rock.

THE GREAT SITES OF AFRICA

This vast continent contains some of the most spectacular and important archaeology in the world. There is the stunning prehistoric rock art of the Sahara, for example, with its depictions of crocodiles and elephants bearing witness to more clement and humid times in that region; and the equally beautiful but different rock art found in southern Africa. In South and East Africa are the numerous sites that have yielded so many fossil specimens of our earliest ancestors – the hominids. The continent also has astonishing and impressive structures, such as the rock-cut churches of Lalibela and the tower of Great Zimbabwe. Above all there is Egypt, whose temples and tombs have enchanted the world for centuries and whose ancient remains have given rise to an entire branch of archaeology.

Large parts of this continent remain virtually unexplored archaeologically, so there are bound to be many more exciting discoveries still to be made.

Rock art The Tassili N'Ajjer range in the Sahara is known for rock art made over a long period.

Valley of the Kings Egypt's New Kingdom rulers were buried in rock-cut tombs.

The Great Sphinx The colossal statue guards the entrance to the mortuary complex at Giza.

Sterkfontein, Swartkrans and Kromdraai

The fossil sites of Sterkfontein, Swartkrans and Kromdraai, north of Johannesburg, South Africa, are known as 'the cradle of humankind' and have been accorded World Heritage Site status. These sites are especially rich in australopithecine fossils.

The cave system at Sterkfontein has revealed a sequence of deposits with fossils dating from 3.5 to 1.5 million years ago. Between 1936 and 1947 excavations were carried out by Dr Robert Broom. He was following in the footsteps of Raymond Dart, who in 1924 described the first *Australopithecus* specimen – the Taung child – in South West Province, South Africa. In 1936 Broom found the first adult *Australopithecus africanus* fossil at Sterkfontein. In 1938 his work revealed more *A. africanus* specimens at Kromdraai.

Excavations at the nearby Swartkrans cave provided evidence of another species of australopithecine. It was

Right Mrs Ples is the most complete cranium of an Australopithecus africanus **ever** found in Africa.

named 'Paranthropus', but it is now usually classified as *Australopithecus robustus*, because of its heavier, more muscular build. It differs from other australopithecines, as well as humans, on account of its larger teeth and jaw and the presence of a sagittal crest – a ridge of bone along the top of the skull to which powerful jaw muscles were attached.

One of Broom's most celebrated finds was a well-preserved skull, around 2.7 million years old. It was discovered at the Sterkfontein Caves in 1947 and was originally classified by Broom as belonging to the genus *Plesianthropus*, (meaning 'almost human'). The skull was dubbed 'Mrs Ples' by the media. Today it is recognized as *Australopithecus africanus*. It is also thought that the skull may, in fact, have been that of a young male. Working at Swartkrans with John Robinson, Broom also discovered *Homo erectus* (or *ergaster*) remains. *Homo habilis* fossils have also been identified at Sterkfontein.

Further finds

Researchers have built on the work of Broom and his contemporaries. Almost two decades of work at Swartkrans by Dr Bob Brain have been celebrated in both the scientific arena and in the popular imagination – for example in Bruce Chatwin's book *The Songlines*. Brain's finds included over 120 hominids belonging to the genera of *Australopithecus* and *Homo*.

Brain's careful analysis of the australopithecine bones revealed a pattern of tooth marks. The shape and

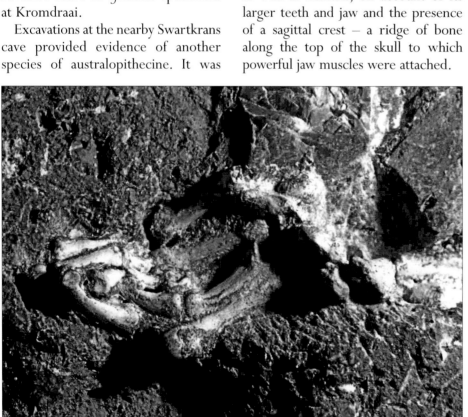

Left These are the hand bones of a 3.3 million-year-old australopithecine fossil, found at Sterkfontein in 1998.

Left The hand (top), arm (middle) and skull (bottom) of Clarke's 3.3 million-year-old find, embedded in the rock at Sterkfontein.

The first use of fire

Brain and his colleagues also noticed that a number of the bones from Swartkrans had been burnt. Using a technique known as electronic spin resonance, they were able to estimate the temperatures at which the bones were burnt. Some of the bones were burnt at the high temperatures often associated with campfires, rather than at the low temperatures normally linked to bushfires. So the Swartkrans bones may represent the earliest hominid use of fire, although it is not clear which of the species present at Swartkrans — *A. robustus* or *H. erectus* — might have been responsible.

'Little Foot'

In 1994 Dr Ron Clarke was examining boxes of fossils excavated from Sterkfontein in the 1970s, when he discovered four australopithecine foot bones that fitted together. The bones displayed both human and ape-like features. Clarke and his colleagues concluded that this hominid (Stw 573) might have been adapted for both bipedal (upright) walking and tree-climbing. The boxes contained several more foot and leg bones from the same individual, and Clarke wondered whether the remainder were still in situ in the cave.

Amazingly, a search located more bones from the individual, including an arm, hand and complete skull. It is likely that a near-complete skeleton may be assembled. The hand bones seem to confirm the idea that the creature was at least partly adapted for arboreal (tree) living. This important fossil is probably around 3.3 million years old.

The deposits at Sterkfontein, Swartkrans and Kromdraai are of international importance in studies of human evolution. Continuing work will no doubt reveal further exciting finds that shed light on our ancestors and their way of life.

spacing of the puncture holes were consistent with their having been made by the canine teeth of a large leopard-like carnivore. Brain hypothesized that these australopithecines had been killed by large cats, such as leopards and sabre tooths. Like leopards today, the animals probably dragged their kill into trees. The bones are thought to have fallen into sinkholes, where they became part of the bone-bearing breccias ('breccia' refers to rock composed of sharp-angled fragments within a fine-grained matrix).

Blombos Cave

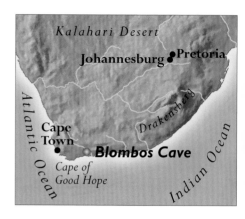

Excavations at Blombos Cave, a site on South Africa's south coast overlooking the Indian Ocean, have uncovered Stone Age finds of international interest. Preservation is unusually good because limestone caves are conducive to the survival of organic materials such as bone.

The deposits, more than 4m (13ft) deep in some places, date mainly to the Middle Stone Age. The uppermost levels indicate that the site was used by Later Stone Age hunter-gatherers in the last two millennia.

Ancient finds

A team of researchers, led by Dr Christopher Henshilwood, have been working at Blombos Cave since 1991. The artefacts found in the Middle Stone Age levels include the oldest known bone tools, such as projectile points and awls; bifacial tools (shaped on both sides); and perhaps the earliest evidence for fishing. The most exciting finds are pieces of engraved pigment (ochre) and perforated shells that may be the oldest known jewellery.

Modern human behaviour

These important finds at Blombos Cave have contributed to debates about 'modern human behaviour'.

Above Some of the oldest known bone tools have been found in unusually large numbers at the Blombos Cave.

Modern humans, at least anatomically, originated in Africa probably between 120,000 and 150,000 years ago. Some researchers believe that modern human behaviour formed gradually, alongside anatomical evolution, but others believe that there was a more abrupt change, with modern human consciousness emerging only about 40,000 years ago. Researchers regard the capacity for 'symbolic thought' as fundamental to modern human behaviour. In archaeological terms, it is indicated by the making of visual art, decoration of the person (body painting and jewellery suggesting a new awareness of selfhood) and ritual behaviour (for example, attention to death and burial).

The Blombos Cave discoveries suggest that modern human behaviour was in place about 75,000 years ago. The finds include tens of thousands of pieces of red ochre (an iron ore used worldwide as a pigment). Two ochre slabs from Blombos Cave are marked with incised lines. Some researchers believe that this is 'art' – evidence of an emerging human capacity to think abstractly, using symbols. Others remain more sceptical about regarding the marks as 'art' and as evidence for prehistoric peoples intentionally forging symbolic 'meanings'.

Excavations have also revealed a remarkable collection of shells, which seem to have been deliberately perforated, from a tiny species of mollusc that lived in a nearby estuary. The shells, which carry traces of red ochre and show signs of wear, may be the world's oldest known beads.

The Blombos Cave finds have raised new questions about the timing of the emergence of modern human behaviour and its relationship to the evolution of the body and brain.

Left The early artist decorated pieces of ochre with an array of carved lines. Many experts regard these markings as being early evidence of the human ability to think symbolically.

Saharan rock art

The Sahara Desert is extremely rich in ancient rock paintings and petroglyphs (rock carvings). This rock art is testimony to a time when the environment of the region was wetter and the landscape was home to hunting and herding peoples.

There are tens of thousands of rock-art sites in the moutainous areas, with Algeria's Tassili N'Ajjer range being particularly rich in paintings and Libya's Messak range in engravings.

Subjects and dating

These paintings and petroglyphs are among the most spectacular in the world; however, they are difficult to date. Paintings seldom contain sufficient amounts of carbon for radiocarbon dating, and the technique cannot be applied to petroglyphs. Accordingly, the dating of Saharan rock art has depended largely on

Above A rock painting from the 2nd millennium BC, featuring people and cattle.

subject matter and style, which are correlated with environmental and economic changes.

The subjects chosen by the ancient rock artists are diverse, although – as in other African rock-painting traditions – human figures and animals predominate. A few specialists believe that some of the images date to the end of the last Ice Age, more than 10,000 years ago. Most, however, attribute the earliest figures to the Bubalus period, from the late 6th to the mid-4th millennium BC. Subjects from this period include animals that are now extinct, such as the buffalo *Bubalus antiquus*. The Cattle period follows, a period lasting to the mid-2nd millennium BC, and linked to the introduction of pastoralism (herding). The images feature not only cattle but also various wild animals. The next phase has been dubbed the Horse

Above The sandstone outcrops of the Tassili N'Ajjer range present a barren scene today, but once this was savannah landscape, populated with an abundance of animals.

period, and in later phases camels are also depicted, as are chariots and charioteers. It is hoped that this general chronological scheme will eventually be refined by direct dating.

Interpretations

As with rock art elsewhere, interpreting these images has been difficult. A variety of strange and fanciful ideas have been applied to Saharan rock art, from the existence of 'Martians' in the Tassili to recent notions about 'shamans', 'trance' and hallucinogenic mushrooms. It is far more sensible and plausible, however, to relate the images to mythologies and rituals, such as rites of passage.

Giza

The three pyramids at Giza represent the pinnacle of tomb architecture. King Khufu's Great Pyramid is the oldest and last-surviving Wonder of the Ancient World. For more than 4000 years it was the tallest monument ever built. To this day it is still the largest stone monument in the world.

The Giza cemetery lies on a plateau by the Old Kingdom capital, Memphis. First used in Early Dynastic times, it became a royal necropolis when the 4th Dynasty King Khufu (Cheops), who reigned from 2551 to 2528 BC, chose the site for his pyramid complex.

The Great Pyramid

Khufu's Great pyramid has sides that vary by less than 5cm (2in) and the base is almost completely level. The pyramid was once cased in Tura limestone, but it was removed in the Middle Ages and reused in the building of Cairo.

The 12th-century writer Abou Abdallah Mohammed Ben Abdurakim Alkaisi claimed that the first modern pyramidologist, Caliph El Ma'mun, forced his way into the pyramid with a battering ram and discovered Khufu's mummy. However, the pyramid had been looted centuries ago, so this is unlikely. The first significant investigation was led by the astronomer John Greaves, who published his results in 1646. In 1763 Nathaniel Davison explored the well that dropped from the Grand Gallery, and in 1817 Captain Giovanni Battista Caviglia connected the well to the descending passageway.

The chambers

Three chambers inside the pyramid are linked by passageways. From the entrance on the north face a steep passageway drops to enter the Subterranean Chamber, an unfinished underground room of ritual significance. The ascending passageway leads to the Grand Gallery, a corridor with walls made from seven layers of limestone blocks. The west wall of the Gallery includes the entrance to the horizontal passageway leading to the Queen's Chamber. This chamber had a ritual purpose but was not used for a queen's burial. The Grand Gallery leads upwards to an

Below The three pyramids dominate the skyline to the west of Cairo. The original casing stones are still visible at the top of Khaefre's pyramid (centre).

antechamber, then to the red granite burial chamber, known as the King's Chamber. 'Air-shafts' (long, narrow passageways), which are orientated towards the northern pole star and the constellation of Orion, lead from the King's and the Queen's Chambers.

Boat pits

Khufu's pyramid was surrounded by a narrow courtyard defined by a limestone wall. The only access to this area was via a walled causeway, which linked the pyramid mortuary temple to the valley temple – now lost under the modern suburb of Nazlet el-Simman. Five boat-shaped pits were excavated close to the causeway and mortuary temple, but these were empty when opened. Two narrow, rectangular pits dug parallel to the south side of the pyramid outside the enclosure wall, discovered in 1954, held dismantled wooden boats. One boat remains sealed in its tomb, but the other boat has been conserved and fully reassembled, and it is displayed in a museum near the pyramid.

Queens' pyramids

A small satellite pyramid lay outside the enclosure wall to the south-east of Khufu's pyramid. Three larger queens' pyramids, with mortuary chapels, lay to the east of this satellite pyramid. All three were robbed in antiquity, but a shaft discovered to the east of the Great Pyramid in 1925 has yielded the burial equipment and jewellery of Queen Hetepheres, mother of Khufu. Although the shaft held Hetepheres's canopic jars and sarcophagus, there was no sign of the queen's body.

Khaefre's pyramid

Khufu's son, Khaefre (reigned 2520-2494 BC), built his mortuary complex to the south of the Great Pyramid. His pyramid is smaller than Khufu's but is built on higher ground, and this, together with its steeper angle, makes it appear the larger of the two. Khaefre's pyramid had a subterranean burial chamber that was built, lined and roofed in a large, open trench before the pyramid was erected on top. The entrance, about 11m (35ft) up the northern face, was well hidden. In 1818 Giovanni Battista Belzoni realized that the entrance was not in the centre of the northern face. When he

Right An armchair, adorned with gold, was included in the grave goods provided for Queen Hetepheres.

Left The Great Sphinx faces due east, the direction of the rising sun. The statue is crumbling today because of the wind, humidity and the smog from Cairo.

Beyond this a horizontal passage, guarded by three granite portcullises, leads to a rectangular antechamber that may have once been intended to serve as a burial chamber. A descending corridor drops from the anteroom floor to the burial chamber and a ritual 'cellar'. From the northern wall of the antechamber, directly above the entrance from the horizontal passage, a corridor led up through the bulk of the pyramid before petering out, unfinished, in a rough upper chamber.

Human remains

The burial chamber yielded a basalt sarcophagus carved with elaborate panelling. In 1838 it was dispatched to the British Museum in London, but it was lost when the ship carrying it foundered off the Spanish coast.

The sarcophagus had been empty when rediscovered, but the chamber at the end of the blind upper passage yielded a wooden coffin with some human remains: a pair of legs, a lower

reached the burial chamber he found a graffito scrawled by 'The Master Mohammed Ahmed, stonemason'.

Today, Khaefre's complex (pyramid, mortuary temple, causeway and valley temple) is the most complete of the Giza three and is the only one to retain some of its Tura limestone casing.

The Great Sphinx

Looking towards the rising sun, the Great Sphinx crouches beside Khaefre's Valley Temple. It is an awesome 72m (236ft) long and 20m (65ft) tall and is Egypt's largest statue. Its human head, which is perhaps Khaefre's own, is about 22 times life-size, with eyes 6ft (2m) high. Today, the Sphinx is clean-shaven, but it would have sported a long, plaited, curved beard of the type worn by gods and deified kings. As the Great Sphinx is carved from a natural rocky outcrop covered in places with a stone block veneer, the statue has sustained differential weathering due to the three limestone strata in its body.

Menkaure's pyramid

Khaefre was succeeded by his son Menkaure (reigned 2490-2472 BC), who also chose to build at Giza. His

pyramid was aligned with those of Khufu and Khaefre but, as space was now somewhat limited, it was built on a smaller scale. To compensate, the bottom layers of the pyramid were cased in expensive red granite. The pyramid casing was removed by Mohammed Ali Pahsa (1805-48); the first European to enter the pyramid was Colonel Howard Vyse (1837).

From the pyramid entrance on the north face, a passageway drops down through the masonry and into the bed-rock before opening into a chamber.

Below A papyrus dating from about 1000 BC shows workers dragging a shrine towards a tomb. The workmen who built the pyramids at Giza would have used a similar dragging technique to move large blocks of stone.

ANCIENT EGYPT TIMELINE

Periods/dynasties	Dates
Late Predynastic Period	3100-2950 BC
Early Dynastic Period (1st-3rd Dynasties)	2950-2575 BC
Old Kingdom (4th-8th Dynasties)	2575-2150 BC
1st Intermediate Period (9th-11th Dynasties)	2125-1975 BC
Middle Kingdom (11th-14th Dynasties)	1975-1640 BC
2nd Intermediate Period (15th-17th Dynasties)	1630-1520 BC
New Kingdom (18th-20th Dynasties)	1539-1075 BC
3rd Intermediate Period (21st-25th Dynasties)	1075-715 BC
Late Period (26th-30th Dynasties, 2nd Persian Period)	715-332 BC
Greco-Roman Period (Macedonians, Ptolemies and Romans)	332 BC-AD 395

torso, and some ribs and vertebrae wrapped in cloth. These remains have been dated by radiocarbon analysis to the Roman Period. The wooden coffin, which is inscribed for 'Osiris, the King of Upper and Lower Egypt, Menkaure, living forever' has been dated, based on stylistic grounds, to the 26th Dynasty Saite Period. The coffin is more than half a millennium older than its bones, and neither is dated to the time of Menkaure.

Khentkawes's tomb

The late 4th/early 5th Dynasty Queen Khentkawes I built her tomb to the south of Khaefre's pyramid and connected it by a causeway to Menkaure's valley temple. This imposing structure, complete with its associated 'pyramid village', was initially misclassified as a pyramid. Further investigation has revealed it to be a mastaba-style superstructure perched on top of a natural rock base, cased in fine Tura limestone.

Inside Khentkawes's tomb a granite-lined chamber allows access to a descending passage leading to the antechamber, burial chamber and a series of storerooms. Here were recovered the fragments of a smashed alabaster sarcophagus but no other signs of burial. A granite doorway

Above A statue of Menkaure with the goddess Hathor on his right and a goddess representing the seventh nome (administrative district) of Upper Egypt on his left.

names Queen Khentkawes, lists her titles and then adds a cryptic phrase which can, with equal validity, be translated either as 'King of Upper and Lower Egypt and Mother of the King of Upper and Lower Egypt' or as 'Mother of the Two Kings of Upper and Lower Egypt'. It is clear that Queen Khentkawes was an important woman, who was rewarded with a regal-style burial close to Egypt's most prominent funerary monuments.

Saqqara

The extensive necropolis at Saqqara, situated near the cult centre of the sun god Re of Heliopolis, was built in the western desert of northern Egypt near Memphis, capital of the Old Kingdom. Sculptural reliefs in the underground chambers provide a rich source of information on life in the Old Kingdom.

During the 1st and 2nd Dynasties, Egypt's elite built their mastaba tombs at Saqqara. Named after the Arabic word *mastaba*, meaning 'low bench', these were low, flat, mud-brick super-structures covering burial chambers that were cut deeper and deeper until they passed through the desert sand into the bedrock. Although occasionally packed solid with sand and gravel, the super-structures were usually filled with storerooms for the grave goods needed in the afterlife.

By the end of the 1st Dynasty the number of rooms had been reduced in favour of more subterranean storage galleries. Eventually, the mastaba became a solid mound with two false doors at each end of the eastern wall. Around the largest mastabas were single rows of smaller, brick-lined tombs. These tombs were built for the artisans who worked for the deceased.

The Step Pyramid

Djoser, who was first king of the 3rd Dynasty, raised his mortuary complex on the high ground of the Saqqara

Above This is a statue of Imhotep, the legendary architect of Djoser's pyramid. Imhotep was also revered as the founder of Egyptian medicine.

Right Djoser's six-step pyramid was the prototype of the more sophisticated pyramids built by his successors of the 4th Dynasty.

cemetery. This was Egypt's first stone building. Working in limestone, the royal architect Imhotep designed an unusual square, solid mastaba-like structure with corners orientated to the points of the compass and a burial shaft cut beneath. This structure was subsequently extended on all four sides and upwards until, after several stages, it evolved into an impressive six-step pyramid. Today this pyramid is 60m (197ft) high and has a ground plan of 121m x 109m (397ft x 358ft).

The Step Pyramid's interior was explored by Napoleon's soldiers, von Minutoli and Segato (1821), John Shae Perring and Colonel Vyse (1837), and Richard Lepsius (1842). It was not until 1924, when Pierre Lacau and Cecil M. Firth started to excavate around, rather than beneath, the Step Pyramid that the true complexity of the site was realized.

The substructure was accessed by a shaft descending from the courtyard of the mortuary temple that ran along the lower step of the northern pyramid wall. The burial chamber lay at the base of a wide shaft that dropped from the centre of the original mastaba. The compact granite-lined burial chamber could be entered only via a 1m- (3ft-) wide hole in the ceiling; after the funeral, this hole was sealed with a stone plug.

The burial chamber lay at the centre of a maze of corridors and rooms. In the 'king's apartment' over 36,000 blue-green tiles were stuck onto sculpted limestone to replicate the ridged reed walls of Djoser's palace. Shafts for the burial of lesser members of the royal family were provided along the original mastaba, but they were abandoned when the building extension covered their entrances.

Around the pyramid was an enclosure defined by a limestone wall, measuring more than 1600m (5249ft) long and 10.5m (34ft) high. The wall was equipped with 14 false doors, plus one true entrance. The best-known and most fully restored buildings in the complex are in the southern and eastern sections of the

enclosure, and in the area around the pyramid. Here were built a series of inaccessible symbolic buildings — replicas of Egypt's most important shrines whose carved stone doors could never be opened.

The Apis burials

A further 14 royal pyramids from the Old and Middle Kingdom were raised at Saqqara. From the New Kingdom until the Ptolemaic Period the mummified sacred Apis bulls were buried in the Saqqara Serapeum, or bull cemetery. Before the 19th Dynasty reign of Ramesses II, the carefully selected bulls were interred in individual tombs; subsequently, they were buried in enormous stone sarcophagi in underground galleries. The Serapeum became a place of pilgrimage for late dynastic Egyptians. It was rediscovered by Auguste Mariette in 1851.

Above The interior of the mastaba of Irukaptah – a court official, one of whose titles was Head of the Butchers of the Great House – houses figures of his family in the niches.

Below A limestone statue of an Apis bull from the 4th century BC was found in Saqqara's bull cemetery.

Abydos

As cult centre of the god of the underworld Osiris, Abydos became an important 'national' cemetery and place of pilgrimage, with a wealth of tombs and monuments. The vast necropolis is situated on the desert edge on the west bank of the Nile in Upper Egypt.

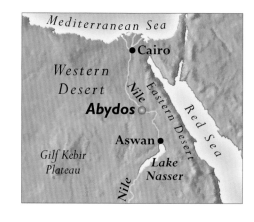

The Abydos graveyard was used for over 3000 years, from Prehistoric times until the Roman age. Initially, it had been used by all, irrespective of rank or wealth. By late Predynastic times, however, the part of the necropolis known today as the Umm el-Qa'ab had evolved into one of Egypt's most exclusive burial grounds, where Egypt's early kings built their tombs. As many generations of Egyptians continued to build tombs and occasional temples, Abydos developed into a rich multi-period archaeological site.

Abydos has been the site of virtually unbroken excavation from the first serious work conducted by Auguste Mariette (in 1859) onwards. Archaeologists from the German Archaeological Institute in Cairo, led by Gunther Dreyer, are currently involved in a thorough long-term reappraisal of the site and are discovering much that was missed by its early excavators.

Early writing

The most impressive of the late prehistoric tombs, which measures almost 67sq m (721sq ft) in area, is a 12-chambered structure known today as Tomb U-j. Traces of a wooden structure (possibly the remnants of a shrine) in the burial chamber, plus the discovery of an ivory crook-style sceptre, suggest that this is the tomb of a regional king.

Although Tomb U-j was looted extensively in antiquity, modern excavation has uncovered large quantities of Egyptian and imported Palestinian wine jars, small-scale ivory and bone artefacts and a series of inscribed labels. These labels — apparently torn off the now-vanished grave goods — provide the earliest known examples of hieroglyphic

Left A portico from the temple of Seti I, a 19th Dynasty pharaoh, was built with columns that show Seti's son, Ramesses II (who completed the temple) making offerings to the gods associated with the Osiris cult.

Left Plant motifs traditionally adorned the capitals of Egyptian columns. The column shafts were originally designed to look like a tree trunk or a bundle of plant stems.

Below An ivory statuette of an unknown king of the 1st Dynasty was found at Abydos. The king is wearing the crown of Upper Egypt.

writing. Some of these brief texts have been translated; they mention agricultural estates and the Delta settlements of Buto and Bubastis.

Tombs of the first kings

Umm el Qa'ab, or 'Mother of Pots', was so named because of the heaps of shattered ancient pottery found covering the ground. It was here that Egypt's first kings built their mud-brick mastabas (flat-topped, free-standing tombs).

Both Émile Amélineau (in 1897) and Flinders Petrie (in 1899) excavated here. They discovered that Cemetery B on the Umm el Qa'ab housed three double-chambered tombs dated to the Dynasty 0 kings Iri-Hor, Ka and Narmer, plus the tomb complex of the 1st Dynasty King Aha. The remaining kings of the 1st Dynasty built their tombs to the south of Cemetery B.

These tombs all shared a similar plan. The underground burial chamber was surrounded by storage chambers and covered by a low, brick-covered mound that was hidden beneath a larger mound. Above ground, two stelae (upright slabs or pillars) recorded the name of the deceased king.

Early excavators considered the Abydos tombs of the 1st and 2nd Dynasty kings to be disappointingly small. So small, in fact, that it was speculated that they were cenotaphs rather than actual burials. It is now realized that the tombs were merely one element in the kings' much larger funeral complex. Less than 2km (1¼ miles) to the north-east of their Umm el Qa'ab tombs, closer to the cultivated land, they built massive rectangular ritual enclosures defined by mud-brick walls. The precise purpose of these funerary enclosures is unknown.

The 1st Dynasty tomb complexes included long, narrow trenches sub-divided into subsidiary graves. These were provided, not for the royal family, but for the king's personal retinue: his servants, minor courtiers, harem women and, occasionally, favourite animals, including dogs and lions. The deceased – partially mummified in a cloth coated in natron (a carbonate salt) – were buried in short wooden coffins with their own grave goods. Their names were engraved on small, crude limestone stelae. The funerary complex of King Djer included 318 of these subsidiary graves. Of the 97 surviving stelae, 76 bore women's names. As most of the subsidiary burials were disturbed in antiquity, it is impossible to determine how these women died. But it seems likely that they were human sacrifices – servants who were either murdered or persuaded to commit suicide at the time of the king's death. If this is the case, it was only a short-lived ritual. The 2nd Dynasty tomb complexes of Peribsen and Khasekhemwy lack any form of subsidiary burial.

Hidden in a hole in the wall of the tomb of Djer, Petrie found the earliest known example of mummification – a linen-covered arm dressed with four gold and bead bracelets. The arm was subsequently lost in Cairo Museum, but the bracelets survive to testify to the skill of the ancient craftsmen.

Later royal monuments

Khentamentiu, 'Foremost of the Westerners', was the original, local god of the necropolis. His temple was an important religious site during the earliest dynasties. By the late Old Kingdom, however, Khentamentiu had become identified with Osiris, and the Umm el Qa'ab had become

recognized as the burial place of Osiris, with the 1st Dynasty tomb of King Djer being transformed into the god's tomb.

Ideally, every pious Egyptian would have liked to be buried close to Osiris, but that was clearly impossible. Instead, Abydos became an established place of pilgrimage. Many ordinary Egyptians visited the necropolis to witness the 'mysteries of Osiris', which included a re-enactment of the god's violent death and subsequent rebirth. The pilgrims dedicated either statues or *mahat* (mud-brick shrines holding limestone stelae that could act as small-scale cenotaphs or dummy burials). Today, these stelae, which have survived in their hundreds, are our most important source of information for the funerary beliefs, occupations and family connections of non-royal Egyptians living during the Middle Kingdom. The statues were placed in the cult temple of Osiris, while the

mahat were set up overlooking the processional way linking the temple of Osiris to his 'tomb'.

Kings, too, established *mahat* at Abydos, although their monuments were on a far larger scale. The 12th Dynasty king Senwosret III built a cenotaph temple that may even have replaced his pyramid as his final resting place. The 18th Dynasty king Ahmose continued this tradition by building a cenotaph for his grandmother, the 17th Dynasty queen Tetisheri, and other New Kingdom monarchs followed suit.

The most impressive surviving *mahat* are the temples built by the kings of the early 19th Dynasty. Seti I built a small *mahat* for his father, Ramesses I, and an enormous one for himself. His son, Ramesses II,

Below The falcon-headed sky god, Horus, is depicted offering life to the dead pharaoh Ramesses II.

Right The hypostyle hall, which is common in Egyptian temples, has massive columns supporting a high roof. Each column is topped with a lotus-bud capital.

Below This section of the King List from the temple of Seti I is one of 76 of these oblong cartouches listing Seti's predecessors.

completed Seti's temple and built his own smaller version. Seti's Abydos temple has Egypt's best-preserved King List. Here the Ramesside scribes recorded an unbroken line of kings stretching from Menes, the legendary founder of the 1st Dynasty (who is probably to be equated with Narmer), down to Seti himself. The heart of the Seti temple incorporated seven sanctuaries dedicated to Osiris, Isis, Horus, Amen-Re, Re-Harakhty, Ptah and the deified Seti.

Immediately to the west of his temple, Seti excavated a dummy tomb. This was a curious subterranean structure whose central hall, roofed in granite, was accessed by a descending corridor. This structure is today known as the Osireion. Although the Osireion never housed the king's mummy, a room opening off the central hall was shaped and decorated like an enormous sarcophagus. A channel surrounding the hall acted as a moat for ground water, and perhaps allowed the hall to symbolize the mound that rose up from the sea of chaos at the moment of creation.

Karnak

The toponym Karnak is a modern one, referring to the site of a series of temples built in the northern part of the southern Egyptian city of Thebes. The Egyptians called this site Ipet-Swt, 'most select of places', since it was the home of Amen-Re, the great imperial god of New Kingdom Egypt.

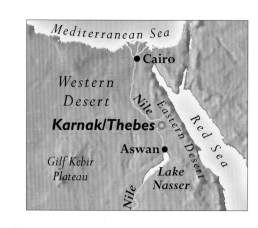

The Amen-Re temple is the heart of the Karnak site. Its impressive remains were never lost (early explorers mistakenly believed that Karnak was a great royal palace), and they have been the subject of almost ongoing exploration and excavation from the early days of Egyptology, which has involved the work of many people.

Colossal monuments

There was almost continuous building works at Karnak from the early Middle Kingdom up to Roman times – a period of almost 2000 years – as successive kings expanded and re-modelled the temple complex. Karnak grew into an extensive, multi-period site of bewildering size and complexity, representing the achievements of many ancient builders.

Above A relief from the White Chapel of Senwosret I, showing the king paying homage to Min, the god of fertility.

Below This 19th-century view of the ruins at Karnak was painted by the Italian archaeologist Giovanni Battista Belzoni.

Much of what is now visible was erected during the three centuries covering the period from the early 18th Dynasty to the mid 19th Dynasty (*c.*1550–1250 BC). In order to demonstrate their piety to Amen-Re, the Theban kings enlarged and embellished the god's house with impressive colossal structures. Especially notable in this context are the monolithic granite obelisks erected in the early 18th Dynasty by Tuthmosis I, Hatshepsut and Tuthmosis III, the multiple pylon gateways built by Amenhotep III in the late 18th Dynasty, and the hypostyle hall decorated by Seti I and Ramesses II in the early 19th Dynasty. Most of the stone for this huge building programme came from the riverside sandstone quarries upriver at Gebel el-Silsila.

the Amen-Re temple via a series of courtyards and pylons. A branch of this southern axis also bypassed the Mut enclosure and ran along a sphinx-lined road southwards, to Amen-Re's 'Southern Harim' temple at Luxor.

Later building works

Later kings were unable to build on the same vast scale as their New Kingdom predecessors. Their interest in Karnak, however, prompted them to carry out minor works of repair and improvement in most parts of the temple structure, and they erected smaller temples for 'guest' deities within the Amen-Re enclosure. The last major building project at Karnak seems to have been the replacement of the central sanctuary of Amen-Re with one built by the Macedonian king Philip Arrhidaeus, who reigned from 323 to 316 BC.

Below A colossal statue of Ramesses II, with the diminutive figure of a princess, possibly one of his daughters, standing at his feet.

Above These two rows of columns once supported the roof of an immense hall in the temple of Amen-Re. There are 134 columns in all, arranged in 16 rows.

Demolition and reuse

In order to build, many kings demolished the monuments of their predecessors. The most striking evidence for this can be seen in the pylon gateway (pylon three) built by Amenhotep III. The rubble fill of his pylon included blocks of exquisitely carved, fine limestone taken from a dismantled chapel originally erected by the Middle Kingdom monarch Senwosret I. This chapel, the White Chapel, is the most significant remnant of the large, and now almost entirely lost, Middle Kingdom temple. Like other examples of dismantled but recovered buildings at

Karnak (most famously the quartzite Red Chapel built by Hatshepsut), the White Chapel now stands, rebuilt, in the open-air museum within the Amen-Re enclosure.

The main axis of the Amen-Re temple was aligned westwards, so that it formed part of a processional route linking Karnak with the royal mortuary temples situated on the Theban west bank.

It is from the reign of Amenhotep III that the intention to develop the Amen-Re temple as the nucleus of a series of related, satellite structures becomes most clear. To the south of the Amen-Re enclosure, Amenhotep III enlarged a temple enclosure for Mut, divine wife of Amen-Re. Mut's temple enclosure was joined to the Amen-Re enclosure by a second processional axis running south from

The Valley of the Kings

Egypt's New Kingdom monarchs (Dynasties 18-20) were southerners loyal to the god Amen of Thebes. Abandoning the northern pyramid cemeteries favoured by the kings of the Old and Middle Kingdoms, they were buried in the cliffs on the west bank of the Nile, opposite the Karnak temple of Amen.

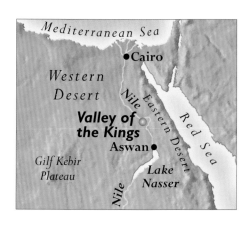

The kings' funerary monuments were divided into two separate elements. A highly visible mortuary temple was built on the edge of the cultivated land. Here the cults of the dead kings could be maintained for all eternity. Meanwhile, their rock-cut tombs were hidden in a remote dry valley known today as the Valley of the Kings (Biban el-Moluk). The elite workmen employed to construct these tombs lived in the purpose-built village of Deir el-Medina.

The royal mummies

As the New Kingdom plunged into economic decline, thieves targeted the rich royal burials. Eventually, the High Priests of Amen emptied the tombs, stripping the kings of their grave goods and storing their mummified bodies in caches dotted about the necropolis. Two major royal caches have been discovered – one in a tomb in the Deir el-Bahari cliffs (DB320) and one in the Valley tomb of Amenhotep II (KV35).

The royal tombs

The classical historian Diodorus Siculus, writing in the 1st century BC, suggested that there might be as many

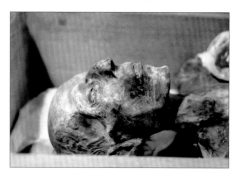

as 47 tombs in the Valley. However, it was not until 1707 that Claude Sicard recognized the true nature of the royal necropolis. The first significant work in the Valley was conducted by Belzoni who, in 1816, found the tomb of Tutankhamen's successor Ay (WV23). The following year he discovered the tombs of Mentuherkhepshef (KV19)

Left The mummy of Ramesses II, who died at the age of 92. His mummy was discovered at Deir el-Bahari in 1881.

Above The Valley of the Kings today. The monarchs' tombs were made by boring into the limestone walls of the valley's cliffs.

and Seti I (KV17). Commencing excavations in 1898, Victor Loret discovered the tomb of Tuthmosis III (KV34), the cache in the tomb of Amenhotep II, the tomb of Tuthmosis I (KV38), and 14 private tombs.

Theodore Davis, a wealthy, retired American lawyer, was determined to find an intact tomb. In 1902-3, working with Howard Carter, he discovered the tomb of Tuthmosis IV (KV 43). They then excavated KV20, the tomb of Tuthmosis I and his daughter Hatshepsut. On 5 February 1905 Davis, this time working with James Quibell, discovered the almost intact double burial of Yuya and Thuyu (KV46), who were the parents of Queen Tiy, wife of Amenhotep II. On 6 January 1907, working with Edward Ayrton, Davis found KV 55, a secondary Amarna burial. In 1908 Davis and Ayrton discovered KV57, the tomb of Horemheb who succeeded Ay.

During their excavations, Davis's team were able to uncover several components of Tutankhamen's burial: a faience cup (1905-6); a small pit holding the remains of the king's embalming materials (1907); a small chamber that yielded a model servant figure; and the gold foil from a chariot harness, which was inscribed with the names of Tutankhamen and Ay (1909).

On 1 November 1922 Howard Carter, financed by Lord Carnarvon, discovered the tomb of Tutankhamen himself (KV62). More recently, the 1989 rediscovery of KV5 by the Theban Mapping Project, led by American Egyptologist Kent Weeks, has led to the identification of an enormous tomb prepared for the burial of the sons of Ramesses II. Work on the tomb is still in progress; so far more than 100 chambers built on different levels have been revealed.

The Valley of the Queens

Also known as 'the Place of Beauty', the Valley of the Queens was the last resting place of many New Kingdom queens, princesses, princes and nobles. The cemetery was first recorded by Robert Hay in 1826, although official excavations did not start until 1903, when Ernesto Schiaparelli, Director of Turin Museum, set to work. Schiaparelli opened several tombs in the Valley, but his most important discovery was made in 1904, when he found the

empty, but beautifully decorated, tomb of Queen Nefertari, who was the consort of Ramesses II (QV66). The paintings on the tomb walls depict the queen's journey after death to the afterlife, guided by various guardian-spirits and deities, including Isis, Hathor and Osiris.

Left The gold mask ot Tutankhamen, one of the priceless treasures discovered in his tomb by Howard Carter and his team in 1922.

Below Part of the hall from the tomb of Seti I in the Valley of the Kings. The ceiling shows the stars and constellations of the northern sky.

Amarna

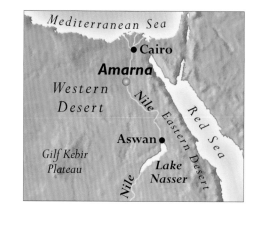

*The city of Amarna (ancient Akhetaten) was a purpose-built capital
in Middle Egypt designed by the 18th Dynasty pharaoh Akhenaten
(c.1353-1335 BC) as a suitable home for his favoured god, the Aten.
Excavation has revealed a wealth of secrets from the New Kingdom.*

The city, situated on the east bank of the Nile, almost equidistant between the southern capital Thebes and the northern capital Memphis, was defined by a series of massive inscriptions carved into the limestone cliffs of the east and west banks.

Amarna was occupied for little more than 25 years before being abandoned during the reign of Tutankhamen. The site has been excavated by a series of archaeologists including Flinders Petrie, Ludwig Borchardt and John Pendlebury. The workmen's village is currently being investigated by the Egypt Exploration Society, led by Barry Kemp. Norman de Garis Davis recorded the tombs of the nobles, and Geoffrey Martin has recorded the royal tomb.

The city

Amarna may be divided into three disparate areas: the main city, the workmen's village, and the tombs. The city was laid out along the Royal Road, or Sikket es-Sultan, a long, fairly straight road that ran parallel to the river. The Royal Road linked the North Riverside Palace, the fortified private home of the royal family, to the southerly Maru-Aten cult centre.

The southern suburb, home of some of Amarna's most luxurious villas, was also the site of a large glass factory and the sculptors' studios. One of the sculptors who worked here was Thutmose, who created the painted limestone bust of Akhenaten's wife, Nefertiti. This masterpiece of Egyptian sculpture was discovered by Borchardt in 1912 and is now housed in the Berlin Museum.

Left This is the bust from a colossal statue of Akhenaten, one of a series from the Great Temple of the Aten.

Right A touching depiction of Akhenaten holding his daughter on his lap and kissing her, but the statue was never finished.

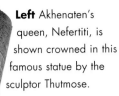

Many merchants lived in the northern suburb of Amarna, within easy reach of the quay and where there was working-class housing. The city centre housed the Great Palace, administrative buildings and two significant temples: the Great Temple to the Aten and the Lesser Temple. The King's House was opposite the Great Palace and linked to it by a mud-brick bridge that passed over the Royal Road. Surrounding the House were the offices and archives of the civil service. It was here, in 1887, that a local woman discovered the 'Amarna letters' – a series of clay tablets representing the remains of Akhenaten's diplomatic archive.

The workmen's village

A valley in the cliffs to the east of the main city was the location for the workmen's village. The houses were for the labourers employed to cut the elite tombs. In contrast to the city proper, the village was laid out with a strict regularity and enclosed by a wall with a single gate. Within the complex each workman was given a small unit, measuring 5m x 10m (16ft x 33ft), and 63 houses stood in six straight terraced rows facing onto narrow streets.

The tombs

The main cemetery – the one that was provided for the ordinary people of Amarna – lay to the north of the city; the investigation of this cemetery is currently in progress. A separate small cemetery was associated with the workmen's village.

The royal tomb, and a series of subsidiary royal graves, lay in a dry valley, or wadi. It was discovered by locals sometime during the early

Above Akhenaten and members of his family present offerings to the Aten. The relief comes from the Great Palace at Amarna.

1880s; when archaeologists entered the tomb, they found that it had been thoroughly looted. Two groups of rock-cut tombs were provided for Amarna's elite, with 18 tombs lying to the north and 27 tombs to the south of the royal wadi. Only 24 of the elite tombs were inscribed and none has yielded a mummy, suggesting that few of the tombs, if any, were ever occupied. The elite decorated their tombs with images of the royal family going about their daily duties. The most elaborately decorated tomb was built for Ay, father of Queen Nefertiti. This tomb contains the lengthy poem known today as *The Great Hymn to the Aten*.

Abu Simbel

The twin temples at Abu Simbel, which were carved out of the mountainside and adorned with colossal statures, were built as a triumphant statement to the power of the 19th Dynasty pharaoh Ramesses II (c.1290–1224 BC) and his favourite queen, Nefertari.

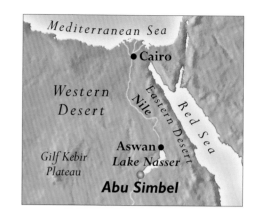

The Great Temple and the Small Temple, as the twin temples are known, project from a vertical rock face at Abu Simbel, on the west bank of the Nile, in Nubia, 64km (40 miles) north of the Second Nile Cataract. They were re-discovered by the explorer Johann Ludwig Burckhardt, and cleared of sand by Giovanni Battista Belzoni (1817).

The Great Temple

The façade of the Great Temple is adorned with two pairs of colossal seated statues of the king. Each statue is about 22m (72ft) tall. An earthquake during Year 30 of Ramesses' reign caused the statue to the north of the entrance to lose an arm (later restored) and the statue to the south to lose its upper body. Above the doorway stands the god Re-Herakhty. To his left is the goddess Maat and to his right

is the sign for 'User', so that the statue is a rebus reading 'User-Maat-Re', the throne name of Ramesses II.

The Great Temple extends 48m (157ft) into the cliff. The first pillared hall is decorated with scenes of Ramesses displaying his military triumphs. The second hall includes images of the divine Ramesses. Beyond the halls, four gods sit in a niche in the sanctuary: Ptah of Memphis, Amen-Re of Thebes, Re-Herakhty of Heliopolis and Ramesses of Per-Ramesse. Twice each year (on the 20th February and the 20th October), the rising sun would illuminate the four statues.

The Small Temple

A local form of the goddess Hathor, the sacred cow, was strongly identified with Ramesses' consort Nefertari, and

Left A statue of Ramesses depicted as the god Osiris, from the interior of his Great Temple.

Above The four colossal figures of Ramesses II flank the entrance to the Great Temple. The smaller figures between his legs are members of the royal family.

the Small Temple was dedicated to the goddess. The façade shows two colossal figures of Nefertari and four of Ramesses. The images on the internal walls include scenes of temple ritual and of Hathor and Taweret, protectors of women in labour.

Rescue mission

When, in 1954, the decision was taken to build the Aswan High Dam, the Abu Simbel temples had to be moved clear of the water. Between 1964 and 1968 the temples and statues were dismantled and reconstructed on higher ground at a site nearby.

Egypt's fortress

Located on Egypt's Mediterranean coast, 280km (174 miles) to the west of Alexandria, Zawiyet Umm el-Rakham is the largest and best-defended fortress to survive from Egypt's imperial age, the New Kingdom. It was designed to intimidate local Libyan tribes.

This large fortress-town was founded by the pharaoh Ramesses II in around 1280 BC in order to defend Egypt from the growing incursions of Libyan tribesmen, and to protect international trade routes in the eastern Mediterranean.

Fortified staging post

It was discovered by chance in 1948, and the site has been excavated since 1994 by a team from the University of Liverpool, led by Dr Steven Snape. A combination of seasonal rainfall and the large-scale use of mudbrick by Ramesses' architects has meant that little of the fortress has survived above ground level. However, the site has produced a series of important structures, together with artefacts, which are either unique or of outstanding quality.

The site was built with impressive fortifications, and among them there is a single, heavily defended gateway. Notable structures were also found within the fortress walls, which includes the 'Governor's Residence'. This multifunctional building served as both a production/administrative centre, as well as being the private

Above The remains of some of the mud brick enclosure walls at Zawiyet Umm el-Rakham still survive today. The walls were originally 5m (16ft) thick.

quarters of Neb-Re, who was 'Troop Commander, Overseer of Foreign Lands'.

Discoveries indicate that the huge garrison was sustained by a combination of self-sufficiency – a major bakery/brewery has been excavated, as have a series of wells – and exchange with local nomads, which can be attested by finds of animal bones and ostrich egg shells. The role of Zawiyet Umm el-Rakham as a defended staging post for international trade in the Late Bronze Age is confirmed by a range of ceramic vessels originating from many points on this trade circuit, including Canaan, Mycenae and Cyprus.

Right In this statue of Neb-Re, he is holding a standard bearing the lion head of the goddess Sekhmet.

Abandonment

The fortress was abandoned, probably early in the reign of Ramesses II's successor, Merenptah, as a result of increased pressure on the part of the Libyans. Today, Zawiyet Umm el-Rakham has the 'frozen-in-time' character of sites that have been suddenly destroyed, such as the near-contemporary Ulu Burun shipwreck off southern Turkey. On-going investigations at Zawiyet Umm el-Rakham will no doubt reveal much more about life in the garrison.

Meroe

Although the memory of Meroe was preserved in the Bible and by the classical authors who recorded a land ruled by a 'Queen Candice', the city remained lost until, in 1772, the explorer James Bruce came across ancient remains near the village of Begarawiya in the Nile Valley.

The second independent kingdom of Kush (Upper, or southern, Nubia) lasted for more than 1000 years. Although one political and cultural continuum, the period is divided into two phases on the basis of the royal burial ground.

In the Napatan empire (*c.*900-300 BC) burials were made south of the 4th Nile cataract at Gebel Barkal, Kurru and Nuri. During the Meroitic empire (*c.*300 BC-AD 300) burials were carried out further south, beyond the 5th cataract on the east bank of the Nile at Meroe, in present-day Sudan.

Taking advantage of a period of Egyptian weakness, the Kushite kings were able to rule Egypt as the 25th Dynasty. However, eventually Meroe fell to Ezana of Aksum, and the city was abandoned and forgotten.

The Royal City

In 1910 John Garstang excavated the 'Royal City', the walled royal residential quarter of Meroe. He discovered what had been a prosperous industrial city, whose temples were dedicated to a mixture of Egyptian and

Above The steep-sided pyramids that mark the tombs of the kings and queens of Meroe were built on a smaller scale than their Egyptian counterparts.

non-Egyptian gods. Chief among the latter was the lion-headed hunter god Apedemak. The imposing Temple of Amen included a large outer court and a series of pillared halls. The Sun Temple featured a pylon gateway and a sanctuary that was walled and floored with blue-glazed tiles.

The cemetery

More than 40 kings and queens of Meroe were interred in rock-cut burial chambers beneath small, steep-sided pyramids. Accompanying the royal family into the afterlife were hundreds of sacrificed servants. In 1834 the Italian doctor turned archaeologist Guiseppe Ferlini partially dismantled the pyramid of Queen Amanishakheto to recover a collection of grave goods, including gold and beaded jewellery. The pyramid cemetery was subsequently formally excavated by George Reisner (1920-23).

Above These gold panels engraved with Egyptian hieroglyphs were part of a piece of Kushite jewellery.

The Zimbabwe tradition

The Later Iron Age sites of Mapungubwe and Great Zimbabwe represent the first two phases of the Zimbabwe Tradition in South Africa. These sites provide evidence for the emergence of complex societies that developed into large and powerful states almost 1000 years ago.

Sites in the Limpopo River Valley, South Africa, dating to the last centuries of the 1st millennium, were typical of the Late Iron Age economy, founded on cattle-keeping and agriculture. The Limpopo River linked these settlements to east coast commerce and its important trading hubs, such as Sofala.

Findings from excavations – such as ivory and glass beads, and later gold items – suggest that subcontinental and intercontinental trade became increasingly important to the economy of the Limpopo Valley.

Mapungubwe

The hill site of Mapungubwe, which was rediscovered in 1932, lies in the Northern Province of South Africa, close to the borders of Zimbabwe and Botswana. Mapungubwe provides evidence of a stratified society that had both elite and commoner classes. Many researchers consider it the centre of southern Africa's first 'state'. The elite occupied stone structures on the summit. The ordinary classes lived in homesteads at the hill's foot and on the surrounding plateau. Excavations of the hilltop burials of the elite have revealed prestige goods, including items of copper and gold. Most famous is a golden rhinoceros, a small wooden sculpture clad in thin sheets of gold foil.

Mapungubwe was established by the early 1200s and flourished in the 13th century. Yet it was abandoned by the mid-14th century. Its decline has been attributed to a colder climate and to the limited capacity of the local environment to sustain a population of several thousand people. Changes in the city's place within the trading networks of the time may have been a factor too. Precisely as Mapungubwe waned, Great Zimbabwe, in the southeast of contemporary Zimbabwe, was on the rise.

Great Zimbabwe

At its pinnacle, Great Zimbabwe had become the capital of a vast Shona empire. The word *Zimbabwe* is from the Shona term meaning 'stone houses', or 'venerated houses'. The stone structures at Great Zimbabwe are

Right The Great Enclosure is one of the most impressive of Great Zimbabwe's remains. With walls up to 12m (39ft) high and 6m (20ft) thick, the Great Enclosure is Africa's largest single ancient structure south of the Sahara.

walling would have enclosed *daga* (mud and grass) huts and structures, and perhaps maintained separation between categories of person, distinguished by class, kinship and gender. Several types of walling, including a decorative style that incorporates a herringbone design, have been identified from different time periods.

Early investigations

Portuguese travellers were the first Europeans to visit the site in the 16th century. In the 1870s a German geologist named Karl Mauch revealed the ruins of Great Zimbabwe to the western world and in 1891 Theodore Bent carried out the first excavations.

These late-Victorian visitors speculated that it was the work of Phoenicians, Sabaeans and other incomers into the subcontinent, fuelling romantic myths about 'lost cities'. They denied that it could be the work of indigenous peoples, supporting contemporary prejudices about the inability of African peoples to produce great civilizations and justifying European colonization.

Archaeological work sponsored by the British Association for the Advancement of Science provided

Above Two rows of chevrons adorn the top of the Great Enclosure's outer wall, an example of the fine craftsmanship of the stonemasons.

reminiscent of those at Mapungubwe, but the site is larger, covering an area of about 50ha (124 acres). Like Mapungubwe, it comprises settlements on a hilltop as well as in the fertile valley below. It was the centre of a greater state, with scores of smaller *zimbabwes* linked to it. Occupation of Great Zimbabwe precedes and post-dates the distinctive stone walling, much of which dates to the city's heyday in the 14th and 15th centuries.

Rather than serving a defensive purpose, the dry-stone walls are thought to have delineated both functional and social spaces within the complex. The walls, creating a series of passages, were not built according to a preordained design, but were apparently added to as circumstances required – joining living areas, demarcating cattle enclosures and perhaps protecting areas of special social or symbolic importance. The

another view. In the 1900s David Randall-McIver investigated both Great Zimbabwe and similar smaller settlements in the area. Although he failed to provide irrefutable archaeological evidence for his findings, he was convinced that the site dated to the earlier part of the 2nd millennium and was an indigenous African settlement. He was succeeded in the late 1920s by Gertrude Caton-Thompson, whose own excavations provided firm evidence to support Randall-McIver's findings.

Caton-Thompson's work provided crucial links between structures and finds in the deposits and located in situ materials. Aided by further analysis of datable imported goods, such as Chinese ceramics, she was able to revise earlier chronologies. Caton-Thompson argued that far from being the work of Phoenicians, 'Every detail in the haphazard building, every detail in the plan, every detail in the contents, apart from the imports' indicated that Great Zimbabwe was an African achievement. However, myths about the 'mystery' of Great Zimbabwe persist to this day.

From the Eastern Enclosure, which is associated with the hill settlement – and hence the city's elite – came the discovery of six of eight carved soapstone birds that stood atop carved pillars. Their symbolic significance is unknown, but they may have symbolized chiefly strength and authority, and/or the power of the ancestors. Today, the Zimbabwe bird is the emblem of the contemporary Zimbabwean nation.

Decline and fall

Like Mapungubwe, Great Zimbabwe was a trading centre with a population of skilled farmers and craftsmen, but on a far larger scale than its more southerly predecessor. At its zenith, Great Zimbabwe's population has been estimated at 10,000, or perhaps even twice that – at least double the size of Mapungubwe. Yet by the middle of the 15th century Great Zimbabwe had declined, as had Mapungubwe before

it. Again, environmental factors have been invoked as an explanation. Did the population density exhaust local resources, such as the wood needed for the kilns? Were pastures over-grazed and degraded? Had the goldmines been exhausted? Alternatively, was there some upset in the trading network in which the success of Great Zimbabwe was embedded? Excavations at other sites indicate that the centre of trading moved north and, over the next two centuries, to sites in the south-west.

In contemporary Zimbabwean archaeology, researchers lament the fact that romantic myths about Great Zimbabwe still circulate. Current archaeological interest focuses more pointedly on understanding the cultural and social lives of the Great Zimbabweans, rather than on neutral description or on the establishment of dates and sequences. The scientific studies of many archaeologists, from Caton-Thompson to the more recent work of Peter Garlake and Tom Huffman, among others, have laid the foundations for new questions to be addressed by a new generation of researchers.

Below This conical tower may represent a grain bin, symbolizing the king's key function of ensuring a reliable supply of grain.

Ife and Benin

The cities of Ife and Benin, in the south-west of present-day Nigeria, are known for their extraordinary sculptures, principally in terracotta and metal. Both cities flourished before the arrival of the first Europeans in the late 15th century.

Archaeology in Nigeria is a recent development and has focused on artefacts of artwork. The most significant findings are from early 2nd millennium sites at Ife and Benin.

Ife

The city-state of Ife is of great importance in the traditions and origin myths of the Yoruba people. Ife no doubt owed a great deal to its trade networks, with the domestic economy probably based on yam cultivation. The people of Ife were producing their artworks by the 12th century, though the site had been inhabited for some centuries previously.

The Ife artworks are known for their naturalism, exemplified by magnificent sculpted heads and human figures, but they also include more stylized works. Some sculptures were associated with Ife royalty, but others may have been placed in domestic shrines.

Benin

The kingdom of Benin dates to the late 12th century. Although associated with the Edo peoples, rather than the Yoruba, the first oba (king) was said to be descended from the founder of Ife. Metal-working, as well as sculpting in ivory, was carried out for the oba and his court. The art of Benin changed over time. Portuguese influence was felt in the late 15th century, and it was at about this time that Benin metalworking reached its greatest heights. Late pieces included new themes, such as Portuguese soldiers. 'Benin bronzes', as they are known – although they are brass – were made using the lost-wax technique, where the sculptor makes a wax model, which is encased in clay. When heated the wax melts, leaving a mould that can be filled with molten metal. When cool, the clay mould is smashed, revealing the metal sculpture.

As well as finely made metal heads of the oba and queen mothers, Benin is also known for the hundreds of brass plaques portraying courtly life, which once adorned the columns of the oba's palace. In 1897 the British sacked Benin, removing thousands of works, exiling the oba and effectively bringing the art tradition to an end.

Left This superb bronze head depicts one of the kings of Benin.

Lalibela

Situated near Lake Tana in Ethiopia, Lalibela is famous for its churches, hewn from the pink-coloured volcanic rock of the Lasta mountains. The site is principally associated with the Zagwe dynasty and named after one of its rulers, who reigned in the late 11th to the early 12th century.

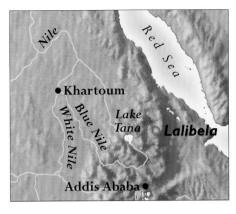

Recent work at the site by the eminent British archaeologist David Phillipson has provided a new perspective on the history of Lalibela. The site is thought to have come into being in the 7th or 8th century, at a time when the power of Axum to the north was in decline and the political environment was unstable. Some structures dating to this phase, namely the churches of the Ethiopian saint Merkurios and of the archangel Gabriel, may have been part of a fortress and palace complex.

A second developmental phase probably dates to the 10th or 11th century. The buildings – or, more properly, sculptures – of this time are unquestionably inspired by Christianity. These later churches self-consciously utilized features that refer to the architecture, and by implication, the legendary power that

Axum had enjoyed. Churches dating to around the late 12th century and early 13th century are attributed to King Lalibela. As with other African sites there has been unwarranted speculation that Lalibela's churches were not built by indigenous peoples, but were the work of foreigners, such as the Knights Templar.

Lalibela's vision

According to legend, Lalibela was poisoned by his brother and fell unconscious for three days. During that time he travelled to heaven, where he saw churches cut from the rock. Another explanation is that he travelled to Jerusalem and was

Left The Bet Giyorgis church, built in a deep pit with perpendicular walls, can be reached only by a tunnel.

Left One of the 12 apostles was carved into the rock in the church of Golgota-Mikail.

inspired to recreate it. Whether or not Lalibela aimed to create a 'New Jerusalem', the references to the Holy City are abundant. A stream running through the site was named after the River Jordan and Lalibela himself is said to be buried beneath the church of Golgota-Mikail, named after Golgotha (the hill of Calvary where Jesus was crucified).

The structures

Some of the churches are free-standing, detached from the rock on all sides. Others remain attached to the mountain from which they have been carved, and yet others extend underground. The rock churches and their courtyards are joined by a labyrinth of tunnels and passages, with catacombs and hermit caverns. Externally, churches such as that of Bet Medhane Alem – the largest monolithic church at Lalibela – are surrounded by trenches that separate them from the natural landscape.

Two of the churches contain remarkable artworks. Inside Bet Golgota are life-size, bas-relief sculptures of human figures, probably saints. In the same church is a painting of St George, Ethiopia's national saint, slaying the dragon. The rock church of Bet Giyorgis, constructed with a cross-shaped floor plan, is set apart from the others. It was allegedly constructed for St George himself after he complained to Lalibela that no church had been built for him.

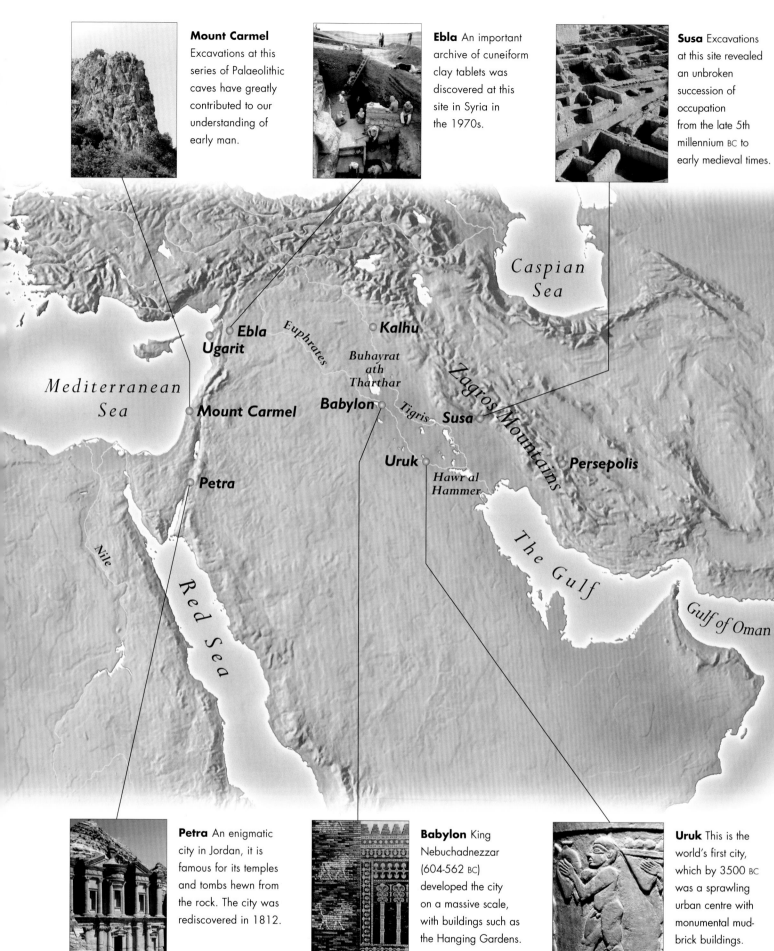

Mount Carmel Excavations at this series of Palaeolithic caves have greatly contributed to our understanding of early man.

Ebla An important archive of cuneiform clay tablets was discovered at this site in Syria in the 1970s.

Susa Excavations at this site revealed an unbroken succession of occupation from the late 5th millennium BC to early medieval times.

Caspian Sea

Ebla
Ugarit
Kalhu
Euphrates
Buhayrat ath Tharthar
Mediterranean Sea
Mount Carmel
Babylon
Tigris
Susa
Zagros Mountains
Uruk
Persepolis
Hawr al Hammer
Petra
Nile
Red Sea
The Gulf
Gulf of Oman

Petra An enigmatic city in Jordan, it is famous for its temples and tombs hewn from the rock. The city was rediscovered in 1812.

Babylon King Nebuchadnezzar (604-562 BC) developed the city on a massive scale, with buildings such as the Hanging Gardens.

Uruk This is the world's first city, which by 3500 BC was a sprawling urban centre with monumental mud-brick buildings.

THE GREAT SITES OF THE MIDDLE EAST

Asia's contribution to world archaeology was initially centred on the Middle East, where work concentrated on exploring the Bible lands for links with the great religions, as well as on understanding the rise of civilization, cities and writing. The pioneering work of archaeologists Layard and Botta in the Assyrian cities revealed a previously unknown culture to the world, with its impressive reliefs and huge winged bull figures. Names such as Ur, Nineveh, Babylon and Sumer lived once again as archaeologists uncovered layers of major settlements. The reconstruction of Babylon's Ishtar Gate in Berlin is testimony to the splendour of these early cultures. Sadly, conflicts in this war-torn region have caused a great deal of destruction. Its museums have been pillaged and many sites have been ransacked.

Ugarit A cosmopolitan Late Bronze Age port in Syria, it occupies a strategic position in the eastern Mediterranean.

Kalhu Excavations at this ancient Assyrian capital in modern-day Iraq have produced a wealth of spectacular finds.

Persepolis Extensive bas-reliefs testify to the importance of this city built by Persian kings during the 6th and 5th centuries BC.

Mount Carmel

Caves and rock shelters along this low limestone range in northern Israel provided habitation sites for early humans. The local fauna and the resources of the coastal plain and sea enabled intermittent occupation over a period of some 800,000 years or more.

Mount Carmel extends south-east for some 32km (20 miles) from the port of Haifa at its northern end. The Palaeolithic cave sites of Tabun, el-Wad, Skhul and Kebara have long since attracted archaeological excavation and are important areas for prehistoric excavation and research.

Excavation

The site's archaeological importance was first recognized in 1928 by Charles Lambert's discovery of the first prehistoric art object to be found in the Levant – a bone animal carving from el-Wad cave from what is known as the Natufian culture (around 10,000-12,500 years ago).

Subsequent excavation in this and other cave sites in the Wadi (1929-34), under the direction of Dorothy Garrod, revealed the Carmel's unique value. Garrod established that the strata in el-Wad and Tabun Caves combine to form a cultural sequence spanning the length of human occupation and activity in the Levant, from the Lower Palaeolithic Acheulian (hundreds of thousands of years ago) to the Natufian.

The discovery of skeletal remains of Neanderthal and Anatomically Modern Humans, in Tabun and Skhul caves respectively, provided the first direct evidence for the intermittent presence of both these Mousterian (Middle Palaeolithic, c.180,000-30,000 years ago) populations in the Near East.

Kebara Cave in southern Mount Carmel was first excavated by Stekelis (in 1927) and briefly by Garrod and McCown (in 1928). Then the Natufian, Kebaran and Aurignacian levels were excavated by Turville-Petre in 1931. With absolute dating of the site available, the Israeli archaeologist Bar-Yosef and others (excavating from 1982-89) shed further light on the Levantine Mousterian with the discovery of a Neanderthal burial. This was an adult male who lived around 62,000 years ago and whose intact hyoid (at the base of the tongue) and throat bones implied this species' capacity for speech.

Excavation at the Mount Carmel sites continues, mainly under the auspices of the University of Haifa.

Below Exposed limestone can be seen in this view of Mount Carmel. Cave sites such as Tabun, el-Wad and Skhul have occupation deposits inside the cavern and at the top of the talus slope that formed at the cave's entrance.

Uruk

Located on a branch of the Euphrates River in southern Mesopotamia (Iraq), Uruk was continuously inhabited for nearly 5000 years, until the early centuries AD. The remains at Uruk provide evidence for the emergence of the world's first cities.

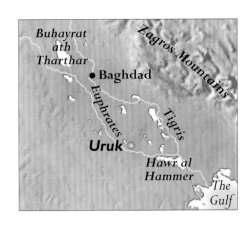

The first excavations at Uruk in the mid-19th century produced scattered results, but a prolonged German project – begun in 1912 and continued through much of the 20th century – revealed the city's development and history. The investigations uncovered many important 'late' monuments, including the palace of a local king of the early 2nd millennium BC, an unusually decorated temple from the later 2nd millennium BC and a New Year's Festival temple built in the 6th century BC.

Excavations also yielded archives of cuneiform tablets – a writing system of wedge-shaped characters pressed into clay slabs – that belong to these periods. These monuments, texts and other finds are important, in some cases providing unparalleled glimpses into these late periods.

The world's first city

In Mesopotamian legends, the city of Uruk (Warka in Akkadian, Erech in the Bible) was associated with the

Left A detail of the Uruk Vase (c.3300 BC) shows a file of naked men presenting offerings to the goddess Inanna. The alabaster vase was stolen from the Baghdad Museum in April 2003, but it was returned two months later.

Above An overview of the massive ziggurat in the Eanna precinct.

development of urban life and civilization. Archaeology tells the same story. Uruk initially was a scatter of villages established in the 6th millennium BC, which began to coalesce around 4000 BC. Already by 3500 BC Uruk covered 250ha (618 acres) and by 2800 BC the urban sprawl covered 550ha (1360 acres) enclosed by a city wall, which Mesopotamian stories attributed to the semi-legendary King Gilgamesh.

Excavation in two temple precincts, the Eanna ('the House of Heaven'), associated with the goddess Inanna (Ishtar), and the ziggurat of the god Anu, provided a detailed view of the pivotal period of urbanization (the Uruk period, c.3800-3100 BC).

During this relatively brief span, the residents of Uruk created the monumental religious architecture characteristic of Mesopotamia, including the ziggurat (superimposed terraces supporting a temple). Administrators developed a system of writing, which was initially for recording economic transactions, and used cylinder seals to authenticate their documents. Artisans produced sophisticated works of art in stone, terracotta and other media; the 'Uruk Vase' and the 'Warka Lady' are justly famous, while many cylinder seals are masterpieces in miniature.

Craftsmen developed techniques of mass-production to satisfy the now large market; one form of pottery – the 'bevelled rim bowl' – appears in great quantity and may have been used for doling out rations to workmen.

Ugarit

From around 1550-1200 BC Ugarit was the capital of a Late Bronze Age kingdom in north-west Syria. Ugarit was deeply involved in the international politics and commerce of the time. An early alphabet was used for texts in the local language.

Known today as Ras Shamra, Ugarit lies a short distance from the Mediterranean coast of Syria. This strategic location gave Ugarit access both to the eastern Mediterranean sea lanes and to overland caravan routes.

The long-term archaeological project, begun in 1929 by Claude Schaeffer, shows that Ugarit was first settled in early Neolithic times (before 6000 BC) and grew to become a walled town by the middle of the 3rd millennium BC. Ugarit's foreign

Below The palace quarter, now just ruins, had numerous courtyards, pillared halls and a columned entrance gate.

connections, especially with Egypt, were already evident during the 3rd millennium BC and continued through the 2nd millennium BC.

Two main sources of evidence are available to reconstruct everyday life in Ugarit: the archaeological remains and thousands of cuneiform tablets.

A prestigious centre

The earlier settlements are important in their own right, but the Late Bronze Age town is much better known. This town covered over 22ha (54 acres) and had up to 8000 residents. The acropolis – the mound formed by earlier occupations – held the tower-like temples of Baal and Dagan. The royal palace at Ugarit was laid out around five interior courtyards surrounded by suites of rooms with varied public or private functions; the dead kings were buried in underground chambers beneath the palace. The residential quarters were arranged in irregular blocks laced with lanes, each block encompassing households of different size, apparent wealth and occupation.

Cuneiform tablets from the palace and some private houses reveal Ugarit's political and diplomatic history, social organization, economic structure and foreign trade, as well as other aspects of daily life. Other texts relate myths, religious poetry and cultic rituals that strongly echo practices reported in the Bible. While most texts are written in Akkadian, the lingua franca of the day, many were written in a cuneiform version of the Canaanite alphabets of the Late Bronze Age Levant.

The texts make clear Ugarit's cosmopolitan nature, as does its material culture. Egypt's influence on local art was pervasive, and numerous Egyptian objects also appeared in Ugarit. Imported pottery and other artefacts show connections in other directions, including Cyprus, Minoan Crete and Mycenaean Greece.

The Late Bronze Age world of the eastern Mediterranean came to an abrupt end around 1200 BC, with the cataclysmic upheavals associated with the movements of the 'Sea Peoples'. Invaders sacked the town and the site was not reoccupied.

Susa

From around 4200 BC this ancient city in Iran was a major point of interaction between the Mesopotamian world and the resource-rich uplands to the east. The site provides important evidence for the emergence of civilization in the region.

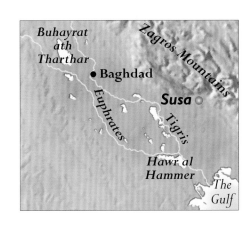

Susa is an enormous mound, sprawling across an area of 550ha (1359 acres) and rising over 35m (115ft) above the surrounding plain, on the Shaur River in Khuzistan in south-west Iran. This location, in the blurred cultural boundary between Mesopotamia and the mountains of western Iran, gave Susa enduring strategic importance. The city in fact looked mainly to Mesopotamia during some periods and to the Iranian highlands during others, but it always maintained ties with both.

Exploration of Susa began in 1884, with the discovery of an Achaemenid Persian *apadana* ('pillared hall'). Excavation resumed in 1897 when a permanent French mission, headed initially by Jacques de Morgan, began its investigation; the French mission continued at Susa, with interruptions for world wars, until 1979.

Gateway city

The excavations reveal an unbroken succession of occupation for some five and a half millennia, from around 4200 BC until the Mongol conquest in the 13th century AD. The first occupations (c.4200-3500 BC) contained elegant painted pottery with highland ties. Of equal significance were burials discovered both in and near a large mud-brick platform; this kind of burial ceremonialism is associated with emerging social complexity in many prehistoric cultures.

The material culture of the period – c.3500-3100 BC – displays very close similarities with the Uruk culture of southern Mesopotamia, including styles of mass-produced pottery, cylinder seals and early writing. Then in around 3100-2700 BC, Susa returned to its mountain orientation – developing a system of writing ('proto-Elamite') found in various sites around the Iranian plateau and enjoying commercial and cultural ties with eastern Iran, western

Left Statuettes made of precious metals depict worhippers bearing offerings. This finely executed gold figure – made 13th to 12th century BC – is carrying a kid. It was discovered at the site in 1904.

Above There are mud-brick remains of the Elamite settlement at Susa.

Afghanistan and Turkmenistan. From the mid-3rd millennium BC until the late 7th century BC, Susa was the major city of the Elamites, a people inhabiting south-west Iran from the southern Mesopotamian borderlands to Fars. The city then passed into the hands of imperial powers; the Achaemenid Persians kept Susa as a major administrative centre and the Seleucids perhaps implanted a colony of Greeks. Susa's importance declined with the establishment of new regional centres, however, and it was reduced to a village during the early centuries AD.

Ebla

The site of Tell Mardikh, ancient Ebla in north Syria, gained fame in the mid-1970s after the discovery of a large archive belonging to a previously unknown 3rd millennium BC kingdom. The city was also a significant regional centre during the Middle Bronze Age (c.2000-1550 BC).

Tell Mardikh covers an area of approximately 60ha (148 acres). It consists of a lower town and an inner citadel mound rising some 22m (72ft) above the surrounding plain. An Italian team led by Paolo Matthiae began excavating at Ebla in 1964, and work at the site has continued ever since. Although the depth of later deposits obstruct a good view of the early occupations at Mardikh, it is known that the site was first settled late in the 4th millennium BC. By about 2400 BC Ebla had grown to become the capital of a west Syrian kingdom.

Above Many cuneiform clay tablets were found at the site, which provide valuable information about life in the ancient city.

The archive

Knowledge of this kingdom comes mostly from the discovery of an archive of 17,000 tablets and tablet fragments recovered from the royal Palace G on the slope of the citadel mound. The larger tablets had originally been stored on shelves, but they had fallen onto the floor when the palace was destroyed. However, the excavators were able to reconstruct their original position on the shelves and it soon appeared that the tablets were originally shelved according to subject. Unfortunately, the excavations have not yet been able to expose much of the palace, due to the overburden of subsequent occupations at the site.

Left The many excavations have yielded a wealth of archaeological material, including palaces, temples and large religious precincts, tombs and defences.

The texts were written in a cuneiform script borrowed from Mesopotamia but adapted to express a west Semitic language. The archive records a palace economy based on obligatory labour gangs issued food and clothing in exchange for their work, on commercial transactions, and on storage of agricultural and manufactured goods. In addition, the archive reports on the attendance of students at scribal schools in Mesopotamia; gift exchanges of valuable goods between kings and also skilled craftsmen; international agreements to secure trade relations; gifts given to visiting foreign merchants; and other affairs of state.

Revival

Palace G was destroyed during an invasion from southern Mesopotamia, probably around 2300 BC. Ebla's inhabitants rebuilt the city, but around 2000 BC invaders again destroyed it. Revived once more, the city then entered a renaissance during the Middle Bronze Age. The settlement expanded in size and its residents erected a massive rampart wall, some 3km (2 miles) long, around their city. The wall was surmounted by fortresses. The social elites occupied large palaces, often located near temples and funerary cult buildings above royal tombs. Ebla's architecture during this period, notably the ramparts and several temples, has parallels in contemporary sites of the southern Levant, and artefacts indicate frequent interactions with that region and also with Egypt.

Kalhu

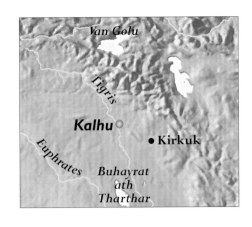

One of the first Mesopotamian sites to be excavated, Kalhu was the capital of the Assyrian empire during the 9th and 8th centuries BC. The city had numerous palaces ornamented with elaborate stone wall-reliefs and filled with sumptuous furnishings; underground chambers held royal graves.

Kalhu, the Biblical Calah, was the capital established by the Assyrian king Assurnasirpal II (883-859 BC), near the Tigris River in northern Iraq. Its modern name Nimrud derives from an imagined association with Nimrod the 'mighty hunter before the Lord' whom the Bible (Genesis 10:8-12) credits with founding Nineveh, Calah and other Assyrian cities.

Expansion

The location was first occupied in prehistoric times, but the oldest cuneiform texts mentioning the place belong to the 13th century BC. King Assurnasirpal greatly expanded the city in the 9th century BC when he laid out the imperial Assyrian capital as a walled enclosure. This covered an area of 360ha (890 acres), with a separate walled citadel in the south-west corner and an arsenal (Fort Shalmaneser) in the south-east corner.

After the Assyrian capital was moved to Khorsabad at the end of the 8th century BC, Kalhu remained a provincial capital until late in the 7th century, when invaders brought the Assyrian empire to an end.

Rediscovery

In 1820 Claudius James Rich, who was the East India Company's resident in Baghdad, visited and provided the first modern description of Nimrud.

Below Layard's vision of what the city of Nimrud might have looked like was presented in this lithograph by James Ferguson.

However, it was Sir Henry Austen Layard, who in 1845 began the first large-scale excavations of the site. It was his results that sparked strong British interest in Mesopotamian archaeology. With the assistance of Hormuzd Rassam, and using local workmen, Layard made significant discoveries, including the walls and southern part of the North-west Palace, including the colossal gateway figures and impressive bas-reliefs that adorned the walls of the palace. He also unearthed the first of the spectacular Nimrud Ivories.

After World War II, the British School of Archaeology in Iraq sponsored renewed excavations at Nimrud under the direction of Sir Max Mallowan – the archaeologist husband

Nimrud Ivories

Excavations have revealed a vast cache of elaborately carved ivory pieces. Originally, much of the carved surface of the ivory would have been covered in gold leaf, which had long been removed. Some particularly fine pieces were found at the bottom of two wells in the southern wing of the North-west Palace, where they had been discarded by looters. Many of the ivories would have been presented to the city as tribute from vassal states to the west of Assyria, where elephants were native.

Above This ivory sculpture, known as the Mona Lisa of Nimrud, was one of the pieces found in the wells.

Above Sculpture decorates the base of an archway at Nimrud.

of Agatha Christie – who discovered important archives of cuneiform tablets and many beautiful carved ivories in the royal precinct.

British teams worked on all areas of the acropolis and also at Fort Shalmaneser, where a large number of ivories were found. From 1987 to 1989 an Italian team of achaeologists surveyed the site and excavated at Fort Shalmaneser. Iraqi restoration work, which began in the mid-1950s, has also revealed significant discoveries.

These excavations carried out over the past 150 years have uncovered portions of over a dozen palaces, temples and administrative centres, but they have touched only small areas of more ordinary residential quarters.

The North-west Palace

Excavations in all the palaces and public buildings at Kalhu have produced some spectacular finds, including works of art, administrative archives and records of state, such as the vassal treaties of Esarhaddon (ruled 680-669 BC). But perhaps most impressive of all is the North-west Palace, built by Assurnasirpal and probably completed between 865 and 869 BC. The palace's inauguration was celebrated with lavish festivities attended by about 70,000 people from all over the empire. An inscription lists what the guests were given to eat and drink, including 1000 ducks, 500 geese, 500 gazelles, 10,000 doves, 10,000 skins of wine and large quantities of beer, fish, eggs and nuts.

The palace lay at the western edge of the citadel, adjacent to that structure's massive mud-brick walls, which were around 15m (49ft) high and 3.7m (12.1ft) thick. The private apartments and possibly the harem were housed in the south wing of the palace, while the administrative offices and storerooms were in the north wing.

The largest of the palace's audience halls was the Throne Room. It was here that the king received foreign visitors, so it was designed to impress. Enormous bas-reliefs, which would have stood about 2.2m (7ft) above the ground level, adorned the walls of the Throne Room.

The North-west Palace has yielded many important discoveries, including the so-called 'Banquet Stela' relating the king's conquests, building projects and the inaugural feast for the palace itself; bronze artwork in the styles of Syria and Phoenicia; and ivory furniture inlays rendered in multiple regional styles. Cuneiform tablets discovered in rooms in the north wing of the palace reveal interesting

Right The Assyrian sphinx, shown on this beautiful ivory plaque, had a human head and the body of a winged lion.

information about the administrative and economic organization of the Assyrian empire.

Fort Shalmaneser

Assurnasirpal's son Shalmaneser III (859-825 BC) built his arsenal along the same lines as a royal palace. The overall architectural plan of the fort is preserved along with the stone foundations of the wall that encircled the 30-ha (74-acre) complex. Archives discovered at the fort provide important details about the Assyrian army's troops, horses and arms. Other records deal with tax collection and legal affairs.

Royal tombs

Between 1988 and 1989 a team of Iraqi archaeologists unearthed the tombs of 9th and 8th century BC queens in vaulted chambers beneath the private apartments of the North-west palace. Three of these tombs contained enormous masses of jewellery and ornaments of gold and semi-precious stones, including a royal crown. Other items included

vessels, seals and ornaments. These rich burials – known as the Nimrud Treasure – give a vivid illustration of Assyrian wealth, amassed through conquest, loot and tribute.

Below A bas-relief from Assurnasirpal's palace includes a figure (left) that represents a protective winged genie, a prominent feature of Assyrian art. Here the genie holds a cone in his right hand and a bucket in his left – both objects are associated with purification and the power to protect.

Babylon

The city, located on a now-dry branch of the Euphrates River in central Iraq, reached its largest and most elaborate state under the kings of the Neo-Babylonian empire (626-539 BC), when the splendour of its buildings surpassed all others of its time.

Its Biblical associations – from the Tower of Babel to the Babylonian exile – ensured that Babylon never faded entirely from memory, but the location of the city was long uncertain. The British Resident in Baghdad, Claudius Rich, presented the first detailed description of the site at the beginning of the 19th century, and visiting archaeologists later in that century added some details.

Excavations

The first systematic exploration of the site was carried out by the German archaeologist Robert Koldewey, who excavated almost continuously from 1899 until 1917, when he retired from the field in the face of the invading Indian army. Koldewey's team published many detailed reports about their work, but some of their results even now remain unpublished. The Germans returned to Babylon during the 1960s and 70s to investigate several specific questions, and the Iraqi government launched a reconstruction programme for parts of the site. However, Koldewey's work remains the baseline for understanding this capital of the Mesopotamian world.

The remains of early Babylon are deeply buried beneath the abundant later construction of the city and there is a high water table, so Koldewey was prevented from digging deeply into

Below In 1982 the Iraqi President Saddam Hussein began reconstructing the 600-room palace of Nebuchadnezzar on top of the original ruins, much to the disapproval of archaeologists. Some of the bricks, which were inscribed with Saddam's name, began to crack after just ten years.

History

Babylon existed by the mid-3rd millennium BC, when the name appears in several cuneiform texts. After the period known as the Old Babylonian dynasty (1894-1595 BC), Babylon was racked with intermittent periods of crisis, occupation and rebuilding for around the next thousand years. In 626 BC the Neo-Babylonian revival began with the expulsion of the Assyrians, who had conquered Babylon a century earlier. The Neo-Babylonian kings, particularly Nebuchadnezzar (604-562 BC), launched massive building projects in Babylon, their imperial capital. This golden period came to an end when Babylon was captured by Achaemenid Persians in 539 BC and the city passed forever under foreign rule. Babylon slowly receded into the backwaters of history and was largely abandoned during the early centuries AD.

the city, apart from one area where he reached an Old Babylonian residential quarter. So Koldewey focused on large exposures of the ceremonial heart of the Neo-Babylonian city.

The city

Neo-Babylonian Babylon covered an area of 8.5 sq km (3.3 sq miles) and had a population of around 150,000 residents. The city, which was surrounded by a massive wall and moat 18km (11 miles) long, spread along both banks of the Euphrates River; fortresses constructed around the edges of the city strengthened its defences. The two parts of the city were connected by bridges. Koldewey documented the piers of one stone bridge that stretched over 100m (328ft) across the river.

An inner city, surrounded by its own rectangular wall on the left bank of the river, formed the civic centre of the Neo-Babylonian empire. The main ceremonial entrance to the inner city was the famed Ishtar Gate – the most spectacular of eight gates that ringed the city's perimeter. This gate was a barrel-arch between pairs of square towers faced with blue-glazed baked bricks moulded with images of bulls and dragons. A walled Processional Way, running along a 15m- (49ft-) high embankment parallel to the river, passed through the Ishtar Gate and into the Inner City.

Once inside the Inner City, the Processional Way first passed Nebuchadnezzar's palace, then blocks of religious architecture that included the temples of the war goddess Ishtar, the wisdom god Nabu, and several other gods. Next came the Etemenanki containing the famed ziggurat of Marduk, and finally the E-sagila, the temple proper of Marduk.

Monumental buildings

The city was famed for two architectural features in particular: the Greek historian Herodotus counted the Hanging Gardens as one of the marvels of the ancient world, while according to the Biblical story God caused people to speak mutually unintelligible languages after seeing the hubris of the Tower of Babel. When Koldewey excavated Nebuchadnezzar's palace, he found massive vaulted chambers constructed of baked bricks laid with natural asphalt. He thought that these were the foundations for the Hanging Gardens – the asphalt protecting the structure

against water seepage from the plants above. However, many scholars today are sceptical of this interpretation.

According to Herodotus, the ziggurat of Marduk was like a stepped pyramid built with six levels, with the seventh level at the top being a temple of Marduk. Only the base of the ziggurat survived until Koldewey's day, so these details cannot be confirmed. The ziggurat was square, about 91m (298ft) to a side at its base, and constructed as a solid core of unbaked bricks covered with a mantle of baked

Above A reconstruction of the Ishtar Gate – built with bricks excavated at the site – is housed in the Pergamon Museum, Berlin. The top of the gate is crenellated (notched) and would have provided cover for archers defending the city.

bricks. The mantle was looted through the ages, leaving only a flattened mound. Koldewey's investigation showed that the Assyrians rebuilt an older ziggurat in the 7th century BC, and that Nebuchadnezzar renewed the ziggurat during the following century.

Left The head of a dragon sculpted in bronze represents Marduk, Babylon's patron god. The bronze is in the Louvre Museum in Paris.

Persepolis

The royal seat of the Achaemenid (Persian) empire, Persepolis was founded by Darius the Great (522-486 BC). The impressive palace complex, built on an immense terrace, was later destroyed by Alexander the Great in 330 BC during a drunken party in celebration of his conquest of that empire.

To create his new palace at Persepolis (in south-west Iran) – and for building another massive palace at Susa – Darius ordered that skilled craftsmen and valuable materials be assembled from all parts of the empire.

Persepolis became the ceremonial centre of the Persian dynasty, and although the kings spent much of their time in other cities, such as Susa and Babylon, they carried out state ceremonies at the new dynastic capital. Persepolis was a vast complex, and Darius did not live to complete its construction, a task that fell to his son Xerxes (486-465 BC) and grandson Artaxerxes (465-423 BC).

Excavating the site

Major excavation work to uncover the half-buried city began in 1930. Among the stonework archaeologists uncovered graphic bas-reliefs that reveal much about the religious and social hierarchy of the city.

In 1935 the first of a series of pioneering aerial survey flights was carried out under the directorship of Professor Erich Schmidt, then field director of the Persepolis expedition. Hundreds of aerial photographs were taken of the site and its environs, at different seasons and at different times of day, giving a valuable overview of the excavations. Documentation and mapping helped to identify areas of the site where digging could begin.

Right An overview of the complex shows the columns of the *apadana* in the background. Although impressive, the ruins only hint at the scale and splendour of the actual city.

Right This detail is from a relief on the staircase leading to the Tripylon palace. The stone carvers adopted the motif of combatant animals – here a lion attacking a bull.

Architectural showpiece

The great complex of halls and palaces at Persepolis was built on a vast stone terrace built against a hill slope at the edge of the vast Marv Dasht plain. This terrace covered an area of 450 x 300m (1476 x 984ft) and was 14m (46ft) high. The visitor reached the top of the terrace via a monumental double-return staircase ornamented with depictions of the royal guard. The platform supported a dense array of imposing buildings, the most magnificent of which was the *apadana* (a high pillared audience hall) built by Darius. The *apadana*, elevated upon its own platform overlooking the plain, was built of finely polished stone and mud brick encased in cedar; colossal columns, each 19m (62ft) high, carried the weight of the ceiling. Its entry staircase is decorated with the famous reliefs portraying emissaries bearing tribute gifts from all corners of the Achaemenid empire.

Next to the *apadana* is the Throne Hall, or the Hundred-Column Hall, which was started by Xerxes. The northern portico of the building is flanked by two colossal stone bulls. Along with other pillared halls, there were also harem quarters and a treasury; these once-sumptious buildings are represented today mainly by rows of stone pillars.

In addition to some important government archives recorded on clay tablets, Persepolis was also a source of trilingual inscriptions – in Old Persian, Akkadian and Elamite. These inscriptions greatly aided the decipherment of the cuneiform script in the first half of the 19th century.

Although Alexander the Great's men had plundered the city, archaeologists have found many artefacts, including weights, tools, weapons, bowls and bottles sent as tribute from Egypt.

Royal tombs

Darius and three of his successors were buried in tombs cut into the cliff face at Naqsh-i Rustam, about 13km (8 miles) north of Persepolis. The tomb entrances were carved as the façade of a columned building, with relief and inscription overhead. The tombs have long since been looted of their treasure.

Right The capture of the Roman emperor Valerian by the Persian king Sharpur I in AD 260 is commemorated in this relief.

Petra

The Nabataeans, an Arabic-speaking people of north-west Arabia, made Petra, in southern Jordan, their capital. By the first century AD the city had become a thriving centre, with magnificent temples and tombs hewn from the rust-coloured rocks.

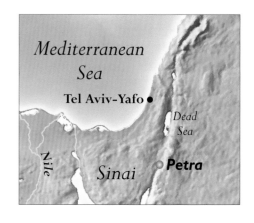

The Nabataeans first appeared in history during the late 4th and 3rd century BC, when they were already middlemen in the caravan trade – their location giving them control of the major routes connecting the Mediterranean Sea with Arabia and the Indian Ocean.

Access to the Mediteranean world meant that the Nabataeans were open to Greco-Roman architectural and artistic influences, which they incorporated into some of their buildings at Petra. The spectacle of classical façades carved into the red stone enchanted European travellers, beginning in 1812 with the Swiss-born and British-sponsored Johann Burckhardt. Although Petra attracted increasing numbers of visitors during the 19th century, the first systematic study came only in 1898 with the work of the German R.E. Brünnow. The first real excavations began in 1929 and have continued ever since. In recent years field work has been carried out by, among others, British, American, Swiss and Jordanian teams.

Desert city

Petra lies within a knot of dry water courses, called wadies, deeply incised into the sandstone of southern Jordan. This location enjoys little rainfall, yet Nabataean engineers created a complex system of dams, cisterns, pipes, aqueducts and other water-control devices. One aqueduct brought water from the Musa (Moses) spring

Below The Monastery is the largest tomb façade in Petra. It consists of two storeys and is topped by a magnificent urn.

Above Two of Petra's rock-cut tombs are the Palace Tomb (left) and the Corinthian Tomb.

into the city through the famous Siq — a gorge up to 200m (656ft) deep and in places only 3m (10ft) wide.

The first sight to greet visitors emerging from the Siq is the magnificent Khaznah (the Treasury), a two-storeyed pillared façade carved into the cliff face, giving entrance to four chambers. The structure was a tomb or, less probably, a temple.

The Siq opens up into a large open area through which run several wadies from the surrounding rugged heights. The Nabataean builders carved many tombs into rock faces along these wadies and upon the hills from which the wadies descend.

This central area housed Petra's urban centre, with its civic heart along the Colonnaded Street — a formal road lined with columns and flanked on either side by temples, markets and other public spaces. A fountain marked one end of the street, and at the other

end a monumental triple arch gave entrance to the great temple known as Qasr al-Bint. This large complex, constructed in the mid-1st century AD and remaining in use until the 6th century, is distinctive for the elephant

heads that ornamented the pillar capitals on the lower platform. The Temple of Winged Lions, a structure built upon vaulted foundations, is named for the lions that decorated the capitals of that building. Recent exploration of the market immediately adjacent to the Southern Temple shows that this open space in fact held a garden with a large pool; the other two 'markets' remain uninvestigated.

The rise north of the Colonnaded Street hosted a cluster of three Byzantine churches and chapels. A building adjacent to the basilica yielded the 6th-century AD personal archive — contracts, wills, sermons and lectures — of a certain archdeacon Theodoros.

Recent excavations on top of a hill south of the Colonnaded Street uncovered the dwellings of well-to-do families, including a mansion decorated with elaborate wall paintings.

Left Visitors to Petra in the 19th century included the painter David Roberts (1796-1864), who captured the city's ethereal beauty.

143

Ostia Excavations at this ancient port have revealed fascinating details about urban life at the height of the Roman Empire.

Delphi The 4th-century BC remains of the Temple of Apollo lie at the heart of a complex of ancient buildings.

Göbekli Tepe A site containing elaborate stone structures carved by hunter-gatherers in about 9600 BC.

EUROPE

Black Sea

Tarquinia
Ostia
The Domus Aurea in Rome
Pompeii and Herculaneum

Pergamon

Göbekli Tepe

M e d i t e r r a n e a n   S e a

Carthage

Delphi
Olympia
Athenian Agora
Mycenae

Ulu Burun

Knossos

Cyrene

Masada

AFRICA

Red Sea

Mycenae This fortified city was one of the major centres of Greek civilization in the 2nd millennium BC.

Ulu Burun The oldest shipwreck ever found has provided a wealth of information about Mediterranean trade in the 14th century BC.

Masada This fortress-palace at the southern end of the Dead Sea was the last outpost of Jews in the Jewish Revolt of AD 66-73.

THE GREAT SITES OF THE MEDITERRANEAN

As the cradle of European civilization, the Mediterranean has yielded a rich variety of archaeological sites. The discovery of Pompeii and Herculaneum in the 1740s was one of the major events affecting knowledge of, and curiosity about, the Roman world. Later, as archaeology was able to extend its investigations back in time, earlier cultures such as those of the Etruscans, Mycenaeans and Minoans were uncovered, thanks to work by pioneers such as Schliemann and Evans. More recently, the Mediterranean Sea has proved a plentiful source of shipwrecks, most notably Ulu Burun, with the latest technology making it possible to detect and study wrecks at great depths.

From the prehistoric site of Göbekli Tepe in Turkey to the exquisite frescoes at Knossos on Crete, the Mediterranean is one of the world's foremost archaeological regions.

Pergamon Successive Attalid kings developed this Turkish city into one of the jewels of the Hellenistic world.

Carthage Founded in 814 BC, this Phoenician colony become one of the leading trading centres of the western Mediterranean.

Pompeii Excavations have revealed a city – its buildings and people – frozen in time after the eruption of Vesuvius in AD 79.

Göbekli Tepe

A ceremonial site of hunter-gatherers, Göbekli Tepe is remarkable due to the fact that its builders used massive blocks of limestone as architectural elements. Even more amazing is that these structures are dated to about 9600 BC, just before the dawn of farming in the Near East.

The low mound of Göbekli Tepe in south-east Turkey was first discovered in the 1960s during a survey. However, it was not until 1994 that Klaus Schmidt of the German Institute of Istanbul realized that it was a prehistoric site and began excavations.

Prehistoric architecture

Using nothing more than flint tools and perhaps fire and water, the builders of Göbekli Tepe carved out blocks of limestone that weighed up to seven tonnes from the local bedrock. They then transported these huge blocks a short distance and set them upright within circular stone buildings cut into the bedrock. At least four such semi-subterranean buildings are known, while others may still lie beneath the hillside. Two pillars were erected in the centre of each building, and several others were placed around the walls.

Each pillar is wider at the top than at the bottom, with some even having a 'T' shape, up to a height of almost 3m (10ft). In the nearby quarry, an unfinished pillar was discovered that dwarfed even those found in the buildings, suggesting that the Göbekli Tepe architects had something more impressive planned.

Images of wild animals, including foxes, boar, cattle, gazelle, herons, ducks and snakes, are carved into the pillars. One even shows a snarling lion. Some of the reliefs have been deliberately erased; perhaps this was in preparation for new pictures.

Hunter-gatherers

There are no traces of domesticated plants or animals among the deposits of animal bones and plant remains. Everything came from wild species, such as gazelle, wild pig, wild cattle, almonds and wild wheat. Thus, the builders of Göbekli Tepe were hunter-gatherers. Moreover, it appears that there was no human habitation at the site, for no traces of houses, hearths or storage pits were revealed.

So what were hunter-gatherers doing at Göbekli Tepe if they did not live there? Klaus Schmidt believes that the site was a ritual centre to which people came to visit. The Göbekli Tepe carvings and architecture show similarities with those at Jerf el Ahmar, about 100 km (62 miles) away in Syria, which suggests a possible range for the people using the site. The question is whether it was a single group or a number of different groups connected through a common belief system.

The archaeologist Stephen Mithen, developing ideas first proposed by the French prehistorian Jacques Cauvin, has suggested that ritual activity of the kind that appears to have taken place at Göbekli Tepe was a catalyst in the emergence of agriculture. In the late 1990s, geneticists identified wild wheat not far from Göbekli Tepe as the closest wild relative of domesticated wheat, thus making the area a strong candidate for the origin of wheat domestication. Mithen hypothesizes that those taking part in the ceremonial rituals at Göbekli Tepe and other nearby sites may have taken seed grain back to their distant homes, where they planted it and thus began domesticating the grain.

Left The pillar carvings at Göbekli Tepe presage the depiction of animals in cave paintings, such as these found at Çatal Hüyük in central Turkey, a Neolithic site dating to about 7000 BC.

Knossos

The labyrinthine palace at Knossos on the island of Crete was the largest and most important of the palatial complexes built by the Minoans during the 2nd millennium BC and is the most thoroughly excavated. Archaeology has revealed delicate wall paintings and unearthed thousands of artefacts.

The Minoans were not Greeks, but their Bronze Age culture became part of Greek history. They settled on Crete during the 3rd millennium BC and became prosperous traders. From about 1900 BC they began to build grand houses and palaces.

Excavations

The first archaeologist to dig at Knossos was Minos Kalokairinos, a Cretan merchant and antiquarian, who in 1878 excavated the west façade and two storerooms and found many artefacts. The person most closely associated with Knossos, however, is the English archaeologist Arthur Evans, who began excavations in 1900. Work at the site was interrupted in 1912-14 by the Balkan Wars but was resumed in 1922 and continued until 1931, when the investigation of the West Court and the Minoan town was completed.

Minoan palaces

Like Kalokairinos, Arthur Evans was certain that he had found the seat of Minos, the legendary king of Crete, and named Knossos the 'Palace of King Minos'. 'Palace' is a misnomer, however, since the site may have been a temple-city dedicated to the cult of the bull. Carvings and images of bulls appear on buildings and artefacts.

Settlements on Crete were frequently destroyed by earthquakes and new ones were built on top of them. Archaeologists have been able to excavate successive settlement layers at Knossos, dating back some 7000 years to Neolithic times. During the 1600s BC earthquakes destroyed the

Below The frieze in the main room of the Queen's apartments depicts dolphins. Marine life was a favourite theme in Minoan art, appearing on pottery as well as frescoes.

first Minoan palaces. This stimulated a phase of rebuilding, and new, larger and more complex palaces arose on the sites of the old. At Knossos, the New Palace effaced its predecessor almost completely and covered an area of 2ha (5 acres). Grand houses and tombs are found beyond its perimeter.

The New Palace

Like other Minoan palace-complexes, Knossos was built around a central Great Court, surrounded by rooms. It also has a West Court – a surviving feature of the Old Palace – and a monumental west façade. There are two storeys below ground and there were perhaps two or more upper storeys. The layout is disorientating: few passages lead directly from A to B but follow a circuitous route and emerge in unexpected places.

The walls of the palace were made of unbaked brick. Wood was also widely used for columns,

Right A rhyton (drinking horn) made from steatite in the shape of a bull's head from Knossos, c.1700-1600 BC. The horns are gilded, the eyes made of rock crystal and the muzzle is crafted from mother of pearl.

doors and window frames, beams and joints. Symbols of the double-headed axe – *labyros* in Greek – appear throughout the palace. The Hall of the Double Axes was a double chamber – an outer room and an inner room – which could be closed off by eleven sets of double doors.

On the west side is the Throne Room with stone benches and a high-backed chair built into the wall. Arthur Evans believed this to be the throne of King Minos, but it may have been the seat of a high priestess. Rooms on a floor situated above the Throne Room may have been used for ceremonies.

A number of storerooms (many with storage jars and vessels, and shrines) have been excavated. The complex also had a theatre, banqueting halls and craft workshops, and an intricate plumbing and ventilation system. There were also grain mills and wine and oil presses.

A number of annexes were built onto the main palace, including the Little Palace and the Royal Villa. To the south of the palace lies the Caravanserai, which was interpreted as a reception hall and hospice. Some of the rooms are equipped with baths and are decorated with wall paintings.

Frescoes

The Minoans decorated their interiors with charming wall paintings, many depicting animals and plants. Visitors conducted from the West Door along the Corridor of the Procession Fresco may have been awed by paintings depicting court ceremony, while today's visitors may be delighted by the replica Dolphin Fresco, which Arthur Evans installed in what he thought were the Queen's apartments on the

Left The walls of the Throne Room are adorned with colourful replica frescoes depicting mythological beasts, such as griffins.

Above The west portico of the North entrance to the palace was reconstructed. The red columns were typical of Minoan architecture. Unlike Greek columns, they were made of wood and were wider at the top than the bottom. They had round, pillow-like capitals (tops).

lower floors. The Bull Chamber, near the north entrance, has a replica relief fresco of a charging bull. One of the most famous frescoes at Knossos shows a young man vaulting over a bull.

Ancient writing

Arthur Evans discovered many discs and seal impressions of Minoan writing. Archaeologists call this script 'Linear A' and recognize that the writing of the Mycenaeans, 'Linear B', developed from it. Linear A has never been deciphered.

Conundrums

More than a century of excavation at Knossos and other similar sites has raised questions about the Minoans.

Above Storage containers called *pithoi* were found in a storeroom. Food, grain, wine and oil were stored in these jars. Ropes were threaded through the handles to move them.

Archaeologists disagree, for example, on whether they were warrior people. Knossos has no fortifications, but its position – just inland on a low hill in a valley – is defensive. Many types of swords and axes have been found, but some specialists think they may be ceremonial weapons.

There has also been much debate about whether Minoan civilization was in fact a matriarchal society. The key figure at Knossos may have been a high priestess, with the king acting merely as a figurehead.

Mycenae

The city-states of the Bronze Age Mycenaean civilization, of which the ancient Greek city of Mycenae in the north-east Peloponnese was the richest and largest, were distinguished by fortifications so monumental that later peoples called them 'Cyclopean', after the one-eyed giants of myth.

From about 1500 BC the Mycenaeans, a merchant-farmer-warrior people, dominated trade in the Mediterranean. They began to build a network of palace-citadels on the Greek mainland, of which Mycenae was probably the first to be built. The Mycenaeans eclipsed the Minoans of Crete to become the dominant power in the eastern Mediterrannean.

Palace-citadel

Mycenae occupied a strong, defensive position on a hill that overlooked gorges. It was fortified mainly in the 14th century BC. Its curtain wall was 1km (0.6 miles) in circumference, with two portals and a smaller exit gate. A great ramp led up the hillside to the great Lion Gate, through which visitors entered the citadel. The lions carved above the 3m- (10ft-) high gate symbolized the power of the rulers of Mycenae, and they may once have had heads made of metal and staring eyes of a reflective stone. In case of siege there was a hidden cistern that was supplied via a concealed aqueduct with water from a spring.

The Mycenaean acropolis enclosed a hilltop palace, with a great open court at its centre. The Great Court faced a columned portico, which led into the 'megaron' – the main hall with a vestibule and a huge central open hearth. Four columns positioned around the hearth supported the roof.

Excavations at Mycenae during the 20th century revealed a temple in which were found pottery idols carrying cult objects, a bathing room containing a water jug, a shrine and a cult room. The remains of colourful frescoes adorned the walls of these and other rooms. Recent work has focused on houses in the town that surrounded the citadel, which covers some 32ha (79 acres) and was built mainly in the 13th century BC.

Grave goods

The citadel was built on the site of older settlements. Two grave circles from a cemetery in use between 2000 and 1650 BC lie within and outside its

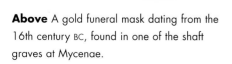

Above A gold funeral mask dating from the 16th century BC, found in one of the shaft graves at Mycenae.

Cyclopean architecture

The terrace wall supporting the great ramp leading into the citadel, the curtain wall and bastions, the monumental gates and the underground passage to the secret cistern are all examples of the Cyclopean building style of the Mycenaeans. They were constructed using massive stones averaging 6-7m (20-23ft) thick in places, and enormous lintels, which were hauled up the hillside or along earth ramps. The large, irregular blocks of stone were roughly finished and laid uncoursed. Small rocks and stones were inserted between them for stability. The curtain wall ranged in height from 4.6m (15ft) to 17m (56ft) on the south-west side.

Above The actual door of the Lion Gate was made of two wooden leaves, which opened inwards.

walls. It was here that Schliemann, the archaeologist who rediscovered Mycenae, began to dig in 1876. The site had long been known, but it was Schliemann who first excavated the site. He was searching for the place, according to Homer's *Iliad*, from where 1000 ships had set sail for Troy under Agamemnon's command.

Schliemann concentrated his search on the deep deposits just beyond the Lion Gate. He soon discovered the shaft graves – deep pits cut through the rock and earth – where the early Mycenaen rulers from the 16th–13th century BC were buried in spectacular style. Here Schliemann unearthed a wealth of gold, silver, bronze, ivory and pottery artefacts, including death masks, diadems, vessels of precious metals and daggers and swords of bronze. The city which Homer had described as 'a city of gold', was living up to expectations.

Schliemann also excavated the large, circular, dome-shaped tholos (or beehive) tombs. The entrance passages to these tombs were cut into the hillside and led into a tall, circular chamber. The most impressive of these tholos tombs is the so-called Treasury of Atreus, constructed in the 13th century BC.

Below Grave Circle A is inside the north-west corner of the citadel walls of Mycenae.

Ulu Burun

A sponge diver working off southern Turkey in 1982 found a shipwreck. It was a late Bronze Age merchant ship with a cargo of precious commodities. The excavation of the ship has provided information about seafaring life, international trade and shipbuilding in the late 14th century BC.

The merchant ship was resting on a slope on the sea floor about 44m (144ft) deep. It had been carrying a cargo of precious commodities, which included copper ingots, ebony logs and ivory tusks, and has provided more than 1200 artefacts. Analysis of its cargo, including jars containing food such as fish, figs, grapes and pomegranates, olives and olive oil, and *pithoi* (storage jars) for carrying water, indicates that the ship may have originally sailed from Egypt or an eastern Mediterranean port such as Ugarit in Syria. From here it then travelled to Cyprus to load its main cargo of copper. The ship may then have headed to the lands of Asia Minor, which at this time were ruled by the Hittites. It was off the Ulu Burun promontory, which is about 8km (5 miles) south-east of Kas, in modern Turkey, that the ship must have run into unfavourable conditions, such as strong winds, and sunk.

Although most of the ship's timbers had been eaten away, computer modelling suggests that to carry its 20-tonne cargo, including up to six oarsmen, 1 tonne of ballast stones for stability, and 24 anchors, the ship must have measured around 15 x 5 x 2m (49 x 16 x 6ft).

Marine excavation

The difficult task of excavating both the shipwreck and its scattered cargo at depths of 44-61m (144-200ft) under water took 11 dive programmes, each one lasting several weeks, carried out between 1984 and 1994. The work was directed by

Copper and tin

Among the objects found scattered on the seafloor around the wreck were what Mehmet Cakir, the sponge diver who discovered it, described as 'metal biscuits with ears'. Marine archaeologists suspected that these were copper ingots with carrying handles.

The Ulu Burun shipwreck was found to carry more than 10 tonnes of copper ingots from copper mines on Cyprus. Also on board was about 1 tonne of tin.

Copper was the basis of the Bronze Age economy: a mixture of nine parts copper to one part tin melts at a lower temperature than pure copper, is easier to cast and the end product – bronze – is a harder metal for tools and weapons. The ship's cargo of copper and tin would have been enough to make almost 11 tonnes of bronze.

Above Each ingot found around the Ulu Burun shipwreck was between 70 to 80cm (28 to 31in) in length. They were made of copper, which was an important metal during the Bronze Age.

US professors George F. Bass, founder and director of the Institute of Nautical Archaeology (INA), and Cemul Pulak. To avoid the bends (nitrogen narcosis) at these depths, the divers were able to work for only 20 minutes at a time.

Treasure trove

The Ulu Burun wreck has yielded the largest and richest collection of Late Bronze Age trading goods and artefacts found to date. Most of the ship's cargo consisted of commodities, notably Cypriot copper ingots, the earliest ingots of glass ever found, and almost 150 jars of resin, perhaps for burning as incense. There were logs of cedar and Egyptian ebony, elephant tusks, hippopotamus teeth (for carving), ostrich eggshells (for containers) and tortoise carapaces (to make musical instruments).

Among the manufactured goods on board were bronze and copper containers, pottery jars and cups, vessels of tin and fine faience and ceramics. There were many commercial weights, some in the shape of animals, including cows, bulls, lions, a sphinx, ducks, a frog and a housefly. The ship was also loaded with bronze woodworking tools and fishing implements, and weapons such as swordheads and arrowheads, daggers and swords.

Priceless commodities

The Ulu Burun ship is most famous for its precious cargo of gold, silver and electrum metal and ornaments; beads of glass and semi-precious

stones, such as agate, carnelian, quartz and amber; and jewellery, including bracelets and pendants. These goods came from far and wide – jewellery and pottery from Canaan (the eastern Mediterranean), fine pottery originating from Cyprus, animal products from tropical Africa and amber from northern Europe.

Some of the most valuable commodities and artefacts of gold, silver and electrum were Egyptian.

One of the most precious items salvaged from the wreck is a gold scarab, which is inscribed with what is believed to be the only surviving cartouche of Queen Nefertiti, wife of Pharaoh Akhenaten. Seals from the royal houses of Egypt, Assyria and Syria have also been found in the wreck. These have inspired a theory that the wreck was once a 'royal ship', perhaps under the patronage of the Egyptian pharaohs. However, other

Above An archaeologist works on a row of copper 'oxhide' ingots, one of four rows in situ. A total of 354 of these ingots have been found on the shipwreck.

objects found that belonged to the crew indicate that the men were from Canaan, Cyprus and Mycenae. These objects and the wide-ranging origin of the cargo suggest to others that the Ulu Burun ship carried commercial and private goods.

Olympia

Located in a fertile valley in the north-west of the Peloponnese in southern Greece, Olympia was the cult centre of Zeus, to whom the Olympic Games, first held in 776 BC, were dedicated. Today, the ruins of Olympia have provided an insight into the glory of the games.

Excavations at the site, which had been covered in silt brought down by the River Alpheios, began in 1875 by archaeologists from the Prussian Academy of Science; this marked the first permit issued to archaeologists from outside Greece. A major series of excavations resumed at Olympia in 1952, which are still continuing.

Sacred site

The understanding of the topography of the sanctuary has been helped by the descriptions of the 2nd-century AD Roman travel writer Pausanias. At the heart of the sacred space lay the Temple of Zeus, which was built during the second quarter of the 5th century BC. Excavations have uncovered marble figures from the two triangular pediments at either end.

The temple housed the gold and ivory cult statue of Zeus, one of the Seven Wonders of the Ancient World. The statue, which stood 15m (50ft)

high, has long disappeared (after being removed to Constantinople). However, the German excavators discovered the

Above A circular design from the interior of a 6th-century BC Athenian drinking cup shows a long jumper using weights.

workshop of the sculptor Pheidias to the west of the sanctuary (later turned into a Christian basilica). Inside were tools, moulds and materials used to craft the statue of Zeus.

To the east of the sanctuary, and joined to it by a tunnel, was the stadium in which some of the races for the original games took place. Remains of the stone starting line have been located. On the stadium's southern slope there is a stone platform for the *hellanodikai* (the judges). Bases for statues of the winners in the competitions have been found across the site. Other finds include a number of tripods decorated with griffins; some are likely to have been given as prizes in the events held within the sanctuary of Zeus.

Below Athletes practised boxing, wrestling and long jumping in the *palaestra*, an annexe of the gymnasium. This was surrounded by colonnades providing shelter from the sun.

Cyrene

The Greek colony of Cyrene, in Cyrenaica, a region in north-east Libya, was established in the late 7th century BC by people from the island of Thera. Today, the many ancient ruins speak of the city's 1000-year period as a flourishing trading centre.

The city was visited by European travellers from the early 18th century, but the first systematic survey was made by British army officers, Robert M. Smith and E.A. Porcher, during 1860-61. Richard Norton made the first scientific exploration by the Archaeological Institute of America. He was granted a permit by the Ottoman authorities in 1910. There appears to have been opposition from Italian interests in the archaeological sites, however, and one of Norton's colleagues was shot and killed. Norton started the exploration of the extensive necropolis of the city of Cyrene and recovered terracotta figures from an extra-mural sanctuary.

The agora

In September 1911 Cyrenaica was annexed by Italy and much of the initial survey work in the region was conducted by Federico Halbherr, who had earlier worked on Crete. The Italians concentrated their work on the main public space of the city – the agora. Remains of the council chamber, or *bouleuterion*, have been uncovered, as well as a shrine sacred to Battos, the founder of the colony. The agora was the area for the display of public monuments, such as a statue celebrating a Ptolemaic naval victory in the mid-3rd century BC.

The Roman influence

As Cyrenaica formed part of the Roman Empire, so the city attracted a series of benefactions. Among them was the construction of a temple to house the imperial cult. Other areas explored by archaeologists include the Temple of Apollo, lying to the north of the acropolis and whose origins lay in the earliest time of the colony. The temple was rebuilt during the reign of Emperor Hadrian after the Jewish revolt of AD 115-117. The *propylaeum*, or monumental gateway, dates to the time of Emperor Septimius Severus (ruled AD 193-211). In 2005 Italian archaeologists discovered 76 intact

Below Carved figures of Herakles and Hermes are from the gymnasium at Cyrene.

Roman statues, dating from the 2nd century AD, which had remained undiscovered since an earthquake occurred in AD 375.

Other discoveries

American excavations have continued at the extra-mural sanctuary of Demeter and Kore to the south of the city on the Wadi Bel Gadir. Substantial amounts of archaic (7th and 6th century BC) material have been found revealing contacts between the city and other parts of the Aegean world.

Delphi

Archaeologists have unearthed the oracle of Apollo at Delphi, the most important oracle in the Ancient World. At its peak in the 6th century BC people came from all over Greece and beyond to have questions about the future answered by the priestess Pythia, who spoke on behalf of Apollo.

The village of Kastri, which had occupied the area of the sanctuary of Apollo since medieval times, had to be relocated several kilometres away before excavations by the French School in Athens, first directed by Théophile Homolle (1848-1925), could begin in 1893. After the removal of huge quantities of earth, the remains of two sanctuaries, dedicated to Apollo and Athena, were uncovered. Outside the sanctuary, the gymnasium, the stadium, the settlement of Delphi and its cemeteries were also excavated.

The Temple of Apollo

The focal point for the sanctuary was the Temple of Apollo. The present remains date from the 4th century BC. However, at least two other temples have been identified. It is thought that the first was probably constructed in the 7th century BC but was destroyed by fire in the mid-6th century BC. Marble pedimental sculpture from this temple, depicting the epiphany of Apollo, has been recovered.

The temple was constructed on a large terrace supported by a massive retaining wall running along the contours. This formed the rear of a long colonnade, known as the Stoa of the Athenians. An inscription

indicates that booty from the Persian wars of the early 5th century BC was placed on display here.

The treasuries

The sanctuary was approached by a sacred way that snaked its way up the hill to the temple. This was lined by dedications and small buildings known as treasuries, which were dedicated by individual cities and housed gold, silver and priceless works of art.

Among the treasuries was one of the Greek island of Siphnos, which was mentioned by the Greek historian Herodotus (*c*.484-420 BC). It has been identified as the structure with caryatids (columns carved in the shape of clothed, standing young women) at the front of the building. Work on the treasury is still ongoing.

At the corner of the sacred way, in a prominent position, stood the treasury of the Athenians, thought to have been erected after the Athenian victory over the Persians at the battle of Marathon in 490 BC. The treasury was decorated with a series of metopes (reliefs) depicting the deeds of Herakles, and the new Athenian hero, Theseus. This building, which was restored by the French excavators in 1903-6, is the best-preserved on the site.

The *kouroi*

Herodotus mentioned the gift of a pair of statues by the people of Argos during the 6th century BC. These have sometimes been associated with the pair of striding male statues, or *kouroi* (plural of *kouros*, the Greek for 'a youth'), which were recovered by the French. A study of the inscriptions on the statues shows that they had indeed been made by sculptors from Argos, and that they represented the *Anakai*, the Argive cult associated with the sons of Zeus (and called the *Dioskouroi* elsewhere in the Greek world).

Now on display at the museum at

Opposite A scene from the continuous frieze around the Siphnian Treasury shows the battle between the gods and the giants (gigantomachy). A lion pulls the chariot.

Above Doric columns are at the eastern end of the Temple of Apollo. The monument was partly restored 1938-41. Excavations are still being carried out at the site to this day.

Delphi, these 2.2m- (7ft-) tall statues may originally have been displayed in an open-plan structure whose architectural elements have been found reused in other buildings at Delphi. There appears to have been a frieze showing scenes from the life of the *Dioskouroi/Anakai*. Researchers believe this building may have been damaged or dismantled when the sanctuary was rebuilt in the 6th century BC.

Bronze tripod

Just east of the temple the base of a bronze tripod, supported by twisted snakes, was discovered. A head of one of the snakes was found in nearby excavations, but the tripod itself had been taken to Constantinople in Late Antiquity, where it remains today. The tripod had been dedicated by the Greek cities that had fought against Persia during the invasion of mainland Greece in 480-479 BC.

Bronze charioteer

One of the most stunning sculptural finds made by the French excavators was the life-size bronze of a charioteer, which seems to have been toppled during an earthquake and landslide. Parts of the base have been discovered, showing that the bronze formed part of the victory monument of Polzalos, the tyrant of Gela on Sicily, who had won the chariot race in the Pythian games during the 470s BC. The group itself would have originally included the four horses pulling the chariot, and possibly two outriders. The sculpture depicts the charioteer at the moment when he presents his horses to the spectators in recognition of his victory.

Left The statue's eyelashes and lips are made of copper, while the eyes are made of onyx. He is wearing the long chiton worn by all charioteers during a race.

157

The Athenian Agora

Lying to the north of the Acropolis, the Agora, or marketplace, first became the commercial, political, religious and cultural centre of life in Athens in the early 6th century BC. The large open square was surrounded by shops, banks, council buildings, law courts and the mint.

In 1890-91 a deep trench cut for creating the Athens-Piraeus Railway revealed extensive remains of ancient buildings. Systematic excavations on the site of the Agora first began in 1931, under the auspices of the American School of Classical Studies at Athens. The location of the Agora had already been known, thanks to the topographical description given by the 2nd-century AD Roman travel writer Pausanias.

The heart of democracy

Excavations have uncovered buildings associated with Athenian democracy along the west side of the Agora. These include the *bouleuterion*, or council chamber, where 50 members of each of the 10 tribes of Attica met. Next to it was the *tholos*, a circular building where the presiding tribe for each of the months resided. In front of these buildings was a long stone base surmounted by statues of the heroes, after whom each of the Athenian tribes was named (more were added in the Hellenistic and Roman periods), and alongside which notices relating to each tribe could be displayed.

On the hill behind the public buildings is the well-preserved Temple of Hephaistos. The discovery of planting pits dating from the 3rd century BC indicate that the grounds of the temple were fully landscaped.

On the north side of the Agora was the 'Royal' stoa, or colonnade, where the laws of Athens were placed. Next to it was another stoa decorated with painted panels, showing scenes from the famous Athenian victory at the battle of Marathon in 490 BC. Remains of one of the law courts have been found, including ballots for making decisions in trials.

The Agora received a number of benefactions in the Hellenistic period, including the stoa given by Attalos II, a king of Pergamon. The Romans added a concert hall (the *odeion*) to the open square at the end of the 1st century AD, and Emperor Augustus seems to have moved a redundant temple of Ares, the god of war, from the countryside round Athens and reconstructed it in the open space.

Left The reconstructed Stoa of Attalos, built in about 150 BC, is now a museum.

Tarquinia

Beautiful frescoes adorn some of the 6th-century BC burial tombs found in Tarquinia, in modern Tuscany. These scenes, which include figures playing sports, hunting and banqueting, provide an important insight into the culture of the Etruscans, who dominated the area north of Rome.

The cemeteries of Etruria drew increasing interest in the 19th century. The rock-cut tombs were opened and their contents – bronzes and fine figure-decorated pottery, such as the Athenian pottery with local metalwork found by Signor Rispoli in the late 1880s – were transported to museums.

The excavations of the Monterozzi cemetery (1958-63) was sponsored by the Lerici Foundation. It uncovered some 5500 tombs of the 6th and 5th centuries BC. The Foundation also backed excavations of the Hellenistic Villa Tarantola cemetery in the 1960s.

Excavations in the cemeteries suggest that there was contact with the eastern Mediterranean from the 8th century BC. One of the tombs had a faience vase bearing the cartouche of the Egyptian pharaoh Boccohoris (late 8th century BC); a scarab of the same pharaoh was found in a grave on the island of Ischia in the Bay of Naples.

In recent years archaeologists have carried out photographic probes of the tombs at Tarquinia, by inserting a camera into a small hole dug into the tomb. This provides a photographic record of the contents of the tomb before they are exposed to the light.

Painted tombs

A burial chamber of the mid-6th century BC, known as the Tomb of the Bulls, includes a fresco depicting the ambush of Prince Troilus by Achilles during the Trojan War. Sporting events, including discus-throwing, are portrayed on the walls of the Tomb of the Olympic Games. The natural

Above A banqueting scene in the Tomb of the Leopards shows one man holding an egg, the symbol of life after death. All are wearing crowns of laurel for the festive occasion.

world is represented in the decoration of the Tomb of Hunting and Fishing, dated to about 520 BC, which includes scenes of birds and dolphins and fishermen casting their nets. The Tomb of the Leopards (early 5th century BC) shows a banqueting scene.

One of the features of the tombs was the inclusion of false architectural details, so that the tombs resemble the rooms of a house. This technique can be seen in the Tomb of the Augurs (late 6th century BC), where a double door is flanked by two figures with arms outstretched.

Left This gold Etruscan earring is dated to the 3rd century BC. Etruscan goldwork was of an exceptionally high standard. One technique was granulation, which involved the soldering of tiny beads of gold.

Pergamon

In the 3rd to 2nd centuries BC, Pergamon, in north-west Turkey, developed into a major power. Successive Attalid kings transformed the city into one of the most important architectural and cultural centres of the Hellenistic east. Its library was second only to Alexandria's.

The city of Pergamon was established by Philetairos in 283 BC and continued down to 133 BC when King Attalos III bequeathed it to Rome. It stands on a steeply sloping hill, with the royal buildings at the highest point. With its combination of monumental sculptures, Temple of Athena and theatre, the acropolis at Pergamon seems to have been designed to evoke the acropolis at Athens.

The Altar of Zeus

Antiquities had been removed from the site since the 17th century. The first scientific investigation was instigated by Carl Humann in the 1870s. He worked with the support of the Royal Museums in Berlin and came to an agreement with the Ottoman authorities that one-third of the finds could be removed. Humann's initial focus was on the monumental Altar of Zeus at the south end of the site. The altar, which measured 36.4 x 34.2m (119 x 112ft), had been constructed by Eumenes II (197-159 BC) to commemorate the defeat of the Gauls, who had arrived in Anatolia in the early 2nd century BC. The altar was surrounded by a continuous 120m-(394ft-) long marble relief frieze – perhaps inspired by the frieze on the Parthenon at Athens – showing a gigantomachy (battle between the Greek gods and giants). The iconography of the frieze also included scenes about Telephos, the mythical forefather of the Attalids.

The precinct of Athena

To the north of the altar was the Doric temple of Athena. This was surrounded by a series of colonnades, or stoas, which carried relief carvings of the weapons of the defeated enemies of Pergamon. The bases of a number of sculptural groups were found in the open space before the temple. These may have included the famous statue groups known from ancient classical authors, such as Pliny the Elder, which commemorated the defeat of the Gauls. It is likely that the

Left In 1871 the front of the Altar of Zeus was shipped to Germany, where it has been reconstructed in the Pergamon Museum, Berlin.

'Dying Gaul' and a group showing the suicide of a Gaul after killing his wife, which were known from Roman copies, were derived from Pergamene originals displayed in this area.

The library

The north stoa of the precinct of Athena also provided access to the celebrated library of Pergamon. Study of the holes for mounting the shelving has allowed scholars to estimate that the reading room alone would have stored some 20,000 papyri, perhaps one-tenth of the total for the library. Inside the reading room was a colossal statue of Athena, which may have been a copy of the Athena Promachos from the Athenian acropolis.

The Trajaneum

At the northern end of the acropolis was the Trajaneum. Built in the Corinthian style with 6 x 9 columns, this temple was the focus for worship of the deified Roman emperor Trajan, completed by his successor Hadrian (ruled AD 117-138). In the excavation of the site, remnants of sculptures of both emperors were found.

Above Only ruins survive of the Trajaneum, which originally stood 18m (60ft) tall.

Theatre of Dionysos

On the western slope of the acropolis, below the Temple of Athena, was located the steeply raked Theatre of Dionysos, god of wine. The top row was some 36m (118ft) above the level of the actors. The theatre provided a focal point for the acropolis to anyone approaching the city from the west. The 80 rows of seats would have held an audience of about 10,000 people. The bottom of the theatre was level with a long terrace, which provided access to the Temple of Dionysos. Plays were performed on a portable wooden stage, which was removed between performances and stored in the theatre terrace's lower floors. Three rows of quadrangular holes remain in the floor of the theatre terrace that once held the wooden support beams for the temporary stage.

Sanctuary of Asklepios

In the lower city there was a major Sanctuary of Asklepios, the healing god. This seems to have been established in the 4th century BC and was one of the three main healing centres of the god in the Aegean, alongside Kos and Epidauros. The sanctuary received a number of benefactions during the Roman period. One of the most notable was the domed temple itself, given by the Roman consul Lucius Cuspius Pactumeius Rufinus in the middle of the 2nd century AD. The design appears to have been based on the Pantheon at Rome.

Below An aerial view of the acropolis shows the Trajaneum at the centre, with the columns at the rear outlining the northern portico.

Carthage

Founded as a Phoenician colony on the Tunisian coast near Tunis, ancient Carthage rose to become one of the great powers of the Mediterranean and Rome's most dangerous rival. In 146 BC the city was destroyed by Rome. However, archaeologists have still been able to make discoveries.

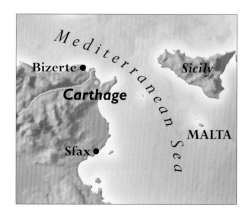

The site was excavated by Charles Ernest Beulé from the 1850s. In 1925 Francis W. Kelsey excavated the *tophet*, the sanctuary sacred to the deities Tanit and Baal Hammon, and found it to contain the remains of children who had been sacrificed. This was the subject of a series of rescue excavations in the 1970s supported by UNESCO.

The German archaeologist F. Rakob uncovered the earliest levels relating to the Phoenicians. These date to the 8th century BC, which roughly corresponds to the traditional foundation date of 814 BC given in ancient texts.

The city

Details about the range of religious temples has come from Punic (Phoenician) inscriptions, although the evidence of religious structures is slight and reflects the efficiency of the Roman destruction of the city. Rescue excavations have revealed information about the housing. Some of the wealthier buildings, for example, had internal colonnades.

The cemeteries of the Phoenician city were discovered by the Frenchman Father Delattre in 1878. Some of these were accessed by vertical shafts and the lowest levels can be more than 30m (98ft) underground. Further work on the cemeteries is being undertaken by the University of Georgia.

The harbours

The western Phoenicians spread across much of the western Mediterranean. Their strength lay in their ships and there were two main harbours for the city. The circular harbour appears to have been used for the war fleet. British excavations there have revealed evidence for activity as early as the 5th century BC. The second rectangular harbour seems to have been used for commercial shipping. Other significant Punic harbour facilities have been excavated at Motya, in western Sicily, which was destroyed by the people of Syracuse in the early 4th century BC.

Roman Carthage

By the middle of the 1st century AD, Carthage was established as a thriving Roman colony. Named Colonia Julia Carthago, after Julius Caesar, it became the hub of the prosperous Roman province of North Africa, with a population peaking at approximately 500,000. Among the remains of the Roman city are elements of a massive bath complex, which appears to have been constructed in the middle of the 2nd century AD. The Romans also built an aqueduct stretching over 130km (81 miles) to supply the city's demand for water.

Left Stone stelae, such as these in the *tophet* sanctuary, were set up over urns containing the ashes of human sacrifices.

The Domus Aurea

Following a devastating fire in Rome in AD 64, Emperor Nero seized a large area of the ruined city to create a huge palace. Named the Domus Aurea, or Golden House, because of its gold-covered façade, its extravagance shocked the citizens of Rome and amazed the archaeologists who later excavated it.

The remains of Nero's extravaganza remained buried until the late 15th century, when some chambers were discovered by accident. The scale of the project to the north-east of the Palatine was vast: conservative modern estimates suggest it may have covered at least 50ha (124 acres). It included pavilions, reception rooms, gardens and an artificial lake. At the entrance, Nero placed a colossal statue of himself that was intended to evoke the Colossus of Rhodes. The palace was described by the Roman biographer Suetonius, who mentioned ivory fittings and inlaid jewels in the ceilings. The Domus Aurea was probably the intended setting for works of art that Nero had removed from various cities and sanctuaries in the empire.

After Nero's suicide in AD 68, successive emperors attempted to obliterate the Golden House. The main parts were filled in with earth and built over. Part of the western end is covered by the Baths of Trajan. The artificial lake was drained and became the site of the Flavian Colosseum.

A palace fit for a feast

Excavations beneath the Baths of Trajan have revealed parts of Nero's building. Just over half of the length of the building has been explored, and originally it must have been approximately 400m (1312ft) long. One of the major features of the palace was the provision made for huge banquets. Some 50 dining rooms have been found arranged round a rectangular courtyard in the western end of the complex.

Above The Domus Aurea still lies under the ruins of the Baths of Trajan.

Below The octagonal room has smaller rooms that radiate from it.

At the centre of the western wing was an octagonal courtyard covered by a concrete dome with a central oculus (opening) to let in light. This was surrounded by five dining rooms, each with a water feature. On either side would have been two polygonal courtyards; the western one, which still survives, is itself surrounded by 15 dining rooms.

Although the palace was stripped of its treasures by subsequent emperors, fine frescoes and mosaics on the walls and ceilings have survived, and they provided inspiration for Renaissance artists such as Raphael. One of the long connecting corridors had apparently just been plastered, probably in preparation for a fresco, when the palace was abandoned.

Ostia

Located at the mouth of the River Tiber, Ostia became Rome's principal port in the 1st century AD. Many of its buildings, including apartment blocks, amphitheatre, shops and baths, remain to this day, providing important clues to urban life in the Roman Empire.

Rome's growing population meant that it became increasingly reliant on imported foodstuffs, especially grain. The harbour at Ostia was too shallow for the larger ships to enter, so their goods had to be transferred to smaller vessels to be brought on shore. Grain convoys waiting to be unloaded were occasionally wrecked, leading to shortages and the threat of political unrest. In AD 42, during the rule of Emperor Claudius, work began on the construction of a new permanent and secure harbour, which was completed by his successor Nero (AD 54-68).

The port's facilities underwent further improvements under Emperor Trajan, who ruled AD 98-117, with the construction of a hexagonal harbour. There was space for at least 100 ships, and cargoes could be offloaded into

Below A mosaic shows ships entering the harbour of Ostia, represented by the central lighthouse. The inscription reads: 'Here ends every pain'.

a series of warehouses built behind the harbour front. Grain and other materials could then be transported to the city of Rome via a specially constructed canal, which has been identified by a geophysical survey conducted by British archaeologists from the University of Southampton.

With the end of the Roman Empire, Ostia fell slowly into decline and was effectively abandoned in the 9th century AD. The city became a source for building materials and its marble was used in the construction of St Peter's basilica in Rome.

Renewed interest

In the late 18th century Ostia attracted the interests of dealers in antiquities – among them the Scotsman Gavin Hamilton – who supplied the European elite on their Grand Tour. As Ostia was part of the papal possessions a series of studies were made during the 19th century, initially at the prompting of Pope Pius VII. One of the

first scientific excavations at Ostia was conducted by Rodolfo Lanciani in the 1870s. The first series of major excavations was conducted from 1907 by Dane Vaglieri. Mussolini encouraged extensive work at Ostia from 1938 in anticipation of the proposed world fair of 1942. The outbreak of World War II, however, meant that scientific excavations did not resume until 1953.

The city revealed

At the heart of the city lay the Piazzale delle Corporazioni. This square was surrounded by a series of small offices for the merchants who used the port. Many of them are named in a series of mosaics. Thus, it has been possible to identify links with Alexandria in Egypt, Carthage in North Africa and Narbonne in Gaul. A theatre, which probably belongs to the early imperial period, was adjacent to the complex. Major public buildings included extensive bath complexes, such as the Maritime Baths. Excavations between

Above The Capitolium, dating back to the 2nd century AD, was built on an unusually high podium so it dominated its surroundings. Six columns used to stand in front of it.

Numerous temples have been discovered, some sacred to standard Roman deities, others to cults introduced from the provinces of the empire. One of the central temples was the Capitolium (Temple of Jupiter, Juno and Minerva). Among the earliest cults to be introduced was that of the Anatolian female deity Cybele, who arrived at the end of the 3rd century BC. A number of *Mithraea* (temples dedicated to the worship of the Persian god, Mithras) have been found in the city. Part of the initiation rites of Mithraism included the ceremonial killing of a bull. Evidence for Egyptian cults, such as Serapis and Isis, have been found, reflecting the close links between Italy and Egypt generated through the trade in grain.

One of Ostia's cemeteries on Isola Sacra – a sacred artificial island – was excavated by G. Calza from 1925-40. The anthropological study of the human remains now forms part of a major project by La Sapienza University in Rome.

1997 and 2001 by archaeologists from the University of Augsburg have made a study of one of the *macella*, or meat markets, of the city.

The excavations have also revealed aspects of domestic arrangements in a Roman city. A number of housing blocks have been explored. These differ from the traditional houses found in Roman cities, and reflect the growing pressure on space in the expanding urban areas of the imperial period. These structures were usually three storeys high, a height restricted by Roman legislation in the face of poor building. Elsewhere, numerous shops, taverns, workshops and some of the city's communal latrines have been uncovered.

Below Traders and craftsmen are buried in tombs in the Isola Sacra cemetery.

Pompeii

Excavation of the ruined city of Pompeii has provided an extraordinary snapshot of Roman life in the 1st century AD. Streets, houses, shops and even people have been frozen in time, just as they were on the fateful summer day in AD 79 when Mount Vesuvius erupted.

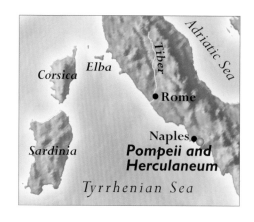

Pompeii lies to the south-east of Mount Vesuvius alongside the Bay of Naples in the Italian region of Campania. The city had been buried under ash during the catastrophic volcanic eruption and the site was effectively lost for 1600 years. Many neighbouring communities, most famously Herculaneum, were also destroyed or damaged.

Rediscovery

Remains of the city came to light in 1748 when the first of a series of excavations of the site began. One of the first buildings to be recognized was the Temple of Isis, which had been restored following an earlier earthquake at Pompeii in AD 62.

The first scientific excavations of Pompeii were conducted by the Italian Giuseppe Fiorelli. He had already prepared studies of the history of excavations at Pompeii, and had made a plan of the city, dividing it into *regions* — a system still used today. It was Fiorelli's expertise that brought about the creation of a School of Archaeology at Pompeii (1866-75). Fiorelli was also responsible for the reorganization of the finds from the excavations at Pompeii in the museum at Naples.

Life in a Roman town

The excavated town has revealed much about everyday life. The Forum, the baths, the many shops, taverns and houses, and some out-of-town villas,

Below The oldest known amphitheatre, built in 80 BC, could hold 20,000 spectators. The 2-m (6-ft) parapet would originally have been painted with fighting and hunting scenes.

valuable insight into Roman politics at the time. The city was controlled by a series of magistrates, such as *duoviri* and *aediles*, who were elected on an annual basis. One study has reconstructed the list of candidates for office for the nine-year period prior to the eruption. Some of the texts show that individuals supported a package of candidates for office.

The latest research

Recent geological work has been able to explain the pattern of the volcanic eruption and the sequence for the series of flows of volcanic fragments (pyroclastic) that swept down onto the city. This enhances the contemporary eyewitness accounts by the Younger Pliny whose uncle, Pliny the Elder, died during the disaster.

The initial cloud that came up from the mountain contained ash and pumice, and it seems that debris was deposited towards the south of the eruption. Pliny's account mentions that individuals had to tie pillows to their heads to try to protect themselves from the debris, or lapilli.

As ash accumulated at Pompeii, rows of houses would have collapsed, thereby denying the occupants any sense of protection. The earliest pyroclastic flows hit Pompeii on the morning of 25 August, destroying the villas that were situated outside its walls. Around 7.30 a.m. a further surge broke over the city. As many of the bodies were found above the 2.5m- (8ft-) deep layer of pumice, it has been estimated that approximately 10 per cent of the city may have been killed at this point.

One relatively modern approach to the study of Pompeii has been through the work carried out by Wilhelmina Jashemski on the gardens of the city. She was able to study the remains of plant roots alongside pollen analysis to reconstruct the range of plants used in the 1st century AD. Excavation revealed that parts of some of the gardens at Pompeii were given over to the cultivation of vegetables and vines. There is also evidence of the cultivation of citrus trees.

Herculaneum

The neighbouring town of Herculaneum had been buried by a series of pyroclastic flows – ground-hugging avalanches of hot ash, pumice, rock fragments and volcanic gas – in the early hours of the morning of 25 August. There was little warning, and it may have taken as little as four minutes for the flow to travel from the slopes of Vesuvius to the town.

Remains at Herculaneum were first discovered in 1711 when a well was being dug at a depth of 15-18m (50-60ft). Early excavations were conducted by cutting a series of horizontal tunnels and extracting whatever antiquities had been found. Some of the earliest exploration was in the area of the theatre; among the early finds was the larger-than-life-size bronze statue of Lucius Mammius Maximus, who appears to have been a freedman (a slave who has been given his freedom). Excavations were conducted sporadically throughout the 19th century.

The intense heat of the pyroclastic flows had caused rapid carbonization (partial burning). Herculaneum has yielded some of the best examples of organic remains, including timber, furniture, cloth and even loaves of bread. In 1982 excavations by the seafront in a series of boat-sheds uncovered remains of the bodies of victims who had sought refuge during the eruption. Careful excavation has shown how they were smothered as the pyroclastic flows hit the city. Evidence of flying debris was discovered in fractured bones. Studies of the bodies has revealed significant information about the lifestyles and ages of the individuals. This find has challenged earlier theories that few people had been killed in Herculaneum; renewed estimates suggest that thousands may have died in the eruption.

Excavations have uncovered remains of one of the main bath complexes as well as the edge of the forum area. Among the private residences was the Villa of the Papyri, so-called because of the discovery of more than 1000 carbonized papyrus rolls from the library of Lucius Calpurnius Piso Caesonius, an elite member of the community.

Above The excavated buildings at Herculaneum can be seen with Mount Vesuvius looming in the background. Much of the city remains unexcavated.

Masada

Mediterranean Sea

River Jordan

Syrian Desert

Tel Aviv-Yafo •
Jerusalem •
Gaza •
• Amman
○ **Masada**
Dead Sea

Negev Desert

The fortress-palace of Masada, built by Herod the Great (ruled 37-4 BC), is famous as the last stronghold of Jews in the Jewish Revolt of AD 66-73. Facing Roman invasion after a six-month siege, over 960 Jews – men, women and children – committed mass suicide on the rock in AD 73.

Roman activities at Masada were recorded by the Jewish historian Josephus (AD 37-c.100) in his account of the Jewish War. The site, on the edge of the Judean Desert at the southern end of the Dead Sea, was first identified in 1838 by the American scholars Edward Robinson and Eli Smith. In 1867 the site was surveyed by Charles Warren, on behalf of the Palestine Exploration Fund.

Herod's fortifications

An important survey of Masada was made in 1955-56, on behalf of the Israel Exploration Society. This led to

Below The remains of the defensive wall on the plateau of the rock, which rises about 440m (1444ft) above the Dead Sea.

a major excavation made by the Israeli archaeologist Yigael Yadin (1963–65). Among the buildings uncovered was Herod's stunningly constructed palace at the north end of the rocky outcrop.

The palace effectively hangs above the ravine and gives views northwards over the Dead Sea and the Judean Desert. Massive terraces had to be put into place to support the palace.

The decoration of the palace, in Roman style with Corinthian columns and wall paintings imitating panels of fine marble, indicates the strong links between Herod and the Roman world. On the uppermost terrace Yadin discovered a Roman-style bath house – further evidence of how far Roman cultural customs had begun to be adopted by the ruling elite in Judea.

A synagogue was discovered on the western side of the plateau. This had four tiers of plastered benches along the walls and two rows of columns in the centre. Also unearthed were fragments of Old Testament scrolls, containing parts of the books of Deuteronomy and Ezekiel.

The occupation period

During the siege in AD 73 by the 10th Roman legion, Masada was completely encircled by a series of Roman siege walls supported by eight forts. These had been plotted in the 1920s by the British Royal Air Force. Further detailed study was conducted by the British scholar Sir Ian Richmond, who was able to produce a detailed map of the structures.

Qumran

In 1947 the unexpected discovery of biblical scrolls, often called the Dead Sea Scrolls, encouraged the exploration and excavation of a series of caves on the eastern edge of the Judean Desert at the north-western end of the Dead Sea. Nearby was located a complex at Khirbet Qumran, which was excavated by Roland de Vaux from 1951 to 1956.

By the end of 30 BC the site seems to have been the location for a Jewish religious community, which has been linked to a Jewish sect known as the Essenes. Coins dating from the time of the Jewish Revolt suggest that the settlement had been abandoned in AD 68.

Pottery found at Qumran appears to be the same as that found in the caves where the scrolls were discovered. It has been suggested that the scrolls may have been prepared at the main site, where there is apparent evidence of a scriptorium, or writing room, on what must have been an upper floor. Parts of the cemetery have been excavated, which was found to contain the bodies of both men and women; this has raised issues about the prevailing view that this was an all-male community.

Above Fragments of one of the scrolls, known as the Rule of the Community.

The Romans erected a controlling fortress on a plateau immediately opposite the palace; this is likely to have been the camp from where the Roman governor Flavius Silva controlled the operations. Each of the forts was protected by special gateways with an inturned entrance. A massive siege ramp was constructed from the west, protected by the positioning of Roman siege artillery behind it.

Josephus described the drama and tragedy of the mass suicides in AD 73. Rather than fall into Roman hands, first men killed their wives and children, then drew lots to kill the rest of the garrison. However, relatively few bodies have been discovered. Radiocarbon tests on textiles associated with a group of approximately 25 skeletons suggest a date broadly in keeping with the capture of Masada. The presence of pig bones, however, has suggested that these bodies may be linked to the Roman garrison that was located at the site for some time after the suppression of the revolt.

Stonehenge A major complex of prehistoric monuments whose purpose is still shrouded in mystery.

Sutton Hoo An Anglo-Saxon burial ship with a wealth of artefacts discovered in England in 1939.

Biskupin A fortified lakeside settlement of timber-built buildings dating back to the 8th century BC.

Skara Brae

North Sea

Baltic Sea

Newgrange

Biskupin

Mezhirich

Sutton Hoo
Stonehenge

EUROPE

Carnac

Heuneburg

Bay of Biscay

The Alps

The Iceman

Bla Se

Lascaux

Adriatic Sea

Pyrenees

Lascaux A cave, rediscovered in 1940, with the most spectacular collection of Palaeolithic wall art yet found.

The Iceman The body of a prehistoric man, with some of his belongings, frozen in time for around 5,300 years.

Mezhirich These extraordinary Ice Age dwellings were constructed from the bones and tusks of the woolly mammoth.

THE GREAT SITES OF EUROPE

Archaeology as a subject really began in Europe, as educated people tried to learn more about impressive monuments, such as Stonehenge in England. As the world of scholarship in the mid-19th century began to realize that humankind had a very ancient past, the study of prehistoric sites got underway, including the decorated caves of the last Ice Age. We now know that there were people in parts of Europe, such as Atapuerca (Spain), up to a million years ago, so the time scale of the continent's prehistory is immense.

Europe is home to a fascinating and diverse range of important sites and material – from the unsurpassed cave paintings of Lascaux to mysterious stone circles, and from mammoth-bone houses to Iron Age forts. These discoveries – as well as the magnificent ship burial at Sutton Hoo in England and the wonderfully preserved Iceman found in the Tyrolean Alps – provide important clues about our past and ancestors.

Carnac The landscape of this region is studded with impressive Neolithic monuments, including alignments of standing stones.

The Heuneburg The site of a Celtic fortress provides a fascinating glimpse of life in Iron Age Europe.

Skara Brae A unique Neolithic settlement of stone-built houses on Orkney, preserved for thousands of years beneath the sand.

Mezhirich

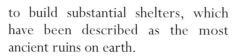

The Ice Age inhabitants of Mezhirich, in the Ukraine, built their dwellings from the bones and tusks of the woolly mammoth. These extraordinary mammoth-bone houses — along with others discovered at sites in Eastern Europe — represent the world's oldest human architecture.

We often think of the Ice Age people of Europe as having lived in caves, and it is true that when caves were available they were usually the first choice. In many parts of Europe, however, there were few or no caves, and the Palaeolithic (literally meaning 'old stone age') hunters had to live in the open. This required the construction of shelters from whatever materials were available. Although trees were scarce on the steppes of southern Russia and Ukraine, fortunately the bones of mammoths were plentiful, and the Ice Age inhabitants used them to build substantial shelters, which have been described as the most ancient ruins on earth.

The mammoth-bone houses of this treeless plain were built after the last maximum deep freeze of the Ice Age that took place about 20,000-18,000 years ago. Since the number of individual mammoths represented by the bones in these sites is immense, it seems unlikely that they were obtained solely as the result of hunting. Instead, most were probably gathered from the natural accumulations of bones that were found on the periglacial landscape as mammoths died natural deaths over the centuries. When people reoccupied the area as the ice sheets retreated northwards, around 17,000 years ago, they would have found the bones lying about and selected the ones most suitable for construction. Jaws, tusks, shoulder blades and long bones were lugged back to the settlement sites — no mean feat since mammoth bones can be extremely heavy.

The bone-house dwellers

Along with mammoths, the inhabitants of Mezhirich also hunted bison, bear, reindeer, horse, hares and Arctic fox, along with rodents and birds. They either ranged over vast areas or had a wide network of trading contacts, for crystal, ochre and amber found at Mezhirich came from dozens — even hundreds — of kilometres away. Bone and ivory were worked into beads and pendants, and some of the mammoth bones had traces of paint.

Archaeologists believe that the mammoth-bone houses at Mezhirich and other sites in the Dnieper and Don valleys served as base camps during the long winter on the periglacial steppe. About 25-50 people may have lived at each of these sites for several months at a time. During the short summer, their inhabitants probably dispersed to temporary camps in pursuit of game. As well as serving a functional purpose, these mammoth-bone structures would have provided a strong visual signal about the presence of their inhabitants on the landscape.

Below The plan shows the mammoth bones at the excavation of Mezhirich Dwelling 4. The long tusks are clearly visible.

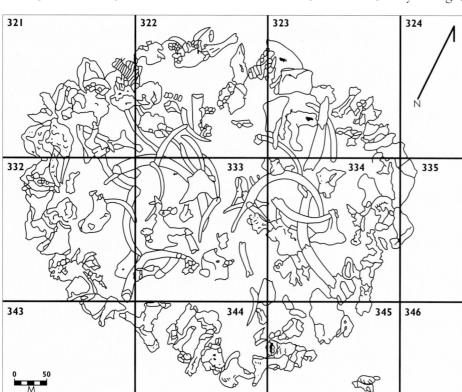

The Mezhirich site

Located along a tributary of the Dnieper river southeast of Kiev, Mezhirich is one of the best-studied and best-preserved Ice Age sites. The mammoth-bone houses here were built about 15,000 years ago.

In 1965 a farmer digging his cellar, almost 2m (6ft 6in) below ground, struck the massive lower jaw of a mammoth with his spade. The jawbone was upside down and had been inserted into the bottom of another jaw.

A year later, the first of several excavation campaigns at the site revealed the traces of four circular structures, each measuring between 6m and 10m (20ft and 33ft) in diameter, plus associated hearths, pits and habitation refuse. Other structures may be present in unexcavated parts of the site. The presence of refuse layers and hearths confirms the residential nature of these structures.

When excavated the structures appear as jumbles of bones, but careful mapping and study permit the reconstruction of the architecture. Jaws were stacked up to form walls, supplemented by long bones. In one house, 95 mammoth jaws were carefully piled several deep to make an interlocking herringbone pattern of structural bone. Tusks and shoulder blades formed the roof framing, which was probably covered over by hides. Such shelters would have been necessary to protect the inhabitants from the bitter winds that swept across the steppes at

Above It is thought that the red design on this painted mammoth skull may represent the flames and sparks of a fire.

Above This reconstruction is of a Mezhirich mammoth-bone dwelling.

the end of the Ice Age. A hearth inside each hut kept the occupants warm and permitted the cooking of meat.

Spadzista Street

The remains of mammoth bones were also found at a somewhat earlier site in southern Poland, named Spadzista Street B. Recent studies have shown, however, that there are key differences between this site and Mezhirich. At Mezhirich, large bones useful for building were selected from natural accumulations. At Spadzista Street, however, many small bones from extremities, skulls and tails were found. As it seems unlikely that people would have transported such small bones any distance for construction, Spadzista Street has now been interpreted as the site of a mammoth butchery site, possibly a killing site.

Lascaux

Discovered in 1940 by four teenage boys, the cave of Lascaux, situated on a hill above the town of Montignac in Dordogne, France, houses one of the biggest collections of Palaeolithic figures, including about 600 painted animals and abstract signs and almost 1500 engravings.

No proper excavation was ever carried out in Lascaux, and much of the archaeological layer was lost when the floor was lowered and the cave adapted for tourism. Nevertheless, it is clear that this was never a habitation site, and people merely made brief periodic visits for artistic activity or ritual. Charcoal fragments have provided radiocarbon dates around 15,000 BC.

Dazzling imagery

The Palaeolithic entrance of the cave may have been close to the modern artificial entry leading into the great Hall of the Bulls, whose walls are covered in painted figures. They were apparently outlined, and then their infill was done by spraying or with a pad and dampened powder.

The hall's frieze is dominated by a series of four enormous black aurochs bulls (now extinct), over 5m (16ft) in length, as well as smaller horses and tiny deer. The frieze begins at the left with an enigmatic imaginary animal, with two straight horns, known oddly as the 'Unicorn'.

The hall is prolonged by the Axial Gallery, which has a keyhole shape in cross section, and whose upper walls and ceiling were decorated with more paintings of cattle, deer and horses, as well as dots and quadrilateral signs. The figures include the so-called Chinese horses (named because of their superficial resemblance to the style of horses in some Chinese art) and a jumping cow.

Right A detail from one of the paintings of aurochs bulls at Lascaux.

Above The painter of the back-to-back bison has managed to convey a sense of movement.

At the far end is a falling horse, painted upside down around a rock; photographic reproduction has revealed that, although the artist could never see the whole animal at once, it is in perfect proportion. The Lascaux artists also conveyed perspective simply and cleverly by leaving the far limbs of the animals unattached to the bodies.

Leading off to the right from the Hall of the Bulls is the Passage. Here there are almost 400, often small, engravings, dominated numerically (like all of the cave's art) by horses, depicted in the same style as the other paintings. To one side is the Great Apse, which contains over 1000, often superimposed, engravings.

Within the Apse is the entrance to the shaft, 5m (16ft) deep, containing the famous scene of a bird-headed man (the cave's only human figure). He has an erect phallus and is falling backwards in front of an apparently speared bison with its entrails spilling out; a bird on a stick stands nearby, and a rhinoceros painted in a different style walks off to the left.

Beyond the Apse is the Nave, with its frieze of five black deer heads, each 1m (3ft) high and usually described as swimming; the nave also has two painted male bison, facing in different directions, with overlapping rumps. The cave ends with the narrow, 25-m (82-ft) long 'Gallery of the Felines', into which one can only crawl; it is covered in engravings, including six felines.

Techniques

Stone tools suitable for engraving were found only in the engraved zones. Many lamps were recovered. The cave contained 158 mineral fragments, together with crude mortars and pestles stained with pigment. There are scratches and signs of wear on many of the mineral lumps. Black dominates, followed by yellows, reds and white. Chemical analysis revealed sophisticated uses of heating and mixing of different minerals to produce a variety of hues.

For much of the decoration, ladders or scaffolding must have been used. In the Axial Gallery there are sockets cut into the rock on both sides, which probably held branches forming joists for a platform, to provide access to the upper walls and ceiling.

Although seen in recent decades as a homogeneous cave, whose art was produced within a few centuries of 15,000 BC, Lascaux is currently undergoing reappraisal. Its history now seems far more complex, with a number of decorative episodes, possibly scattered through millennia.

Motivation

Many different theories have been put forward to explain the phenomenon of Ice Age cave art, from being used as hunting magic to depicting fantasies involving shamans and trance imagery. There is no doubt that some cave art — though by no means all — had a strong religious motivation of some kind, and much of it was probably linked to mythology, and the transmission of information of different kinds.

Lascaux II

The cave opened to the public in 1948, but it had to be closed again in 1963 when it was realized that the numbers of visitors (eventually reaching 100,000 per year) were having a radical effect on the cave's micro-environment, and causing the proliferation of algae and bacteria. These problems have now been largely overcome, and although the public is no longer admitted, a facsimile of the cave and its paintings has been made nearby. Opened in 1983, Lascaux II receives 300,000 visitors per year.

Stonehenge

Located on Salisbury Plain in Wiltshire in southern England, Stonehenge is Britain's most famous and enigmatic prehistoric monument. The original purpose and meaning of this complex structure of stone and earth, which first began to be built around 5000 years ago, is still shrouded in mystery.

Excavations and radiocarbon dating carried out at the site over the years have revealed that Stonehenge is the remnants of at least three different circles. The first monument, dated to about 2950 BC, was a simple circular enclosure – an earthen bank with a ditch on the outside, and two entrances at north-east and south. Such ritual structures, called 'henges', are well known in Britain, although their ditch is usually on the inside. The depth of the Stonehenge ditch was about 2m (6ft 6in), and the chalk excavated from it was piled up to form the interior bank, which was also about 2m (6ft 6in) high.

A circle of 56 holes was dug within the henge. These holes are known as Aubrey holes, after their 17th-century discoverer, John Aubrey. The holes do not seem to have contained posts or upright stones, and they were later filled in – many contained cremation ashes. Also at this time, two great stones were erected at the entrance. One of them, known as the heel stone, still survives.

The second and third stages

In around 2600 BC the so-called bluestones were erected in a circle, after probably being transported 322km (200 miles) from the Preseli Hills of South Wales. Some specialists insist that the bluestones arrived in the vicinity of Stonehenge as erratics, through natural glacial action during the Ice Age. However, there is a total absence of such rocks in Wessex except in prehistoric monuments. So unless one argues that prehistoric people used every single large bluestone in the area, the only other explanation is that the rocks were brought to the area through human transport, despite the great distances and efforts required.

Finally, around 2300 BC, the great blocks of sarsen stone (a hard sandstone), weighing 25 to 45 tonnes, were hauled by hundreds of people more than 32km (20 miles) to the site. These enormous sarsen stones were set up as a ring of uprights with their unique lintels. Within this circle was an inner horseshoe setting of five trilithons ('three stones'), each

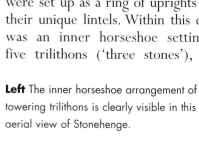

Left The inner horseshoe arrangement of towering trilithons is clearly visible in this aerial view of Stonehenge.

Above The standing stones and trilithons cast shadows across the surrounding grassland of Salisbury Plain.

comprising two uprights with a horizontal stone on top. The lintels, weighing 9 tonnes, were held in place with mortise and tenon joints.

In 1953 some petroglyphs (carvings on rock) of prehistoric daggers and axe-heads were discovered on one of the sarsen uprights in the horseshoe, and more were detected recently, thanks to laser scanning.

Excavations at Stonehenge have recovered an abundance of sarsen 'mauls', battered round stones ranging from tennis- to soccer-ball size. These were used to bash and

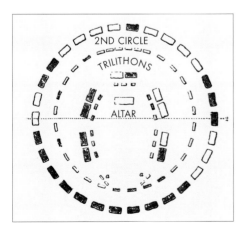

Above This 19th-century engraving shows a plan of Stonehenge, during a time that saw many, often damaging, excavations by amateurs.

shape the surface of the sarsens and bluestones, and to carve the mortises and tenons.

The monument, approached by an 'avenue' of twin banks 12m (39ft) apart and 2.5km (1¹/₂ miles) long, was abandoned in about 1600 BC, after 1400 years of continuous use. The finished monument would have been visible from kilometres around, and many of the clusters of Bronze Age round barrows (burial mounds) were placed on ridges that were visible from the ceremonial site.

What was it for?

Nobody knows who built these monuments or why. In the 12th century the English writer Geoffrey of Monmouth claimed that Merlin had removed the stones from Ireland and rebuilt them in England. The 17th-century architect Inigo Jones saw it as a Roman temple, while in the 18th century the antiquarian William Stukeley attributed it to the Druids – as do many people today. Yet Druids had nothing to do with building the monument, since they emerged in Britain more than 1000 years after Stonehenge was finished.

Stonehenge was likely a ritual site for ceremonialism. It had some astronomical or calendrical function, since the sun rises over the heel stone on midsummer's day and the

monument's north-east/south-west axial alignment is upon the midwinter sunset. In the 1960s and '70s the astronomical aspect was exaggerated by astronomers who thought the monument had been a sophisticated eclipse predictor. These claims have been criticized by recent researchers.

A monumental landscape

Stonehenge was surrounded by a monumental landscape of tombs, enclosures and ceremonial sites, including the famous megalithic tombs known as the Kennet long barrows, and Silbury Hill, the greatest prehistoric mound in Europe. But above all, there is Avebury, 32km (20 miles) away from Stonehenge. The largest stone circle in Europe, enclosing an area of 11 hectares (28 acres), Avebury comprised numerous 20-tonne sarsen stones, which were erected about 5000 years ago in a circle within a massive circular ditch and bank earthwork. The monument was under construction and in use for about 1500 years, and the whole of Stonehenge could easily be fitted inside either of Avebury's inner circles. Like Stonehenge, Avebury defies attempts to unlock its mysteries.

The Iceman

In 1991 a German couple hiking in the Tyrolean Alps spotted a yellow-brown human body emerging from the ice near the Similaun glacier in the Ötztaler Alps. The Iceman, Similaun Man, or 'Ötzi', as the body was named, is the oldest fully preserved human to have survived from prehistory.

The corpse, which lay at an altitude of more than 3200m (10,500ft), was crudely excavated because nobody had any idea of its age or importance. It was taken to Innsbruck University, Austria, while the many objects and garments later found in the vicinity were taken to Mainz, Germany, to be preserved. Because measurements taken at the spot proved that the body

Below The desiccated body of the Iceman was photographed at the spot where he was discovered in 1991, near the Similaun glacier.

had been lying 93m (305ft) inside the Italian border, in 1998 Ötzi was transferred to a museum in Bolzano, where he is displayed today in a chamber with constant humidity and a temperature of -6°C (21°F), along with all his restored equipment.

The first assessment of the Iceman's axe was that it had a bronze blade, and that the body was probably 4000 years old. Subsequent examination, however, showed that the metal was almost pure copper, and radiocarbon dating of the body, of grass from its

garments and of artefacts placed the Iceman to about 5350 to 5100 years ago, the Copper Age (Late Neolithic) in this region.

Clothes and toolkit

Analyses of the Iceman's well-preserved equipment and garments have revealed much about the tremendous range of materials and techniques used in prehistoric life. For example, 18 types of wood have been identified in the 70 artefacts. These include a flint dagger with an ashwood

shaft in a woven grass sheath and an unfinished yew-wood long-bow. The Iceman's axe, 60cm (24in) in length, had a yew-wood handle and a copper blade glued in place with birch pitch and leather straps. A deerskin quiver held 14 arrows of viburnum and dogwood. Two sewn birch-bark containers held what may be embers for starting a fire, while a short rod of linden wood, with a piece of antler embedded at one end, was probably used for working flint tools. Two round pieces of birch fungus, attached to leather slips, are thought to have some medicinal purpose. There was a marble disc with a perforation at its centre, which was attached to a leather strip and a tassel of leather thongs. The Iceman was also carrying what could have been a fur backpack with a frame of hazel and larchwood.

Microscopic analysis of the tool surfaces revealed traces of animal hair, blood and tissue, suggesting that the Iceman had recently killed or butchered a number of animals, such as chamois, ibex and deer. Deposits of large, partly cooked or heated starch grains on the axe blade imply that one of his last acts was to repair or refit the shaft while eating porridge.

The Iceman's clothing comprised much-repaired leather shoes (with bearskin soles and deerskin uppers) stuffed with grass for insulation; goat-hide leggings and loincloth; a calfskin belt and pouch; a cape of woven grass or reeds; a coat made up of pieces of tanned goat hide, sewn together with animal sinews; and a bearskin cap. The supposed backpack may, in fact, be the remains of one snowshoe.

How did he die?

Much speculation concerns the Iceman's identity and his cause of death. DNA analysis of his intestinal contents revealed that his last meal consisted of red deer meat and possibly cereals, while earlier he had also eaten some ibex. Hornbeam pollen in his stomach shows that he probably died in June. The pollen (inhaled about six hours before his

death), as well as the kinds of flint in his equipment, show that he came from the Katarinaberg area, to the south in Italy.

The man was in his mid- to late 40s (quite old for the time), dark-skinned, around 1.57m (5ft 2in) in height, and weighed about 50kg (110lb). He was not in good shape. His lungs were blackened by the smoke from fires; he had hardened arteries; his teeth were worn (probably from coarsely ground grain); his toes showed traces of frostbite; and some of his ribs had been fractured and healed. There are small tattoos – short lines and a cross – on his lower back, knees, ankles and left wrist, which were made by rubbing charcoal into small cuts. These marks may be therapeutic, aimed at relieving arthritis.

One of the Iceman's fingernails was recovered, and dark lines in it have revealed that the man suffered regular periods of severe disease or malnutrition (which affects nail growth) during the months before his death. So he was an already enfeebled individual, perhaps caught by a storm on the mountain, who succumbed to the elements.

Above The Iceman's well-preserved belongings – including his well-worn shoes packed with grass for insulation – have provided a unique time-capsule of the kinds of objects made from organic materials that were used by prehistoric man.

A CT scan taken in 2001 revealed the presence of a stone arrowhead in the Iceman's upper left shoulder, but it is unclear whether this arrowhead was responsible for killing him – if it did, where is its shaft? His own arrows were beautifully preserved, so why did the shaft of this one disappear? Could it be the vestige of an old hunting accident?

Two deep wounds have also been detected on the Iceman's right hand and wrist, and it appears that something sharp penetrated the base of his right thumb, causing a serious wound not long before he died. These marks have led to speculation about hand-to-hand fighting.

In short, even after 15 years of study, the Iceman is still presenting us with enigmas and surprises, and we still do not know exactly how he died, let alone what his occupation was or why he was on the mountain.

Carnac

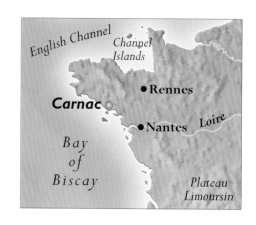

The landscape around the French seaside resort of Carnac, on the Morbihan coast of southern Brittany, is studded with Neolithic ritual monuments. The region has the greatest concentration of megalithic monuments, including spectacular standing stones, in all of Europe.

The area, covering around 300 sq km (116 sq miles), is filled with a profusion of long mounds, passage graves and standing stones known as menhirs, which occur singly and in groups. Yet the archaeological fame of this area comes from the remarkable parallel rows of standing megalithic stones that stretch in some cases for over 1km (0.6 miles).

The Carnac stones had long been the subject of myth, but it was a Scottish antiquary, James Miln, who made the first extensive excavations from around the 1860s.

Carnac mounds

Some of the earliest megalithic monuments to be built at Carnac were the great menhirs and the long mounds, which date from before 4000 BC. The long, low Er-Grah mound was almost 200m (656ft) long when it was built, while Carnac's most impressive mound, Saint-

Below A section of the alignment of standing stones at Le Menec. The stones are smaller at the eastern end, at around 1.5m (5ft), rising to around 4m (13ft) at the wider western end.

Michel, is still 125m (410ft) long today – large enough for a chapel to be built on top of it. Along with several others, they form a distinctive regional type of monument known as 'Carnac mounds'. The mound at Er-Grah originally lacked a central stone chamber, but one was added later, while Saint-Michel contained a small stone cist. Excavations at Saint-Michel, which first began in 1862, yielded remarkable grave goods, including 39 stone axes. Several of the stone axes were made from jadeite, which comes from the Alps.

The Grand Menhir Brisé

Adjacent to the Er-Grah long mound is the Grand Menhir Brisé, a huge granite pillar that stood 20m (66ft) high when it was upright. Now toppled, its four pieces weigh a total of 356 tonnes, making it the largest standing stone known from prehistoric Europe. On one of the pieces is a carving of an enigmatic object that archaeologists have called an 'axe-plow', although recently it has been suggested that this figure, which is repeated on other Carnac megaliths, might represent a whale of the sort seen in the nearby ocean. Archaeologists found a number of holes close to the Grand Menhir Brisé where other large menhirs had stood, although the stones themselves are now missing.

Passage graves

Carnac's great menhirs were pulled down during the 4th millennium BC. The Grand Menhir Brisé was simply too large to be reused, but fragments of others found their way into the next type of monument to be constructed in the Carnac area – the passage graves. Two of the most famous are La Table des Marchand, which is adjacent to the Er-Grah long mound and the prostrate Grand Menhir Brisé, and Gavrinis, which is on a small island just offshore.

The remarkable fact is that pieces of the same menhir found their way into both of these megalithic monuments. Observant archaeologists noticed that horns that had been carved on the enormous stone slab, which formed the roof of the Gavrinis tomb, matched the body of an animal carved on the capstone of La Table des Marchand tomb. Closer examination showed that the broken edges of the stones matched, proving that they were originally one enormous stone, possibly one that had stood near the Grand Menhir Brisé.

The Gavrinis tomb is further known for the profusion of carvings on its stones, including curved lines and concentric semi-circles.

Alignments

The long mounds, great menhirs and passage graves were merely a prelude to the crowning achievement of the Carnac megalith builders – the rows of standing stones known as alignments. These are multiple rows of irregularly spaced menhirs, each several metres tall, which were erected starting just before 3000 BC and ending around 2500 BC. Over the years many of the stones have disappeared, and others have fallen over, but the surviving menhirs give a

Above The passage of the Gavrinis tomb is extensively decorated with patterns of concentric semi-circles and parallel lines.

good impression of how these monuments would have looked to their Neolithic builders.

There are several alignments at Carnac, and several more elsewhere in Brittany, but the most important are Le Menec, Kermario and Kerlescan. At Le Menec, 1050 menhirs stand in ten slightly converging rows that stretch for about 1.2km (0.75 miles) from west to east and are 100m (328ft) across at their widest point, while at Kermario 1029 surviving stones run in seven rows for over 1km (0.6 miles). The Kerlescan alignment is shorter, about 350m (1148ft), but it contains approximately 300 stones in 13 rows.

The purpose of the alignments is unknown. Suggestions that they held astronomical significance have not been widely accepted, as the stones are irregularly spaced and the rows bend slightly. More probable is the theory that they were processional paths that led to stone enclosures in which rituals occurred.

Left A carved stone from La Table des Marchand tomb highlights the artisan's skills.

Newgrange

The Neolithic inhabitants of Ireland constructed enormous burial monuments from large stones (megaliths) that were then covered with smaller stones or earth. The Boyne valley is particularly rich in prehistoric tombs, of which the huge mound of Newgrange is the most famous.

Such megalithic tombs take different forms, but some of the most impressive are the passage tombs, in which a burial chamber is entered by going through a narrow tunnel-like corridor. Passage tombs are found in many parts of Ireland, and they often occur in clusters that form vast cemeteries. In the Boyne valley, the tombs of Knowth, Dowth and Newgrange are the focal points of a huge mortuary and ceremonial complex that existed around 3000 BC.

Newgrange

The tomb was first rediscovered in 1699 by labourers who were looking for building stones. It was at this time that the entrance to the tomb was discovered. A major excavation and restoration project was carried out between 1962 and 1975.

The circular mound is around 85m (279ft) across and 11m (36ft) high. The perimeter is marked with 97 large stones, many of which are decorated with engraved spirals. A passage 19m (62ft) long and lined with upright stone slabs leads into the main burial chamber. The central part of the chamber is roofed with flat stone slabs in circular courses, each one set closer to the centre to form a beehive-shaped ceiling, which reaches its peak 6m (20ft) above the chamber floor. Smaller chambers open off the central part of the chamber to form a cross-shaped plan.

Every year, at the time of the winter solstice, on 21 December, the sun shines directly along the passage into the chamber for about 17 minutes as it rises. The alignment is too precise to have occured by chance. The sun enters the passage through a specially contrived opening, known as a roofbox, directly above the entrance.

Not much was left for archaeologists to find in the chamber other than a few cremated human bones. Based on evidence from other Irish megalithic cemeteries, the chamber would have contained the cremated remains of multiple individuals, along with pottery and other artefacts. The area in front of the entrance would have been the scene of communal ceremonies, while the whole tomb would have been visible from a great distance to reflect the importance of the ancestors whose remains it contained.

Below An impressive façade of white quartz, using stone found at the site, greets the visitor to Newgrange, although its reconstruction has been the subject of archaeological debate.

Skara Brae

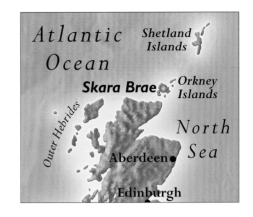

Farmers first settled the Orkney Islands off the northern tip of Scotland around 3700 BC. By 3100 BC a large settlement was established at Skara Brae. Scarcity of timber meant the settlers built their houses and furniture of stone, much of which has survived to this day.

After being occupied and rebuilt for centuries, the sandstone houses at Skara Brae – on Mainland, Orkney's largest island – were abandoned and slowly covered over by drifting sand and turf. In the 1920s the eminent prehistorian V. Gordon Childe cleared the sand and exposed the houses in one of his rare excavation projects. The remarkable architectural detail he revealed resulted in Skara Brae becoming one of the most famous Neolithic settlement sites in Europe.

The houses

A trash dump, or midden, had existed on Skara Brae before the Neolithic farmers built their houses. The farmers scooped large pits in the midden, which they then lined with sandstone slabs to form at least eight houses. Each house had a rectangular open area 4m to 6m (13ft to 20ft) across and 3m (10ft) deep. In the centre of each house was a sunken, stone-lined hearth, which would have been used for heating and cooking. Some of the houses had alcoves that open from the central area, and tunnels roofed with stone slabs joined the houses. We do not know how the open areas were roofed. It has been suggested that whale ribs covered with hide were used in place of timber.

Furniture

Stone slabs and blocks were stacked to form shelf units that appear to have been used for storage. Larger bins along the sides may have been filled with straw and furs to make beds. Stone-lined square pits in the house floors had their seams packed with clay to make them watertight, perhaps for storing shellfish.

Above A shelved stone 'dresser' was postioned on the wall opposite the doorway.

Life at Skara Brae

The inhabitants of Skara Brae kept cattle, pigs, goats and sheep, and they fished. They also cultivated barley and wheat on a small scale. Deer and stranded whales yielded additional meat, and sea-bird eggs were gathered.

Bone was used to make beads for necklaces and awls for working hides. Some of the most distinctive artefacts at Skara Brae and other Neolithic sites on Orkney are carved stone balls, which may have served as symbols of status and prestige.

The windswept Orkney landscape has yielded several other such sites of this period, although none as well preserved as Skara Brae. Circles of standing stones and immense passage graves complete the dramatic Neolithic scenery.

Left Each of the dwellings shares the same basic layout, with a central hearth.

The Heuneburg

Situated along the upper Danube in south-west Germany, the Heuneburg was a prosperous early Iron Age hilltop fortress. The powerful chiefs who ruled there controlled the trade with the Greeks in the region. The mud-brick fortifications were evidence of contact with the Mediterranean.

Beginning around 800 BC, central Europe was inhabited by the Celts, whose lands were divided into complex chiefdoms. Between 650 and 450 BC the Celtic chiefdoms in west-central Europe began trading with Greek merchants. This led to remarkable accumulations of wealth and demonstrations of status. One especially prosperous chiefdom was Heuneburg. Built on a hilltop, its fortification system – begun in the late Bronze Age – enclosed an area of 3.3ha (8 acres). Systematic excavations, which began in 1950, have yielded an exceptional amount of artefacts relating to the Celts on the Upper Danube.

The hillfort

During the early Iron Age, around 650 BC, a substantial part of the wall was constructed with Mediterranean-style, sun-dried mudbrick, which ostentatiously demonstrated that the chief had contacts with distant lands and could imitate their building style. The mud-brick wall was suddenly and violently destroyed late in the 6th century BC. Apparently, the hillfort was then rebuilt under new leadership using the standard Celtic method of timber framework and stone.

The interior of the hillfort had the remains of structures that housed the local nobility and specialized pottery and jewellery workshops. Imported goods included Greek black-figure pottery, coral and amphorae (large jars) from the region of Massilia (Marseille), which had contained wine brought up the Rhône valley. An outer settlement covering about 20 hectares (49 acres) stood outside the ramparts. Many of the structures in this settlement were houses, while others were workshops for working bronze and weaving cloth.

The fortress succumbed to a great fire in about 450 BC, after which it seems to have been abandoned forever.

Burial mounds

Further afield, and dating back to the same time as the hillfort, lie several burial mounds where Celtic chieftains were interred. Among these is the Hohmichele tumulus, which at a height of 13m (43ft), is one of the largest in central Europe. Excavations at Hohmichele began in 1936. In the centre was a large burial chamber built of massive oak beams. Although this had been looted in antiquity, archaeologists found grave goods, including a bronze cauldron, a four wheeled-wagon, numerous small ring beads of green glass and even a piece of silk, probably from China.

Below The hillfort has revealed important clues about life in a Celtic settlement over time.

Biskupin

The lowlands of northern Poland are dotted with lakes connected by streams. It was by one of these lakes, at Biskupin 60km (37 miles) north-east of the city of Poznan, that the waterlogged remains of a fortified settlement dating to the 8th century BC was uncovered.

In 1933 a local schoolteacher named Walenty Szwajcer noticed timbers sticking out of the peat at Biskupin. Szwajcer had heard of the famous Swiss Lake Dwellings and thought these might be the traces of a similar find. He reported his discovery to the museum in Poznan and excavations, led by Professor Józef Kostrzewski, began the following summer.

The settlement

Over the following several years, Kostrzewski's excavations revealed the waterlogged remains of a large settlement in which the outlines of timber houses along log streets were clearly visible. A rampart constructed from timber boxes filled with earth and stone surrounded the settlement. At its base, a breakwater of oak logs prevented the lake water from

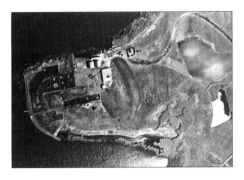

undermining the walls. A gate in the rampart provided the main entrance to the settlement.

The houses at Biskupin were set in continuous rows. They were strikingly uniform. Each consisted of a large central area with a stone hearth, which was entered through a vestibule with a storage area. If there were 7 to 10 inhabitants per house, and a total of about 100 houses, then the population of Biskupin was somewhere between

Left Excavations at Biskupin were technically advanced for their time. In 1935 aerial photographs of the peninsula were taken from a balloon borrowed from the Polish army.

700 and 1000 people. Narrow streets made from timbers ran between the rows of houses, with a larger open area situated just inside the gate.

The inhabitants of Biskupin grew mainly millet, wheat, barley, rye and beans. Pigs provided most of their meat, but they also kept cattle for milk and pulling wagons and ploughs. Wooden wagon wheels and plough-shares have been found in the waterlogged sediments, along with a range of items made from wood, cloth and other perishable materials. The inhabitants of Biskupin were also part of a trade network that extended as far as Italy and Ukraine.

Dating

Accurate dating of Biskupin has been provided by the study of the tree rings of the timbers. Virtually all the trees used in the construction of Biskupin were cut between 747 and 722 BC, and over half of them were cut during the winter of 738-737 BC. The actual duration of the settlement is unclear, but there were several episodes of reconstruction.

Right Reconstruction of the rampart and some of the streets and houses began in 1968. The interiors of the houses have been furnished to show how the inhabitants lived.

Sutton Hoo

The excavation of mounds at Sutton Hoo near the English Suffolk coast in the late 1930s unearthed an Anglo-Saxon boat burial, with a spectacular number of preserved grave goods. Sutton Hoo remains the richest burial site ever discovered in Britain.

The round burial mounds were on the estate of Mrs Edith May Pretty, who had an interest in the past. She hired a local antiquarian, Basil Brown, to excavate them, and in June 1938 he and two helpers began opening the mounds. Although the first three that they excavated had been robbed in ancient times, enough remained in them to show that the mounds contained cremation burials from the Anglo-Saxon period. In addition, Brown found a number of iron objects that he identified as the rivets used to hold together the planks of ships.

Discovery of the ship

Another excavation campaign in 1939 was concentrated on a single large mound. Here Brown discovered row upon row of iron rivets. He quickly deduced that he had found a buried boat, whose wood had decayed but whose regular pattern of rivets survived. The boat had been used as the tomb of an elite individual. He traced the rows of rivets downward

Above This exquisite gold buckle would have been used to fasten the king's waist belt.

Right This is an extremely rare example of an Anglo-Saxon helmet. It was fitted with decorative foil panels of tinned-bronze, which depict animal motifs as well as scenes from German and Scandinavian mythology. The nose has two small holes cut into it to allow the wearer to breathe freely. The bronze eyebrows are inlaid with silver wire and garnets.

and found that the boat had been 27 m (88ft) long. Word of this discovery spread, and several professional archaeologists soon arrived to give Brown help in documenting the find.

Burial goods

Work proceeded to the central burial chamber in the middle of the boat. Over 17 days of excavation in July and August 1939, an astonishing collection of 263 burial objects was found. Armour and weapons included an iron helmet, a coat of mail, a wooden shield with bronze decoration, a hammer-axe and a sword. Textiles had been preserved, including wall hangings and cloaks. There were gold ornaments and coins; silver bowls, dishes and spoons; bronze hanging bowls; wooden tubs and buckets; and drinking horns with silver decoration. Even traces of a wooden lyre encased in a beaver-skin bag were recovered. The artefacts showed connections with Gaul, Byzantium and North Africa.

Further excavations

Archaeologists have returned to the Sutton Hoo cemetery several times since 1939. More mounds were excavated between 1965 to 1970 and 1983 to 1992, and additional burials have been found recently on the site. A reinvestigation of one of the mounds, originally excavated by Basil Brown in 1938, showed that it too had once contained a ship burial. Some of the burials were cremations with the burnt bones in bronze bowls, while others were uncremated. Under one mound, a young man lay in a coffin in one pit, while his horse lay in another. Several uncremated burials found in the early 1990s are intriguing in that they appear to have met violent deaths – by decapitation or hanging – and were buried face-down.

It was initially supposed that the person buried in the Sutton Hoo ship burial was Raedwald, king of East Anglia between AD 599 and 625, and many scholars continue to accept this attribution. Raedwald had been

baptized into Christianity, but he soon reverted to paganism. While this specific identification is far from certain, the subsequent excavations have established that the Sutton Hoo mounds were indeed a cemetery for the Anglo-Saxon elites between the late 6th and late 7th centuries. After

Above This photograph was taken when the Sutton Hoo ship was under excavation in 1939.

the period of elite pagan burial, the site may have been used as a place for executions, which may account for the victims of violent deaths.

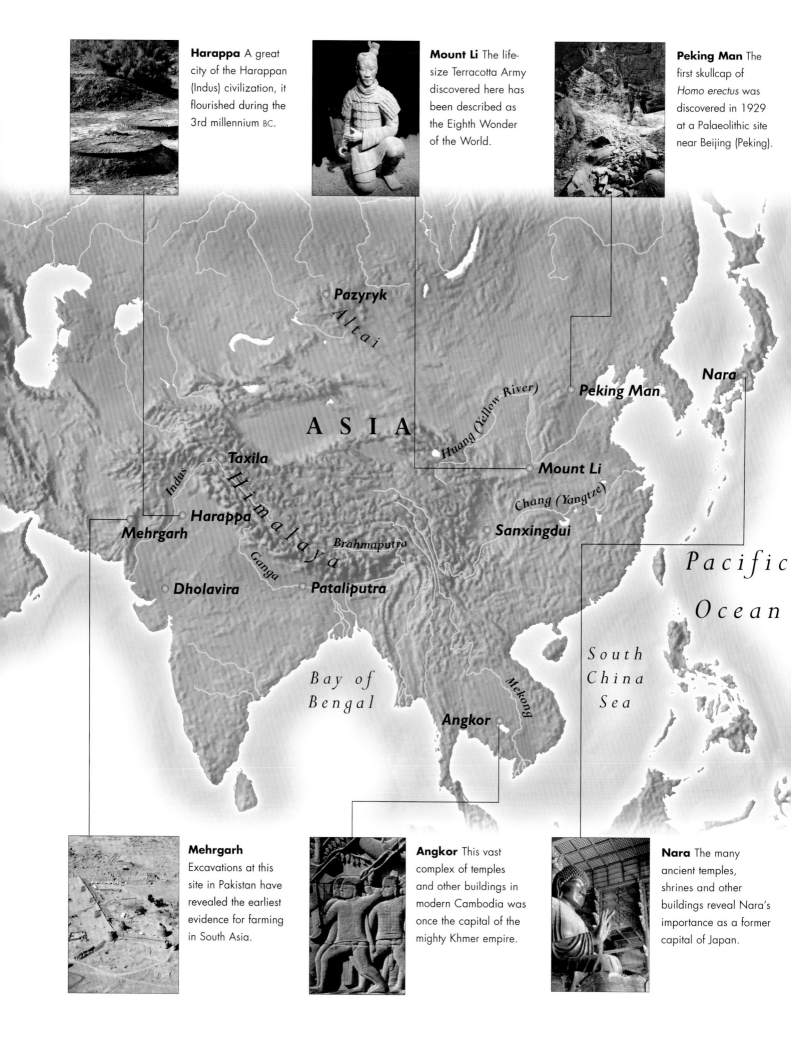

Harappa A great city of the Harappan (Indus) civilization, it flourished during the 3rd millennium BC.

Mount Li The life-size Terracotta Army discovered here has been described as the Eighth Wonder of the World.

Peking Man The first skullcap of *Homo erectus* was discovered in 1929 at a Palaeolithic site near Beijing (Peking).

Pazyryk

Altai

ASIA

Nara

Huang (Yellow River)

Peking Man

Taxila

Himalaya

Indus

Mount Li

Harappa

Chang (Yangtze)

Mehrgarh

Brahmaputra

Sanxingdui

Ganga

Dholavira

Pataliputra

Pacific Ocean

Bay of Bengal

South China Sea

Mekong

Angkor

Mehrgarh Excavations at this site in Pakistan have revealed the earliest evidence for farming in South Asia.

Angkor This vast complex of temples and other buildings in modern Cambodia was once the capital of the mighty Khmer empire.

Nara The many ancient temples, shrines and other buildings reveal Nara's importance as a former capital of Japan.

THE GREAT SITES OF THE FAR EAST

The lands of the Far East are studded with monuments to past civilizations. Archaeologists had long been aware of the importance of many of the region's sites, but other jewels of the Far East have remained hidden until relatively recently. The chance discovery in 1974 of China's Terracotta Army sparked one of the great ongoing archaeological investigations of all time. Most recently, Japan has become prominent not only in exploration of its own past, but also in funding archaeological work in other parts of the world. So much of this vast region – including large areas of Siberia, Mongolia, Central Asia and China – remains relatively unexplored archaeologically. Exciting new discoveries are sure to await us, possibly even including the very timing and location of human evolution. In the meantime, some of the world's most impressive sites – such as the stunning temples at Angkor – bear witness to the awe-inspiring scale of human enterprise in this area of the globe.

Pazyryk Tombs in Siberia have revealed the frozen bodies and possessions of nomads who lived in the 5th to 3rd centuries BC.

Pataliputra By the 4th century BC, this city in northern India had become the spectacular capital of the Mauryan dynasty.

Taxila A World Heritage Site of considerable archaeological importance, it is located in a fertile valley of northern Pakistan.

Peking Man

In the early 1920s two human teeth were found in a cave near the village of Zhoukoudian, not far from Beijing (Peking). Further excavations led to the discovery a few years later of a complete human skullcap. These were the remains of a new genus of human, given the popular name of Peking Man.

Between 1921 and 1966 six nearly complete human crania, or skullcaps, numerous fragments of skulls, 157 teeth, pieces of humerus and various other bone fragments were unearthed from the hills around Zhoukoudian, 42km (26 miles) south-west of Beijing

Below Anthropologists and local workmen dig near the original cave where the Peking Man skull was discovered. The walls are marked in chalk in numbered sections to keep track of what is found.

(Peking). The area had long been a source of ancient animal bones – referred to by local people as 'dragon bones' – which were used in Chinese medicine, and it had therefore attracted the attention of geologists and archaeologists.

Human remains

In February 1918, Johan Gunnar Andersson, a Swedish geologist and mining adviser to the Chinese government, made his first visit to

Zhoukoudian, lured by the rumours of 'dragon bones'. He explored the gullies and caves in the area, and in 1921 he discovered bones and teeth, together with some quartzite cutting tools, which suggested human activity. He sent the collection to Sweden for investigation, and in 1927 announced that two human teeth, one of them a molar, had been discovered among the remains.

The discovery caught the attention of the scientific world as at that time no such human fossils had been discovered in China or any other country in Asia. The Canadian anthropologist Dr Davidson Black, head of the Peking Union Medical College's department of anatomy, identified the find as a previously unknown hominid group, *Sinanthropus pekinensis*, or 'Peking Man'.

More extensive excavations at the Zhoukoudian site began, and in 1929 the Chinese geologist Wenzhong Pei discovered a complete skullcap of Peking Man. Just after this discovery, a second skullcap was found. By 1932 excavation in the area had expanded and employed more than 100 workers. In 1936 another three complete skullcaps were unearthed.

These fruitful excavations came to a halt in 1937, however, when Japan invaded China. They did not restart until 1951.

Who was Peking Man?

Peking Man was classified as a type of *Homo erectus* (upright man) that had inhabited the Zhoukoudian area around 500,000 to 230,000 years ago,

Left Inside one of the caves at Zhoukoudian, archaeologists have identified 13 layers in the excavated deposits.

or charcoal, and researchers concluded that the bones were charred by fire caused by lightning.

The lost fossils

During World War II the more notable fossils, including the five skullcaps, were dispatched to the USA for safekeeping. They disappeared during the journey, however, and have never been recovered. In July 2005 the Chinese government founded a committee to find the bones.

Excavations since World War II have brought to light many more fragments of the Peking Man species, including parts of a skull all from the same person. The pieces were reassembled into a skullcap, and it is now the only original one.

To protect and conserve the site, the State Council of China announced Zhoukoudian to be one of the first State Key Cultural Heritage Units under Protection. The site was placed on UNESCO's World Heritage List in 1987, and since 1997 a joint UNESCO-China project has been set up to preserve Zhoukoudian.

Below A reconstruction of Peking Man's skull shows that his teeth were larger and more robust than those of *Homo sapiens*.

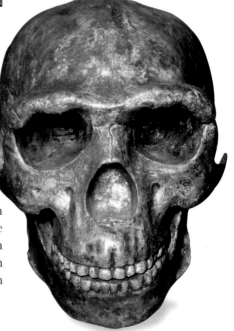

during the Middle Pleistocene. Based on pollen analysis, scientists decided that Peking Man lived at this site during an interglacial period. The climate was a little warmer than it is today, and the area was covered with grassland and trees. Hazelnut, pine, elm and fruit were all part of Peking Man's diet.

Peking Man was a hunter, gatherer, toolmaker and cave-dweller. The discovery of stone scrapers and choppers, as well as several hand axes, indicated that he used a variety of tools for different tasks. Scientific research revealed that the average capacity of his brain was 1088ml (nearly 2 pints). That of a modern man is 1400ml ($2^1/_2$ pints). He was up to 1.56m (5ft) tall.

Early excavators of the site also claimed to have uncovered hearths, and they were convinced that Peking Man had learned to use fire for cooking. As a result, scientists redated the earliest human mastery of fire from 100,000 to more than 400,000 years ago. However, in the 1990s new discoveries and research revealed no evidence for hearths, ash

Mehrgarh

In the 1970s a French team excavating at Mehrgarh in western Pakistan discovered the remains of a village that had been occupied in the 7th millennium BC. Three decades later, Mehrgarh is still the only farming settlement of this antiquity known in South Asia.

The settlement lay above a gorge cut by the Bolan River on the Kachi plain, where the mountains of Baluchistan meet the Indus plain. As part of their work the French team examined ancient deposits in the side of the gorge. They were excited when they found traces of material unlike anything previously known in the Indian subcontinent.

The settlement

The people who lived at the settlement had hunted local game, but they also cultivated wheat and barley and raised sheep and goats, like the farmers whose communities were emerging in contemporary West Asia, Iran and the Caspian region. They also domesticated local zebu cattle.

Archaeologists are still debating whether the people who settled at Mehrgarh originated from West Asia or were local people who had acquired West Asian domestic plants and animals through trade links. Shells from the Arabian Sea and turquoise from Turkmenia found at the site are both evidence that there were wide-ranging exchange networks.

The originally dwellings on the site were simple mud houses, but the buildings took on a semi-permanent nature by 5000 BC, when they were made with mud bricks. By 5500 BC the people of Mehrgarh had begun to make pottery. Mehrgarh's inhabitants were skilled artisans who made beads from many materials, including shells, bone, lapis lazuli, steatite (soapstone), calcite and limestone. One bead has been found made of native copper.

Recently it has been discovered that the tiny stone drills used to perforate their beads had another, surprising, purpose – they were also used for treating toothache. Researchers at the Univeristy of Missouri-Columbia, led by Andrea Cucina, were cleaning the jaws and teeth of fossils found at Mehrgarh when they discovered small holes in some of the teeth. These holes were drilled to relieve the pain in decayed teeth and were probably filled with an organic material.

By the 4th millennium BC the settlement had grown into a major town, becoming a centre of industries that included metal-working and the manufacture of terracotta figurines. These figurines often wear elaborate headdresses and strings of beads

Above The excavated remains at the site include a complex of large, compartmented mud-brick structures, which were probably used as storerooms.

around their necks and waists. Some are shown holding a baby and they are often interpreted as mother goddesses.

During the Harappan (Indus) period (c.2500-1900 BC), however, Mehrgarh appears to have been abandoned for the nearby town of Nausharo.

In the early 2nd millennium BC, burials at Mehrgarh reflected the presence of outsiders, probably from the prosperous culture that had developed in Bactria and Margiana. Similar material was found at Pirak, a new town that developed after the decline of the Harappan civilization.

Harappa

Excavations at the city of Harappa in the Punjab region of Pakistan have yielded a wealth of information about the still largely enigmatic Harappan (Indus) Bronze Age culture, the first great civilization of the Indian subcontinent.

The city of Harappa in the Indus Valley was visited several times by the 19th-century archaeologist Sir Alexander Cunningham. He published a selection of finds from the site, including a steatite stamp seal, although he had no inkling of its great antiquity. Unfortunately in the 1850s the site was used as a brick quarry to provide ballast in the construction of the Lahore to Multan railway.

A large quantity of Harappa's ancient mud bricks had been removed and it was a sadly reduced site when excavations, under the British archaeologist Sir John Marshall, started in the 1920s and its importance began to be realized. A modern town covering part of the settlement has also restricted work here. In spite of these problems, excavations at Harappa and Mohenjo-Daro – the other great city of the Indus Valley, which lay 644km (400 miles) to the south – have provided important clues about the Harappan civilization.

The apparently sudden emergence of the Indus civilization has always been something of a puzzle. Recent discoveries, however, have shown that Harappa evolved gradually from a village settlement established in the mid-4th millennium BC into a thriving town, where the beginnings of a script and a system of weights reflected a growing complexity. Unlike many other contemporary Indus towns, Harappa was not destroyed or rebuilt in the crucial Transition period (2600-2500 BC), but it continued to grow, eventually becoming a city of around 150ha (370 acres).

The city

Excavations in the Marshall era exposed brick-built houses. As at Mohenjo-Daro, these were laid out along streets with excellent drains, although Harappa, located beside the river Ravi (a tributary of the Indus),

Below The streets of Harappa were laid out following the cardinal directions, and the houses were built of bricks of uniform size.

Above A series of working floors built of characteristic Harappan bricks were located north of the citadel. It is thought that the platforms were used for threshing grain. A recently excavated example may have had a wooden mortar in its centre.

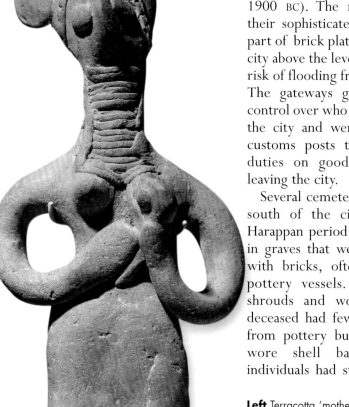

had few wells. As at Mohenjo-Daro there was a raised mound ('citadel') where in the 1940s Sir Mortimer Wheeler excavated massive walls and gateways. The buildings that had once graced the mound's summit had, however, been destroyed. North of the citadel Wheeler also uncovered a large ventilated storage building, which was dubbed 'the granary', but it was more probably a palace or public building. He also discovered a series of circular working floors and small buildings, which he interpreted as the mean dwellings of downtrodden workers. More recent work suggests that these were in fact workshops.

A combined Pakistani and American team conducted modern scientific excavations and field work at Harappa between 1986 and 2001. Their investigations revealed that the city

included at least three, and probably more, separately walled mounds in the Mature Harappan period (c.2500-1900 BC). The massive walls, with their sophisticated gateways, formed part of brick platforms that raised the city above the level at which there was risk of flooding from the nearby river. The gateways gave the authorities control over who came into and out of the city and were probably used as customs posts to extract taxes or duties on goods brought into or leaving the city.

Several cemeteries were uncovered south of the city. In the Mature Harappan period people were placed in graves that were sometimes lined with bricks, often with a layer of pottery vessels. Some burials had shrouds and wooden coffins. The deceased had few grave goods apart from pottery but the women often wore shell bangles, and some individuals had strings of beads. The

Left Terracotta 'mother-goddess' figurines such as this were a distinctive feature of Harappan culture.

196

Dholavira

Contrary to earlier theories that the Harappan civilization gradually expanded south into India's Gujarat region, recent discoveries have revealed early Harappan farming settlements there. Among these was Dholavira, which by 2600 BC was a town surrounded by a substantial stone and brick wall. This grew into a great city, with industrial quarters for shell-working, potting, bead-making and other crafts.

The site, rediscovered in the 1960s, has been under excavation by the Archaeological Survey of India since 1990. Dholavira initially had a raised citadel and a walled Middle Town with a grid pattern of streets and lanes. After a serious earthquake it was rebuilt and extended, creating a Lower Town in the east. An area of the Middle Town adjacent to the citadel was cleared to form a large, open public space. The citadel was divided into two separately walled parts – the lower 'Bailey' and the higher 'Castle', which had a gateway in each wall, and was probably accessible only to the privileged few. A ramp led up to a terrace in front to the main – north – gate.

Local water supplies were inadequate for the city's 5000-10,000 inhabitants, who excavated 16 massive water tanks along the inner face of the city wall. These collected rainwater and were filled by damming two seasonal streams.

One of the most significant discoveries is the remains of a wooden signboard in one of the side rooms of the northern gateway. This board, which would probably have been placed originally above the gateway, was set with ten gypsum signs in the Indus script. Despite decades of study this script still cannot be deciphered, so the board's message is unknown. Its existence, however, shows that writing was an integral part of life.

Left This charming Harappan terracotta is a model of a bird in a cage.

other cemetery, where the graves contained beautiful painted pottery, belonged to a later period when the city was in decline.

A flourishing economy

Harappa was a major industrial centre, with craft activities that were concentrated particularly in the south-eastern mound. Here, pottery was made and fired in sophisticated updraught kilns and decorated with a tin glaze; copper, gold, shell and stone were worked; beads were crafted from many materials; and steatite was cut into seals.

The city was well placed to procure resources from areas to the north, including timber from the Himalayas, which was floated downriver. Some was shipped to Mesopotamia with which the Harappans enjoyed flourishing trading relations. The Harappans established a trading outpost at Shortugai on the Amu-Darya (Oxus) River in northern Afghanistan to access the region's rich mineral resources. These included tin, gold and lapis lazuli, the beautiful blue stone that was one of the most highly prized commodities in the ancient world.

Harappa's location also made good use of local resources: agricultural land in the river valley, pasture for its cattle on the adjacent higher ground, and fish in the river. In addition, it could draw on the produce of other parts of the Harappan realms; for instance, dried marine fish were brought here from the Arabian Sea coast, some 885km (550 miles) away.

There is still much to be learned about the site, most of which remains unexcavated. In 2005 plans to redevelop a site adjacent to the ruins were cancelled when a large quantity of new artefacts was discovered.

Below The Indus people used solid-wheeled, ox-drawn carts to transport goods. This unusual terracotta model from Mohenjo-Daro suggests that they also travelled in ox-drawn chariots.

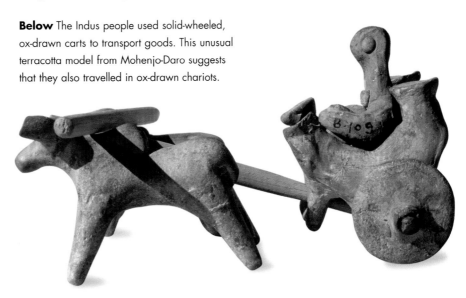

Pazyryk

In the frozen ground of the Altai mountains in Siberia, a group of burial mounds have yielded some exceptionally well-preserved remains from the 5th to 3rd centuries BC: human bodies frozen in the ice along with their possessions, including horses, textiles and leather, gold and silver objects.

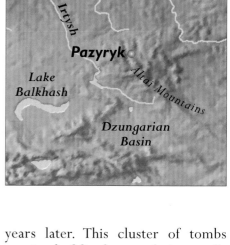

During the first millennium BC the treeless grasslands that lie among the Altai mountains in Central Asia were home to horse-riding nomads who buried their chiefs and other important members of society in timber chambers under large earth mounds. Owing to the area's climate, the contents of the tombs became encased in ice and thus preserved, providing archaeologists with an extraordinary amount of information on this prehistoric society. 'Pazyryk' is the local word for 'burial mound' and it was applied to a series of tombs excavated in the Ust'-Ulagan valley between 1929 and 1949. In the 1990s, several more burial mounds were excavated on the Ukok plateau, near the Chinese border.

Natural iceboxes

The Pazyryk tombs at Ust'-Ulagan were discovered by the Russian archaeologist Sergei Rudenko in 1924. He began work on them five years later. This cluster of tombs consisted of five large and nine small, low earthen mounds covered with stones. The large mounds were 36-46m (118-151ft) in diameter, while the small ones were 13-15m (43-49ft) across. Under the centre of each mound was a shaft 4-6m (13-20ft) deep, filled with logs and stones. At the base of each shaft was a chamber constructed of logs, containing the burial and grave goods.

The secret to the preservation of the contents of the tombs lies in the fact that warm, moist summer air was trapped in the chamber at the time of burial. This warm air rose, and the moisture condensed on the stones in the shaft, trickled back down and saturated the corpse and grave goods. Additional moist air entered from the outside through the earth mound. The following winter, this moisture froze solid inside the tomb. The mound of earth prevented the ice from thawing, and thus the tombs became natural iceboxes.

A double burial

In one of the large Pazyryk tombs, the burial chamber is lined with felt and contained the embalmed bodies of a man and woman. Their coffin was decorated with cut-out leather figures of deer, while the bodies inside were wrapped in a woollen rug. Tattoos on

Left A felt appliqué figure of a horseman was found on a wool wall-hanging in one of the tombs. The horse's tack, trimmed mane and braided tail matched those of the real horses excavated at Pazyryk.

Although tattoos were observed on some of the Pazyryk bodies when they were excavated, the skin of others had turned dark and tattoos were not readily visible. Recent studies with infrared photography at the Hermitage Museum in St Petersburg have revealed that all of the Pazyryk frozen bodies were, in fact, tattooed.

The tattoos were usually found on the shoulders and arms, on the thumbs, and on the shins and back. Almost all the images are of animals, especially tigers, leopards, horses, sheep, deer and imaginary composite animals. A common theme is carnivores attacking herbivores, often in elaborate compositions. The pigment used for the tattoos was soot, probably applied with bone needles.

the man depicted animals such as griffins, rams, birds, snakes and deer. Around the coffin were items of clothing and objects made from leather, wood, gold and silver, including some remarkable mirrors. The Pazyryk tombs also contained horse burials – between 7 and 14 horses per tomb – along with immaculately preserved bridles, saddles and cloth coats.

Recent tree-ring and radiocarbon dating of the Pazyryk timbers suggest that the tomb containing the double burial was constructed between 325 and 275 BC.

Ice maiden

In 1993 the archaeologist Natalya Polosmak found a frozen Pazyryk-type barrow at Ukok. It contained the tattooed body of a young woman, about 25 years old, in a log coffin. Outside the burial chamber were six horses, each killed by a blow to the

Above A detail on the edge of a Pazyryk carpet shows a horse and rider.

head. Their manes, and even their felt saddle-covers, were well preserved. Stylized images of deer and snow leopards carved in leather decorated the outside of the coffin. In 1995, Polosmak and her husband, Vyacheslav Molodin, excavated another frozen tomb, this time of a man. No further Pazyryk-type burials have been excavated since then. The government of the autonomous Altai Republic passed a law barring further excavation because the finds were being taken to distant research institutes.

Ancient riches

The contents of the Pazyryk and Ukok tombs reveal the tremendous wealth of the nomadic aristocracy, while the textiles also demonstrate their contacts with distant lands, such as Persia and China.

Above The chief's right arm from the wrist to the shoulder is decorated with a series of six fabulous animals, their hindquarters twisted around and with branchy horns.

Pataliputra

Occupying a strategic position on the south bank of the Ganges River in north-eastern India, Pataliputra became capital of the vast Mauryan empire under Emperor Chandragupta. Accounts of the glittering city give us an impression of the largest South Asian city of its time.

Pataliputra (modern-day Patna) was founded in the 5th century BC by the kings of Magadha, one of the principal *mahajanapadas* (great states) of the time. Magadha gradually gained control of neighbouring states until in the 4th century BC its ruling dynasty, the Mauryas, united most of India in a great empire, with its capital at Pataliputra, the meeting place of major trade routes to the north-west, north, south and south-west.

Imperial city

Little remains of the city, but clues can be found in carvings on Buddhist monuments known as stupas, especially those at Sanchi in central India.

Eyewitness accounts also help to throw light on the city. An envoy named Megasthenes described Pataliputra in around 300 BC as being long and narrow, enclosing richly furnished palaces. It was fortified by a moat and had timber walls pierced with arrowslits, with 570 towers and 64 gateways.

Kautilya, advisor to the first Mauryan emperor Chandragupta, described his ideal city in a treatise, the *Arthashastra*. Many of the features excavated at Pataliputra in the early 20th century show that Kautilya's vision was based on contemporary urban architecture.

A massive wooden rampart matching Megasthenes' description was uncovered, its timbers preserved by waterlogging. It was built of two parallel lines of huge wooden posts, more than 7m (23ft) high, with a floor of wooden beams between them.

The remains of an open pillared hall, perhaps from one of the palaces mentioned by Megasthenes, were discovered within the city. With its 84 polished sandstone pillars in ten rows, set into a wooden plinth, the hall resembled the public buildings of Achaemenid (Persian) palaces. Ash and other burnt material suggest there had been a massive wooden roof, destroyed by fire. A wooden stair connected the hall with a canal. Other discoveries include brick houses with tiled roofs and soakwells for drainage built of columns of massive terracotta rings.

Left Carvings on the Great Stupa at Sanchi give an impression of early Indian cities.

Taxila

Since the 1st millennium BC, the Taxila valley in northern Pakistan has been a major crossroads for trade and communications between South Asia and the regions beyond the mountains, the Iranian plateau and the west, Central Asia and China. It has provided details about many religious cultures.

The successive cities of the Taxila valley and their associated religious establishments attracted the attentions of many distinguished antiquarians and archaeologists, including Sir Alexander Cunningham, Sir John Marshall and Sir Mortimer Wheeler. Today Taxila is a World Heritage site.

Bhir Mound

Although settlement here dates back to the Neolithic period, it was in the 1st millennium BC that Taxila rose to prominence. In the 5th century BC a settlement known today as the Bhir Mound was founded by people under Achaemenid rule who had strong cultural ties to the emerging states of the Ganges valley. Later, in the 4th century BC, the region was incorporated into the Mauryan empire and Taxila became its provincial capital. The majority of excavated buildings belong to this period, including houses, shops and a pillared shrine.

Sirkap

In the 2nd century BC the valley came under the control of Bactrian Indo-Greeks, who constructed a new walled city at Sirkap. This was laid out in Greek 'chequerboard' fashion, with a walled acropolis and several palaces. Shrines and monasteries constructed in the city and the surrounding valley reflect the diversity of religions practised by Sirkap's cosmopolitan inhabitants under the Indo-Greeks and their Shaka and Parthian successors. These include Buddhist monumental shrines (stupas), a Zoroastrian fire-temple and an Indo-Greek shrine.

Sirsukh

Valuables concealed in the city reflect the troubled period in the 1st century AD when the valley fell to the Kushans, Central Asian nomads, who built a new walled city, named Sirsukh. The Kushans became great patrons of Buddhism, endowing monasteries and encouraging art. Under their rule the famous Gandhara art style, which successfully mingled Indian and Western traditions, reached its apogee. But around AD 460 the valley was overrun by the White Huns, from whose ferocious attacks it never recovered.

Below Beautifully decorated votive stupas at the Jaulian site, which is situated in the hills surrounding the Taxila valley. The main stupa and monastery at Jaulian are among the best-preserved buildings at Taxila.

Mount Li

In 210 BC the First Emperor of China, Qin Shi Huangdi, was buried in a vast burial mound close to Mount Li. Not far away, hidden underground, were more than 7000 life-size terracotta soldiers, together with horses and chariots, to guard him after death. They lay undisturbed for 2000 years.

Born during the Warring States Period (453-221 BC), when ancient China was divided into a number of contending kingdoms, Shi Huangdi became king of the state of Qin in 246 BC. Having ruthlessly obliterated the other states, in 221 BC he unified the whole country under his own rule and gave himself the title of First August Emperor of China.

He established his capital at Xianyang, near present-day Xi'an in Shaanxi province in the heart of China. Here, in an area of about 12 sq km (4¹/₂ sq miles), he had a number of large brick palaces constructed. Unfortunately, the city was set alight by a rebel army in about 206 BC, during the late Qin Dynasty. It is said that the fire lasted three months and destroyed the whole district. Scientific excavation, which started in 1933, yielded hollow bricks and iron, bronze and ceramic objects that testify to the enormous wealth and might of the First Emperor.

The written record

These excavations are not the only source of information about the First Emperor. The historian Sima Qian (c.143-85 BC) recorded that the First Emperor had a huge mausoleum built for himself near Xianyang, with a tomb at its heart laid out like a small universe. This aroused the curiosity of archaeologists, and in March 1974 the first excavations of the area were conducted by Shaanxi Provincial Institute of Archaeology.

The mausoleum

Located north of Mount Li, the mausoleum is 35km (22 miles) east of Xi'an. Its plan is rectangular, with the

Below The terracotta soldiers, discovered in pits not far from the mausoleum, vary in height, uniform and hairstyle, according to rank. This is Pit 1, which contains the largest number of soldiers and horses.

long axis oriented north-south. The mausoleum compound contains several buildings, laid out like the Emperor's palace at Xianyang. It was originally enclosed by an outer and an inner wall made of pounded earth. Except in a few places, the walls have been completely destroyed over the centuries, but remnants indicate that they were 8-10m (26-33ft) high and 8m (26ft) thick. The outer wall measured 2165m (7100ft) north to south, and 940m (3085ft) east to west; the inner wall 1355m (4445ft) north to south and 580m (1900ft) east to west. Gates were set into the walls, and there were watchtowers at each corner.

The tomb itself, which is covered by a mound of earth, or tumulus, has not yet been excavated, but the rest of the

compound has been excavated step by step, including side pits, buildings and attendant tombs. Bricks and tiles provide evidence of the various types of building on the site.

Only 53m (174ft) north of the tumulus are the foundations of a great temple hall. In the north-west corner of the walled area are foundations of smaller, private rooms. On the west side, the remains of three buildings have been excavated and inscriptions on the tiles identify them as provisions offices. The excavation has also revealed a workshop where the stones for the tomb were prepared.

Only 20m (66ft) west of the tomb excavators found two bronze chariots, each drawn by four bronze horses. Large quantities of hay had been placed

Above One of the army's cavalrymen is wearing a breastplate and leading his horse by a copper bridle.

with them, as if the horses were alive. The chariots were badly destroyed but could be restored. They are about half the size of real chariots of the time and illustrate the techniques of chariot-building and harness-making.

Shi Huangdi's tomb

Although the tomb is untouched, again we know something about it from the historian Sima Qian. Excavation and building work had begun at Mount Li as soon as the First Emperor had become King of Qin. By the time he had become emperor, 700,000 conscripts from all parts of the

country were at work there. They dug through three subterranean streams and poured molten copper for the outer coffin; the tomb was filled with models of palaces, pavilions and offices, as well as fine vessels, precious stones and other treasures, including pine trees carved out of jade.

Sima Qian describes fascinating details about the tomb's decoration:

'*All the country's streams, the Yellow River and the Yangzi were reproduced in quicksilver (mercury) and by some mechanical means made to flow into a miniature ocean. The heavenly constellations were shown above and the regions of the earth below. The candles were made of whale oil to ensure their burning for the longest possible time.*'

Crossbows were erected to ensure that any thief breaking in would be shot. And as another precaution, the middle and outer gates were closed to imprison all the artisans and labourers, so that they could not divulge any secrets of the tomb. Trees and grass were planted over the mausoleum to make it seem like a hill.

Perhaps archaeologists have been deterred from excavating the tumulus by the historian's description of booby-traps and rivers of mercury. It is also possible that the tomb itself, like the side pits, was robbed and destroyed with the capital in 206 BC.

The Terracotta Army

In 1974 local farmers drilling a well discovered what was to be one of the world's greatest archaeological treasures – the Terracotta Army.

The spectacular life-size clay figures were found in a cluster of four pits located about 1.2km (³/₄ mile) east of the outer wall of the mausoleum. Pit 1 contains the main battle formation, consisting of more than 6000 clay soldiers and horses. Pit 2 contains cavalry and infantry units and war chariots with horses. The much smaller Pit 3 contains high-ranking

Left This is one of the kneeling archers. Each soldier was given a real weapon, such as a spear, sword or crossbow.

China and its dynasties

For nearly 4000 years, China was ruled by emperors from a succession of dynasties. The first dynasty, the Xia, came to power in c.2000 BC and marks the point when one clan or family took control of every aspect of life in the country. During this dynasty a governing structure and legal system were developed. In 1911, nationalist forces declared China a republic and the Qing dynasty was overthrown.

2000-1500 BC	Xia
1700-1027 BC	Shang
1027-771 BC	Western Zhou
770-221 BC	Eastern Zhou
221-206 BC	Qin
206 BC-AD 6	Western Han
6-25	Hsing (Wang Mang interregnum)
25-220	Eastern Han
220-280	Three Kingdoms
265-316	Western Chin
317-420	Eastern Chin
420-588	South and North Dynasties
580-618	Sui
618-906	T'ang
907-960	Five Dynasties
969-1279	Song (Sung)
1279-1368	Yuan
1368-1644	Ming
1644-1911	Qing (Ch'ing) or Manchu

Right An infantryman with his hair wound into a distinctive topknot is wearing a loose tunic belted at the waist.

officers and represents the command post. Pit 4 is empty and was probably unfinished at the time of the emperor's death.

Pit 1 is the largest of the four and measures 230 x 62m (755 x 203ft). Warriors and horse chariots were placed in 11 columns, separated by stamped earth walls. The walls supported wooden roof beams, which were covered with layers of matting. A layer of earth measuring 3m (10ft) deep was placed over the matting to conceal the army's location. The floor was covered by some 256,000 tiles. It has been calculated that 126,940m³ (4.5 million cu ft) of earth had been moved in order to create the pit and 8000m³ (282,520 cu ft) of timber was used in its construction.

The warriors were placed in the pits when the wooden roofing was finished. As the figures are so heavy, it is possible that they were assembled in the pits, so no one at the time would have seen the army in its entirety.

An ancient production line

Clay is found in loess (a fine-grained silt), which covers large areas of northern China, providing an almost unlimited supply of a raw material that can easily be modelled. The craftsmen of the imperial workshops were divided into teams, with a foreman controlling around ten men. The names of 85 different foremen have been found on 249 figures.

Each part of the warrior's body – head, arms and hands, body and legs – was modelled separately, using standardized castes. Next, the face and hands were individually sculpted and features such as hair and moustaches were added. Then the parts were fitted together. Once the figure was assembled, craftsmen used additional clay to shape details such as those on the shoes or the armour.

The figure was then fired in a kiln. For the process to be successful, the different parts had to be fitted together while the clay contained exactly the right amount of moisture, so correct timing in making and assembling the figure was essential.

Finally, lacquer was used to colour the figures and paint the facial features. Working in this way, the craftsmen maintained a consistent quality of work, while producing several thousand terracotta figures, all with individual features from their faces to the soles of their shoes. It is an army that replicates the First Emperor's guard in his lifetime.

Archaeological excavations are still ongoing. So far over 8000 figures have been found.

Nara

The city of Nara, 40km (25 miles) south of Kyoto, was Japan's capital from AD 710 to 784, when it was called Nara-no-miyako or Heijo-kyo. It formed the core of a centralized state, which thrived under the influence of China's T'ang dynasty. The site has revealed many details of city life.

The site now lies within the central part of the present-day city of Nara. Numerous excavations have been carried out here, which have revealed features of the residences of both noblemen and common people, as well as roads and an abundance of artefacts of different kinds.

The city

Measuring over 4km (2¹/₂ miles) from west to east, and almost 5km (3 miles) north to south, the city was built on the Chinese grid pattern, with avenues running west to east and streets north to south.

The central thoroughfare, Suzaku Boulevard, was 84m (275ft) wide; at its southern end was the principal gate to the city, while at its northern end was the Imperial Palace. It is thought that at its height almost 200,000 people inhabited the city. The grounds of the Imperial Palace covered an area of about 1.25 sq km (¹/₂ sq mile), and contained the Imperial Residence, the Halls of State (including the Great Audience Hall) and various government offices and bureaux. This was the political nucleus of the Japanese nation-state, and it provided direct employment for around 10,000 officials and public employees.

Palace grounds

The grounds of the Imperial Palace were first precisely surveyed by archaeologists at the start of the 20th century, when their extent and layout were ascertained. The first excavations were carried out between 1924 and 1932, but major work began in the 1950s and has continued ever since. Hundreds of thousands of square metres have been uncovered in hundreds of excavations, and these have been thoroughly documented by archaeologists. An earthen wall ran around the palace compound. This was 2.7m (9ft) wide at its base and perhaps 6m (19ft) high, with 12 gates opening out of it.

In 1975 a 1200-year-old imperial villa garden was discovered by archaeologists. Excavations uncovered many features such as buildings, fences, gutters and wells, all located around a magnificent S-shaped pond. Among the artefacts were eaves-tiles of the same kind as those used at the Imperial Palace, and wooden tablets with letters written in ink still visible on them. In fact, tens of thousands of such tablets have been recovered, providing an important written

Below The Buddhist Todai-ji Temple was built on the orders of Emperor Shomu (reigned AD 724-49). The main hall (Daibutsuden) is still the world's largest wooden building, even though it was rebuilt in 1709 at only two-thirds of the original size.

Preservation and tourism

In 1906 the Heijo-kyo Preservation Society was formed, with private donations helping to acquire and conserve parts of the site. The Japanese government designated the whole area of the palace a 'Historic Site' in 1963, and they began to buy and preserve it. Since 1970 the Nara Cultural Properties Research Institute has been in charge of repairs, conservation and presentation of the site to the public, and have exhibited the excavated materials.

record of life in Nara. They comprise documents accompanying the movement of people or goods; government records, accounts and memoranda; and labels, including baggage labels on taxed goods.

A number of the garden's excavated buildings have been reconstructed at the site, some of which have pillars set directly into the ground without base-stones. They all faced east, in order to admire the pond and the view to the mountains. Water is thought to have come from the Komo River, which flowed along the east side of the garden site. A receiving reservoir stood to the north of the pond; from there water flowed into a stone-lined pool through a 5-m (16-ft) wooden conduit, and then overflowed into the pond. At the southern end was a 2.5-m (8-ft) wooden conduit and a stopcock.

Above The bronze Great Buddha is housed in the Todai-Ji Temple. The huge seated figure is 15m (49ft) tall and weighs 500 tonnes.

Ornamental water plants seem to have been grown along the pond's edges, since square wooden planting frames were found there. Rocks – gneiss, granite and andesite – were laid out with great skill, vertically and obliquely, along the banks.

Angkor

The immense complex of temples and other buildings that formed the city that is now called Angkor, in modern Cambodia, was one of the great wonders of ancient Asia. Today, despite years of neglect and damage caused by warfare, it is still one of the world's most impressive tourist destinations.

Rediscovered by a French missionary in 1850, Angkor was studied quite intensively in later decades, and the French colonialists eventually established major programmes to research the archaeology of what was then called Indochina. A restoration programme under the direction of the Ecole Française d'Extrême-Orient began in 1907, which worked to clear away the forest, repair foundations and install drains to protect the buildings from water damage.

In the early 1970s, the Angkor region was captured by the Khmer Rouge, who carried out a 20-year period of neglect and destruction, with sculptures being destroyed or illegally sold, and vegetation allowed to encroach on the buildings.

Restoration work began again after the end of the civil war. Some temples have been carefully taken apart and reassembled on concrete foundations.

The Khmer empire

In the early centuries AD, there seem to have been important political, religious and commercial links between China and India. By the 6th century Chinese records give the name 'Zhenla' to the region of the Middle Mekong River.

Zhenla appears to have denoted a series of regional chiefdoms, each with large, defended settlements, and with temple architecture that displayed a strong Indian influence. Many other elements of Indian culture were also adopted, and the Hindu and Buddhist religions were incorporated. Indian styles of religious art and

architecture became widespread, with new forms and local characteristics also developing at the same time.

By the 9th century AD Zhenla seems to have been consolidated into a single, powerful Khmer empire by King Jayavarman II. At the end of that century King Yasovarmon I moved the capital to Angkor, and from here the empire was the dominant force in South-east Asia until the early 15th century, when Angkor was pillaged by troops from neighbouring Siam (modern Thailand).

Above The towers of the Bayon temple in the heart of Angkor Thom are crowned with massive serene faces.

The Angkor complex

Although the word 'Angkor' comes from a Sanskrit term for 'holy city', Angkor itself was not a city at all, but rather a huge, sprawling complex of temples, monuments, reservoirs and canals that developed in different stages over the centuries. It is not really known to what extent ordinary people lived inside the complex.

The spatial layout of Angkor was based on Indian religious concepts. It was oriented around a central pyramid temple built on Phnom Bakheng, the only natural hill in the area. This temple was linked with Mount Meru, the central mountain in traditional Indian cosmology.

Successive Khmer kings founded temples in which, at first, the central object of worship was the lingam (stylized phallus) of the Hindu god Siva; this also represented royal authority. Gradually, the emphasis of Angkor's iconography changed from the Hindu cult of Siva to Mahayana Buddhism; nevertheless, the constant concern was the desire of Khmer rulers to construct monuments to their own immortality.

Angkor Thom

The Khmer kingdom reached its greatest extent under Jayavarman VII, who built the huge complex of Angkor Thom in the 12th century and which probably remained the Khmer capital until the 17th century. This complex covers 9 sq km (3 1/2 sq miles), and is enclosed by a wall of 3 sq km (1 sq mile). Each side is pierced by a great gateway, which features a tower carved

Above The wonderful bas-reliefs at the Bayon temple capture scenes from everyday life. This relief shows a harvesting scene with workers collecting fruit into baskets.

Below Dedicated to the Hindu god Vishnu by King Suryavarman II, the magnificent temple of Angkor Wat was constructed over a period of 30 years.

with four faces pointing to the four cardinal directions; each gate is approached by an impressive avenue of carved gods (at one side) and demons (at the other) carrying a giant serpent across the moat.

The complex contains a few residential structures (doubtless most dwellings were of wood and thatch and have not survived), but there are numerous temples from various centuries. The most magnificent of these, and one of Angkor's greatest buildings, is the Bayon where the four entrance roads converge.

The Bayon probably began as a Hindu monument, but was converted into a Buddhist sanctuary before being completed, probably in the late 12th/early 13th century. It is characterized by its famous 54 towers, each with four beatifically smiling faces of an Avalokitesvara (a future Buddha), and its extensive bas-relief carvings. These incredible carvings show scenes from Khmer everyday life, as well as events in Khmer history, including great naval battles. The details are highly evocative and include scenes of people cooking, bartering and playing chess, as well as weapons, vessels and cock fighting.

To the north of the Bayon stands the great carved Elephant Terrace, 3m (10ft) high and 300m (984ft) long, with its numerous bas-relief elephants as well as other figures, and many smaller temples.

Angkor Wat

Another very successful monarch was Suryavarman II, who, in the 12th century, built the most famous temple complex of all, Angkor Wat. Situated about 1km (0.6 miles) south of Angkor Thom and covering an area of about 81ha (200 acres), Angkor Wat is the largest and best-preserved temple at the site. This great temple blended Hindu cosmology and architecture with pre-existing Khmer beliefs. The enclosure symbolizes the Hindu cosmos, while the temple itself stood for the five peaks of Mount Meru, the abode of the gods.

One of Angkor's great advantages was its location on the shore of Tônlé Sab, the biggest lake in South-east Asia. In the wet season, water from the Mekong River flows back into the lake and more than trebles its surface area. The lake provided not only a supply of fish, but also water for irrigation. An elaborate complex of reservoirs, canals and moats was dominated by two huge man-made reservoirs. It is known from Chinese

Below An aerial view of Angkor Wat shows the quincunx of towers at its centre. Today, the temple is a symbol of Cambodia, appearing on its national flag.

Above A scene from a Bayon relief depicts the Khmer army going to war against the invading Cham (from Vietnam).

visitors in the 13th century that the people of the Angkor region had three or four rice crops per year, so clearly they had a large agricultural surplus.

Downfall

It also seems likely that a fall in this agricultural surplus – of unknown cause – may have been a factor in the downfall of Angkorian civilization, along with the military expansion of the Siamese. Another possibility is an increase in the incidence of malaria, because if warfare had led to the paddy fields being less well maintained, then the water could have become clear and calm, which is ideal breeding grounds for the most dangerous kind of mosquito.

After the sack of Angkor in 1431, most of the complex was abandoned. However, Angkor Wat was taken over by Buddhist monks, and became a major pilgrimage centre.

Angkor today

As a major international tourist destination, Angkor has many visitors, and five-star hotels proliferate in the nearby town of Siem Reap. This is in stark contrast to the poverty in the neighbouring villages, and the tragic results of the thousands of landmines that were laid in the region. The temple of Ta Prohm is currently one of the most popular tourist destinations in the complex, because its walls are still enveloped by the giant, twisting roots of fig trees, a sight that characterizes the romantic notion of ancient ruins integrated with nature. Another, more remote site is Kbal Spean, a place unique in the world, where rock art occurs within the bed of a flowing river – numerous bas-reliefs of lingams, and figures such as Vishnu and Siva, were carved into the very bed of a river near the top of a hill.

Left Enormous fig trees stretch their roots over the ruins in the central courtyard of the temple of Ta Prohm. When restoration work began at Angkor in the early 20th century, the authorities decided that Ta Prohm should be left as it was. Tourists can still enjoy the beauty of these trees.

HMS Pandora This late 18th-century shipwreck has yielded some remarkably well-preserved contents.

Nan Madol A mysterious ancient complex of man-made lakes separated by a network of canals.

Easter Island This remote volcanic island is studded with hundreds of stone statues called *moai*.

PHILIPPINES

North Pacific Ocean

Pacific Ocean

AUSTRALIA

Easter Island

Nan Madol

Pohnpei Island

I N D O N E S I A

MICRONESIA

MELANESIA

PAPUA NEW GUINEA

Wreck of HMS Pandora

New Caledonia

Lapita

Dampier Archipelago

A U S T R A L I A

Darling

Lake Mungo

Lachlan

South Pacific Ocean

Southern Ocean

NEW ZEALAND

Shag River Mouth

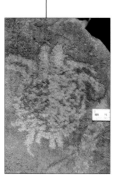

Dampier Archipelago This region is home to probably the largest collection of rock art in the world.

Lake Mungo This now-dry lake in New South Wales has revealed evidence of human occupation dating back 50,000 years.

Shag River Mouth A site rich in cultural material dating back to the earliest days of settlement in New Zealand.

THE GREAT SITES
OF OCEANIA

Parts of this vast region were among the last in the world to be settled, but the colonization of the far-flung Pacific islands is arguably the greatest exploit in human history. The islands produced some remarkable cultures, such as those of Hawaii or New Zealand, but the most extraordinary of all was that of Easter Island, with its stone statues, rich rock art and many other archaeological features. Australia itself has proved a land of great archaeological surprises since its early prehistory was first unearthed only a few decades ago. Often wrongly considered to be very primitive, the Aborigines were in fact extremely well adapted to the often harsh environments in which they lived, and were responsible for some notable cultural achievements, including a wealth of rock art. Archaeologists have also learned a great deal from Aborigines and inhabitants of Papua New Guinea, who still make stone tools and other implements in traditional ways.

Lapita bowl An example of distinctive Lapita pottery, which is named after one of the sites in New Caledonia.

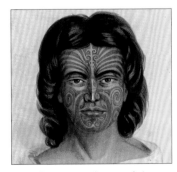

Maori tattoos The art of skin marking – called *ta moko* – has always been an important part of Maori culture.

Ahu Tongariki Easter Island statues were mounted on stone platforms, known as *ahu*. This is the island's largest platform.

Lake Mungo

The now-dry Lake Mungo is part of the Willandra Lakes system in the far west of New South Wales in Australia. The area is rich in archaeological sites and provides an extraordinary picture of Aboriginal occupation stretching back many millennia.

Fifty thousand years ago, the Willandra Lakes had been filled by fresh water from the Lachlan River. Then around 40,000 years ago the climate began to dry out, and the human inhabitants of the region had to adapt their way of life to increasing drought conditions. By 20,000 years ago the lake system was completely dry. Nevertheless, the region does not seem to have been totally abandoned. Although archaeologists have focused mainly on the older sites, evidence of younger sites allows them to explore human adaptation to changing environments over a 50,000-year period.

Cremation

In 1968 environmental scientist Jim Bowler, from the Australian National University, came across burnt bones eroding from dunes at Lake Mungo, where he was studying ancient climates. The remains proved to be those of a young woman, perhaps 19 years old. She had been cremated on the shores of the lake. Her bones had then been gathered and smashed, and finally interred in a small pit. This remarkable find remains the world's oldest evidence of ritual cremation.

Mungo Man

In 1974 a second burial was found nearby. The body of a 50-year-old man had been laid in a shallow grave and covered with red ochre. The original radiocarbon dates suggested that the burial occurred about 30,000 years ago, and the young woman's cremation about 25,000 years ago. In 1999 researchers using new dating

Above The near-complete skeleton of a 50-year-old man, who had been carefully laid on his back with his hands clasped.

methods controversially suggested Mungo Man could in fact be more than 60,000 years old. However, more detailed study of the finds and their context now suggests an age of about 40,000 years for both burials, and dates the earliest human presence in the area, shown by stone tools, at about 50,000 years ago.

Life around the lakes

Hearths and earth ovens, middens, scatters of stone artefacts, and stone quarries around the lakes provide a vivid picture of what life must have been like when they were full. People hunted a range of large and small animals and collected frogs, freshwater mussels and crayfish. They also fished for Murray cod and especially golden perch, which were probably caught using nets.

Stone from local quarries was used to make tools for chopping, cutting and scraping. Analysis of microscopic wear traces on some of these tools shows that they were used for scraping meat from bone and cleaning plant tubers.

The impact of the finds

Lake Mungo occupies an important place in the history of Australian archaeology. The first discoveries there came at a time when archaeologists had only recently demonstrated Ice Age occupation of Australia. The findings firmly established the dispersal of fully modern humans into Australia and provided an unusual insight into the beliefs of ancient people. Surveys and excavations have continued there ever since, and human remains, the bones of extinct animals and camp sites continue to be discovered.

The skeletal evidence remains significant in broader debates about the dispersal of modern humans, as well as the nature of the people who first colonized Australia, while the extraction of ancient DNA from Mungo Man offers new possibilities.

In 2003 the discovery of 20,000-year-old fossilized human footprints added yet another dimension to the archaeological record of the area. This was the first time fossil footprints had been found in Australia. There are at least 124 prints making eight trackways. Study of the sizes and characteristics of the prints suggest they were made by adults and children, some running and some walking. Other marks and indentations are still being studied, but some are thought to be the marks of tools such as spears and digging sticks dragged over the surface.

Indigenous peoples worldwide are concerned about controlling their history and how archaeologists research their past. Lack of respect for human remains has been a particularly contentious issue, and in Australia there has been considerable debate and even conflict between archaeologists and Aboriginal communities. In 1992 the remains of Mungo Lady were formally returned to the care of local Aboriginal communities. This event is an example of increasing partnership between Aboriginal groups and archaeologists in Australia generally.

Left Steve Webb of Bond University, Queensland, examines a series of animal bones – perhaps the remains of a meal – in a 20,000-year-old fireplace.

Below The spectacular crescent-shaped dune formations, which run for 30km (19 miles) along the eastern shore of Lake Mungo, are known as 'The Walls of China'.

The rock art of Dampier

The rugged terrain of the Dampier Archipelago, on the north-west coast of Australia, contains what is probably the largest concentration of rock art in the world. Archaeologists estimate that there may be up to 250,000 individual petroglyphs (carvings made into the rock face).

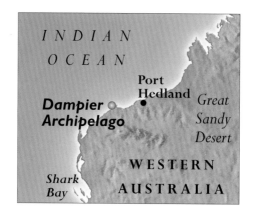

The art at Dampier is extraordinarily diverse both in its subject matter and technique, including human and animal figures as well as a wide range of geometric motifs. Rock art is always difficult to date, but the large number of marine mammals and fish represented at Dampier suggests that much of the art dates to the last 6000 years, when the sea reached its present level and the islands of the archipelago were formed.

Many of the rock motifs can be linked with contemporary Aboriginal ceremonial practices in the wider Pilbara region. However, some heavily weathered designs, such as face motifs, may be much older. They resemble art from elsewhere in Australia, which is thought to date back to the earliest settlement of the continent, up to 50,000 years ago. As well as art, there is also a range of other sites, including shell middens, campsites, quarries and workshops, and stone arrangements.

Threat of destruction

Despite the richness of the area, Dampier is also one of the world's most endangered heritage sites. Industrial development began in the 1960s and continues to this day. Many decorated boulders have been destroyed or moved from their original locations. Those that survive are under threat from future development and emissions from the industrial estate. There is still no proper inventory of the archaeological sites or comprehensive heritage management plan.

Below Tumbled boulders adorned with petroglyphs are a distinctive feature of the landscape of the Dampier Archipelago.

Figures from the Dreaming

The Yaburara Aborigines inhabited the Dampier archipelago and groups from the mainland also visited seasonally. Beginning with the arrival of American whalers in the 1840s, local Aboriginal communities were devastated by European settlement. The impact of introduced diseases and raiding for forced labour for the pearling and pastoral industries was particularly severe. The Yaburara were effectively wiped out in 1868 in the Flying Foam Massacre. Aboriginal communities in the Pilbara today still feel responsible for caring for Yaburara land. They believe that the Dampier petroglyphs were all made by the ancestral creator spirits, or *marga*, during the Dreaming, which they call the 'time when the world was soft'.

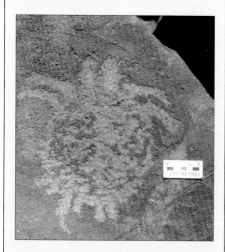

Above Turtles are common in the most recent art phase and are often shown mating, as here, or with eggs.

Nan Madol

Known as the Venice of the Pacific, the mysterious Nan Madol is perhaps the most spectacular site in all Oceania. Situated on the volcanic island of Pohnpei in the Caroline Islands, it is a vast ancient complex of artificial islets linked by a network of canals.

In all there are 93 artificial islets at Nan Madol. These are constructed of massive basalt stones with coral and rubble fill. The whole site covers an area of about 81ha (200 acres) of sheltered reef and is protected from the sea by massive sea walls.

Mapping the site

The first map of Nan Madol was produced in 1910. Since then, archaeological research at the site, most recently led by Bill Ayres, has produced detailed maps of archaeological remains of more than 20 of the islets. Excavations have enabled archaeologists to compile a chronology of the development of Nan Madol, which can be related to the historical accounts in Pohnpei oral traditions.

History

Nan Madol seems to have been the ceremonial and administrative centre of a single state, uniting the whole population of Pohnpei under a single ruling dynasty. The artificial islets

provided both residential and tomb complexes for the ruling elite. The massive tomb complex of Nandauwas is the crowning achievement of the site. Its outer walls, made of enormous basalt slabs, rise more than 7m (23ft) above the level of the canal. These surround a central tomb

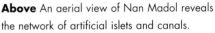

Above An aerial view of Nan Madol reveals the network of artificial islets and canals.

enclosure within the main courtyard. An impressive portal marks the entry into Nandauwas.

Nan Madol was first occupied about 2000 years ago. By AD 1000 the first artificial islets had been constructed. Most of the massive monumental architecture, such as the Nandauwas tomb complex, dates to the period AD 1200-1600. According to Pohnpei oral history, this was the period when Pohnpei was united under the rule of the Saudeleur dynasty. Centralized Saudeleur rule seems to have collapsed about AD 1600, to be replaced by regional chiefdoms. Nan Madol thus lost its role as a political centre and by the time Europeans visited Pohnpei in the 19th century, the vast complex had been abandoned.

Left The heavy basalt slabs, which can be clearly seen in the walls of this ruin, were transported from a quarry on Pohnpei. All the cutting and shaping of the stone would have been done without the aid of metal tools.

The Lapita Culture

A distinctive type of highly decorated pottery marks the appearance of a new cultural complex on several islands in the western Pacific. This cultural complex, which began about 3500 years ago, is called Lapita, after an archaeological site in New Caledonia.

The Pacific Ocean covers about one third of the earth's surface. The settlement of this vast area, with its hundreds of remote islands, involved remarkable feats of voyaging. The western rim of the Pacific, including New Guinea, Australia and the western Melanesian islands, was occupied by about 30,000 years ago. The colonization of the more remote islands of Oceania began around 1500 BC and seems to have been very rapid. How it was achieved has been debated since the earliest European voyages to the South Pacific in the 18th century.

Lapita pottery

Archaeologists first recognized the pottery in 1909 on Watom Island, off New Britain. Lapita sites are widely distributed from the Bismarck Archipelago, off the north-west coast of New Guinea, as far as Fiji, Tonga

and Samoa. The Lapita cultural complex spans a period of about 1000 years and is often linked to the expansion of speakers of Austronesian languages into the region.

Lapita pottery is handmade and poorly fired but is usually very highly decorated, although plain wares were also made. The designs were most commonly stamped into the damp clay using a comb-like tool. Sometimes the potter used a sharp stone or shell to cut

Above Archaeologists excavate a pot-burial site at Teouma. The pots are clearly visible.

Left A flat-bottomed Lapita bowl, decorated with a repeat design of stylized faces.

Lapita settlements

Most Lapita sites are coastal settlements. Marine resources, such as fish, seabirds, turtles and shellfish, made an important contribution to the economy. Lapita colonists introduced domestic pig, dog and chicken to the areas they settled and cultivated tuberous plants and tree crops. Some settlements seem to have been built on piles over the water. As well as the distinctive pottery, Lapita sites often contain shell ornaments and fishhooks, files, bone awls, tattooing needles, and shell and stone woodworking tools known as adzes.

A feature of the Lapita cultural complex is evidence for long-distance exchange between communities. The best indication of the transport of particular materials comes from the study of obsidian, a distinctive volcanic glass. There are several known sources of obsidian in the Bismarck Archipelago, especially on Manus and New Britain. Obsidian from Manus is found as far away as Vanuatu, while obsidian from New Britain is very widely distributed from Borneo to Fiji.

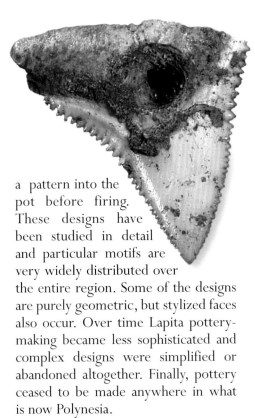

a pattern into the pot before firing. These designs have been studied in detail and particular motifs are very widely distributed over the entire region. Some of the designs are purely geometric, but stylized faces also occur. Over time Lapita pottery-making became less sophisticated and complex designs were simplified or abandoned altogether. Finally, pottery ceased to be made anywhere in what is now Polynesia.

Above and above left Artefacts include this drilled shark tooth and shark vertebra.

Origins of the Lapita

It is widely agreed that the descendants of the Lapita people were the Polynesians. Their culture seems to have developed from the Lapita culture of the Fiji, Tonga and Samoa area. There is, however, considerable disagreement about the origins of the Lapita cultural complex. Some archaeologists argue for local development in the Bismarck Archipelago, while others favour an origin in a South-east Asian island.

The site of Teouma in central Vanuatu is one of the most important Lapita sites and will help to answer these questions. Discovered accidentally in 2003, subsequent excavations at Teouma have revealed a cemetery which, at 3200 to 3000 years old, is the oldest known in the Pacific region. The site is unique in other ways. The distinctive Lapita pottery found there is extraordinarily well preserved. There is evidence of complex burial rites in the form of burials, with the heads removed and the interment of skulls and other human bones in large pots. Such pot burials are unique in the Pacific, but occur from about 5500 years ago in island south-east Asia. Study of these bones, and of DNA extracted from them, will give important clues to the origins of the Lapita people.

Right This fragment of Lapita pottery, which was discovered in 2001, has a unique three-dimensional sculpted face. The stamped designs visible on the face may represent tattoos.

Easter Island

Easter Island is one of the most remote pieces of inhabited land in the world, so remote that it is extremely unlikely that it was ever colonized more than once. Certainly the archaeological record indicates a single unbroken development of culture from the first settlers until the arrival of Europeans.

Easter Island

Santigo

South Pacific Ocean

The 166 sq km (64 sq mile) volcanic island is the easternmost inhabited island of Polynesia. It is situated some 3700km (2300 miles) from South America and 2200km (1367 miles) from Pitcairn Island.

Colonization

People first arrived here in canoes in the early centuries AD. Contrary to the theory of Norwegian Thor Heyerdahl (who in 1947 sailed from Peru to Polynesia in the *Kon Tiki*), the colonists did *not* come from South America, but rather from eastern Polynesia. This is confirmed not only by archaeology and language, but also anthropology, blood groups and genetics.

Once on the island, the colonists were trapped, and it constituted their whole world. Their first known contact with others came on Easter Sunday 1722, when the Dutch navigator Roggeveen encountered and named the island. The Dutch were the first to leave us written descriptions of the inhabitants.

Analyses of pollen from the sediments at the bottom of the freshwater lakes in the island's volcanic craters led British palaeobotanist John Flenley in the 1980s to discover that the island was originally covered by a rainforest dominated by a species of huge palm tree.

It was on this island, which looked totally different from that of today, that the voyagers arrived, bringing with them the domestic animals (chickens, rats) and food plants (bananas, sweet potatoes, taro) with which they transformed the environment of many Polynesian islands.

Constructions

During the initial phase, the islanders seem to have constructed small, simple *ahu* (stone platforms) of normal Polynesian type, with small and relatively crude statues upon or in front of them.

In the middle phase of Easter Island's prehistory (*c.*AD 1000-1500), enormous effort was poured into the construction of bigger ceremonial platforms and hundreds of large statues. As the population grew, there was a need for ever-increasing quantities of food. The decline of the forest, as land was cleared, can be seen in the pollen from the craters. The increasing quantity of statue carving required more timber for rollers and levers to transport the statues.

More than 800 *moai* (statues) were carved, mostly in the soft, volcanic tuff of the Rano Raraku crater, with basalt hammerstones. They depict a human with a prominent nose and chin, and often elongated ears containing disks. The bodies, ending at the abdomen, have arms held to the sides, and hands held in front, with long fingertips meeting a stylized loincloth. They represent ancestor figures.

Over 230 *moai* were transported from the quarry to platforms around the island's edge, where they were erected, backs to the sea. At the most prestigious platforms, the statues were given a *pukao*, or topknot, of red scoria (burnt lava), raised and placed on the head; and white coral eyes, inserted at certain times or ceremonies to 'activate' the statues' *mana* (spiritual power).

Left One of the many *moai* that remain in and around the quarry at Rano Raraku, buried up to their necks in sediment.

The statues on platforms ranged from 2 to 10m (6½ to 33ft) in height, and weighed up to 83 tonnes. The biggest platform on the island was Tongariki, with 15 statues.

The quarry at Rano Raraku still contains almost 400 statues on its slopes, in every stage of manufacture. Finished statues on the slopes are covered by sediments up to their necks, but they are all full statues down to the abdomen.

Collapse

The final phase of the island's prehistory saw a collapse: statues ceased to be carved, cremation gave way to burial, and 1000 years of peaceful coexistence was shattered by the toppling of statues, and an abundant manufacture of *mataa* – spearheads and daggers of obsidian. The conflict was resolved by abandoning the earlier religion and social system based on ancestor worship, in favour of one featuring a warrior elite. An annual chief, or 'birdman', was chosen each year at the ceremonial village of Orongo, perched high on the cliff separating the great Rano Kau crater from the ocean. Each candidate had a young man to represent him. Every spring these young men had to descend the sheer cliff, 300m (984ft) high, then swim over a kilometre (0.6 mile) on a bunch of reeds to an islet. Here they would await the arrival of the sooty tern, in order to find its first egg. The winner swam back with the egg in a headband, and his master would become the new birdman. Orongo's rock art is festooned with carvings of the birdmen, sometimes holding the egg which symbolized fertility. This system ended with the arrival of missionaries in the 1860s.

The causes of the island's decline were probably complex, but the major factor was clearly human colonization. From at least 1200 years ago one can see a massive reduction in forest cover until, by the time Europeans arrived, there were no large trees left. The imported rats fed on the palm fruits and helped prevent regeneration. Without timber, statues could no longer be moved and ocean-going canoes could no longer be built, thus cutting the population off from a supply of deep-sea fish. Chickens became the most precious source of protein. Deforestation caused tremendous soil erosion, which damaged crop-growing. Starvation gave rise to raiding and violence, perhaps even to cannibalism.

Right This statue has been given a separate topknot of red scoria and eyes of white coral.

Above The 15 statues on the Tongariki platform, which were restored in the 1990s, stand facing inland, their backs to the sea.

Shag River Mouth

The Shag River Mouth site, located in Otago on the east coast of New Zealand's South Island, was first discovered in 1872. The site, which has a long history of investigation, occupies an important place in New Zealand archaeology because of the richness and diversity of the cultural remains.

Excavations at the site in the late 19th and early 20th century uncovered a rich and diverse artefact assemblage. Large quantities of the bones of the large, flightless moa, and other faunal remains, were also found, as well as evidence for hearths, houses and refuse areas. The site was generally interpreted as a long-term village site, dating from the earliest period of settlement in New Zealand, and played an important role in early debates about the nature and antiquity of moa hunting and the role of Polynesian settlers in the extinction of the birds.

The settlement

Modern excavations in the 1980s have shown that the site was a short-lived permanent settlement, occupied for about 50 years in the mid-14th century AD. The economy of the site was originally based on the specialized exploitation of large game, such as larger species of moa and fur seals. The focus on big-game hunting seems to have caused depletion in the local resources and later midden deposits indicate that the emphasis later shifted to fishing.

The settlement at Shag River Mouth had a central butchery and cooking area surrounded by midden dumps. Dwellings and workshop areas were clustered in groups around the central area. The excavators estimate a population of 100 to 200 people.

The range of artefacts recovered from the site is remarkable and reflects the diversity of activities that were

carried out at the site. As well as fishing and hunting gear, and plant processing equipment such as grindstones and pounders, there is evidence of bone and stone working. Shell beads and a greenstone tattooing chisel provide evidence of personal adornment. Shag River Mouth is an example of how modern methods of archaeological excavation and analysis can shed new light on old interpretations.

Above Finds of tattooing chisels at sites such as Shag River Mouth show that the distinctive Maori custom of tattooing was part of the culture that the first settlers brought with them to New Zealand.

Left The skull and neck of a moa, one of several species of flightless bird hunted to extinction by the first Polynesian settlers. This bird was mummified in the dry atmosphere of a central Otago cave.

HMS *Pandora*

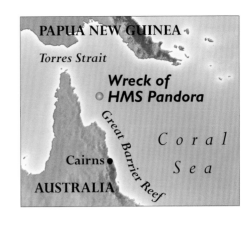

On-going explorations of the wreck of HMS Pandora, *which sank in the deep waters of Australia's Great Barrier Reef in the 1790s, are gradually unearthing a treasure trove of well-preserved artefacts, providing an extraordinary snapshot of life on board at the time.*

The 24-gun frigate set sail from England in 1790 to track down the *Bounty* mutineers and bring them to justice. Her captain, Edward Edwards, caught up with the 14 mutineers who had remained in Tahiti. He failed to find the other mutineers, who had sought refuge on Pitcairn Island, and headed for home with his prisoners. However, the ship struck submerged coral and sank on 29 August 1791 trying to negotiate the Great Barrier Reef. Most of the crew survived, along with ten of the mutineers who were subsequently tried in England.

Excavation

The ship was rediscovered in 1977 and preliminary archaeological surveys showed that she was remarkably well preserved. Much of the ship's hull had been very quickly covered with sand when she sank and therefore survived intact. Systematic excavations began in 1984, led by Peter Gesner of the Queensland Museum.

Excavation work on the *Pandora* has been expensive, difficult and dangerous because it is so remote, and the depth of the wreck allows only relatively short dives. Consequently, only a small part of the site has been excavated so far.

Many of the artefacts found come from the officers' cabins and storerooms on the lower deck. These have yielded a wealth of personal items and equipment, such as surgical instruments, which presumably belonged to George Hamilton, the ship's surgeon. A pocket watch found in the same area

was probably also Hamilton's. Future excavation work in the bow area will reveal details of the lives of ordinary seamen on board the ship.

Below The Pacific claimed many ships at the height of the 18th-century explorations. This painting shows the *Astrolabe*, which sank two years before HMS *Pandora*.

Souvenirs

Among the items found on board are a number of local curiosities that crew members had picked up on their journey. These would have been collected either as souvenirs to take back home or perhaps to sell on to European collectors. These artefacts – including such things as Polynesian clubs and poi pounders, which were used to pound fruits – provide a valuable insight into Pacific culture at the time. First Lieutenant John Larkin seems to have collected many of these curiosities.

Left Many curiosities, such as this whalebone carving of a Polynesian god, were sold on to collectors in Europe.

Little Bighorn Excavations begun in 1983 have uncovered previously unknown details about this famous American battle.

Mesa Verde This location in Colorado is famous for its Anasazi structures, including remarkable many-roomed cliff dwellings.

Chichén Itzá The impressive ruins of this Maya ceremonial centre include a huge stepped pyramid, an observatory and a ballcourt.

Tikal The largest of the ancient ruined cities of the Maya civilization, it included monumental buildings such as step pyramids.

Chan Chan A great mud-brick city in the Moche Valley, it was divided into huge, rectangular compounds by its pre-Inca builders.

Moche Outstanding pots representing life-like people and other subjects provide important clues about the Moche culture that produced them.

NORTH
AMERICA

Little Bighorn

L'Anse aux Meadows

Mesa Verde   Cahokia   Great Serpent Mound
Chaco Canyon

*Atlantic
Ocean*

Tenochtitlán   *Gulf of
Mexico*
Teotihuacán   Chichén Itzá
Cholula   Tikal

*Pacific
Ocean*

Sipán
Chan Chan   Moche

SOUTH
AMERICA

THE GREAT SITES OF THE AMERICAS

Although the earliest-known excavation took place at Huaca de Tantalluc on the coast of Peru in 1765, the New World was otherwise something of a latecomer to archaeological research. But the amazing monuments and cultures of both Mesoamerica and South America soon established the huge importance of this continent to the history of humans. Today, study of the Maya rivals that of Ancient Egypt and the Classical World in popularity and importance. A huge amount of archaeological work has also been carried out in North America – from the Anasazi dwellings of Chaco Canyon in the west to the Viking settlement of L'Anse aux Meadows in the east. In the next few years new discoveries, together with genetic data, should also shed fresh light on how and when the New World was first colonized.

Teotihuacán Archaeologists are still not sure why this once monumental city of Mesoamerica was abandoned.

Great Serpent Mound The precise significance of this huge earthen mound in Ohio is shrouded in mystery.

Tenochtitlán The once vast capital of the Aztec empire is buried beneath modern day Mexico City.

Cholula

One of the most important economic and ceremonial centres of pre-Columbian Mesoamerica, the Mexican city of Cholula is the oldest continuously occupied city in the Americas. The Great Pyramid is the largest in the world by volume.

Situated in the highland Puebla Valley, Cholula first rose to prominence during the Middle Formative period (1000-500 BC), and it continued to thrive through the pre-Columbian era. The city became one of the most important regional centres in pre-Hispanic Central America, and it was also the centre of the cult of the deity Quetzalcóatl.

Archaeological investigations have been ongoing at the site for the last 100 years, with most of the attention focused on the Great Pyramid, which is almost completely buried beneath a layer of soil and vegetation. Due to its long history and monumentality, and the fact that much of the ancient city is covered by modern construction, Cholula remains one of the great enigmas of ancient Mesoamerica.

Prime location

The Puebla Valley, situated between Mexico City and the Gulf Coast, is surrounded by snow-capped volcanoes that supply the alluvial plain with reliable run-off water for intensive agriculture. Located near the convergence of several perennial rivers and a marshy lake, Cholula enjoyed an advantageous environment; colonial Spanish accounts describe it as the most productive zone in New Spain. Another resource was the high clay content in the sub-soil, making it ideal for pottery production. Cholula polychrome pottery was widely traded, and it was noted that the Aztec ruler preferred dining on the beautiful dishes of Cholula. The city is also located on crossroads connecting the highland valleys with the Gulf lowlands, and with the southern highlands of Oaxaca, making it an entrepôt for long-distance exchange.

Early visitors

When the Spanish conquistador Hernán Cortés and his army entered Cholula in 1519, they were amazed at the grandeur of the city, comparable to the Spanish cities from which they had come. The Great Pyramid was taller than the Great Temple of Aztec Tenochtitlán and the marketplace featured an array of exotic goods from throughout Mesoamerica, brought by the long-distance merchants known as the *pochteca*.

Numerous colonial chroniclers described the economic, political and religious organization of Cholula, providing valuable information to complement the archaeological finds. Cholula was also the source of the Mixteca-Puebla stylistic tradition, exemplified in a series of pictorial manuscripts (codices) known as the Borgia group (after the Borgia Codex, which was saved from destruction by Cardinal Borgia and is now housed in the Vatican Library). With their array of gods, kings, mythical creatures and

Left A view of the east side of the Patio of the Altars shows a large head sculpture in the foreground.

abstract designs, these codices depict pre-Hispanic perspectives on the city and its religious groups.

The Great Pyramid

Referred to as the Tlachihualtepetl ('artificial mountain') in Colonial sources, the Great Pyramid at Cholula has been an important religious site for 2500 years, including its current use as the base for a prominent Catholic church.

Dedicated to Quetzalcóatl, work on the Tlachihualtepetl was begun in the Late Formative period (500 BC-0), and construction continued into the Early Postclassic period (AD 900-1200) in at least four major building phases, until it measured over 400m (1312ft) on a side and 65m (213ft) in height. The Great Pyramid was built around sacred principles, oriented to the setting sun at the summer solstice (25 degrees north of west), and standing over a spring, which represents passage to the underworld.

The construction history of the Great Pyramid was explored via 8km (5 miles) of tunnels dug by archaeologists from the 1930s to the 1960s. These excavations revealed different façades and staircases, which had been buried as the pyramid was enlarged and modified. Archaeologists have reconstructed one side of one of the lower segments of the pyramid.

Other excavations have exposed the ceremonial platforms and patios around the base of the pyramid, especially the Patio of the Altars where 10-tonne slabs of onyx form two stela-altar groups oriented towards the setting sun on the longest day of the year. On the platform façade of the patio is the Drunkards Mural, depicting over 100 life-size revellers partaking of hallucinogenic drink and transforming into their animal co-essences.

Other areas

Pre-Hispanic mounds have been found in other parts of the site, although only a few have survived urban development; Cortés counted more

than 400 mounds when he first rode into the city. Salvage excavations have documented residential areas of the ancient city, including changing ethnic patterns as Cholula adapted to the turbulent political events that caused the rise and decline of neighbouring cities, such as Teotihuacán, Tula, Monte Albán and Tenochtitlán. In the

face of these changes, it is significant that Cholula was able to maintain its importance for 3000 years.

Above Full excavation and restoration of the pyramid has been restricted due to the fact that the Catholic church, built at the top by the Spanish in 1594, is a designated colonial monument and place of pilgrimage.

Tikal

Deep in the jungles of what is now Northern Guatemala, the Maya built an astonishing city that was to become one of the largest and most important of the Classic Maya period. The scale of some of its buildings, including steep-sided pyramids, is to this day awesome.

Tikal's roots date back to the Middle Preclassic period (*c.*700 BC), although the nature of this early site is not well understood, as it had been covered by later construction. The city began to grow in the Late Preclassic period (*c.*350 BC to AD 250), with the most impressive architecture located in the *Mundo Perdido* ('Lost World') complex, including a large temple pyramid at its centre. It continued to be important into the Early Classic period (*c.*AD 250-600). The pyramid was modified at the beginning of this period and shows architectural similarities to structures from the Central Mexican city of Teotihuacán. Tikal flourished in the Classic period (*c.*AD 250-900) and then, in common with other Maya cities, went into decline.

For centuries the city had been effectively lost to the jungle until its rediscovery in 1848. Archaeologists later confirmed Tikal to be one of the Maya's main political and ceremonial centres. The first large-scale excavation

Below The Great Plaza at Tikal is dominated by the great step pyramids of Temple I and Temple II (shown here).

Right This detail is from a painted vase, made in Tikal in around AD 700.

and mapping project at the site was carried out by the University Museum of the University of Pennsylvania between 1956 and 1970.

Architecture

Maya construction was accretionary – with new layers added to existing buildings. As a result, the majority of Early Classic architecture at Tikal has been built over by later construction efforts. Much of the architecture that is visible at the site today was constructed during the Late Classic period (AD 600-900). This includes the massive palace complexes (most notably the central acropolis), much of the funerary architecture (Temples I-V and much of the North acropolis), and also the site's ballcourts and *sacbeob* (raised roadways). The area around Tikal also flourished at this time so that at its peak the central district and its rural hinterlands came to encompass an area of over 50 sq km (19 sq miles), much of which is still to be cleared and excavated.

Below Relief carvings on a stela depict a man wearing a ceremonial headdress.

Right This detail is from a painted vase, made in Tikal in around AD 700.

Collapse

Tikal collapsed sometime during the 9th century AD, and the majority of the site was abandoned, with a small squatter population remaining in the area. The last stela, known as Stela II, has the date AD 869. This collapse was part of the broader phenomenon referred to as the Classic Maya Collapse that is represented by a large-scale depopulation throughout the southern Maya lowlands. The cause of this collapse is widely debated, with suggested causes including warfare, internal dissent, disease, drought and famine. Excavated skeletons at the cemetery certainly indicate that disease and malnutrition were widespread.

Teotihuacán

From around AD 100 to 600, Teotihuacán – meaning 'city of the gods' – was the largest city of the Americas. The vast central Avenue of the Dead is still flanked by impressive ceremonial architecture, including the monumental Pyramid of the Sun.

Located in the Basin of Mexico in the central highlands, approximately 40km (25 miles) north-east of Mexico City, Teotihuacán quickly grew to prominence due in part to a volcanic eruption in the southern basin that destroyed the early site of Cuicuilco, its major competitor during the pre-Classic period.

The pre-Columbian Basin of Mexico was filled with an extensive network of lakes that facilitated transportation and supported a diverse biosphere, which included fish and waterfowl. The people of Teotihuacán were able to exploit this environment by using intensive agriculture, hunting and gathering of wild resources. They also mined locally available obsidian for stone tool manufacture.

At its height Teotihuacán had become a thriving economic centre with a population estimated at about 150,000 people.

Abandonment

The ceremonial precinct in the urban core was destroyed by fire in about AD 600. By the time the first Spanish conquistadores arrived in 1519 the pyramids were in ruins and the vast city overgrown except where it was under cultivation. However, this was never a 'lost city' – in fact, the agricultural productivity of the surrounding lands meant that it was never even completely abandoned. The ruins of Teotihuacán were well known to the local people and were a place of pilgrimage in Aztec times. Historical accounts suggest that the Aztec king Moctezuma visited an oracle at Teotihuacán to learn of the strange bearded men (the Europeans), as the conquistador Cortés and his army approached their city.

Minor archaeological excavations were carried out in the 19th century, and in 1905 major excavation and restoration work began under archaeologist Leopoldo Batres; the Pyramid of the Sun was restored to celebrate the centennial of Mexican Independence in 1910. An important mapping project led by René Millon produced detailed maps and plans of the city. Archaeological work at the site continues to this day.

A well-planned city

The layout of the city is a marvel of urban planning and monumental construction. In about AD 100 the city underwent intensive urban renewal, with the streets organized by a strict grid system arrayed around the principal Avenue of the Dead. Stretching for approximately 2.3km (1½ miles) and 40m (130ft) wide, this causeway was probably used for

Left A view along the Avenue of the Dead from the Pyramid of the Moon extends towards the vast Pyramid of the Sun.

Left Heads of the feathered serpent project from the façade of the Temple of Quetzalcóatl.

Another important feature of the ceremonial centre is the Pyramid of the Feathered Serpent (Quetzalcóatl) located within the *ciudadela* (Citadel) enclosure. The pyramid, which was first excavated between 1917 and 1922, was originally covered with a carved façade of undulating feathered serpents, an important supernatural entity found in many Mesoamerican cultures. Excavations into the rubble core of the Pyramid have found nearly 200 sacrificial burials of male and female warriors and attendants, many killed with their hands bound behind their backs and attired in elaborate jewellery of human teeth.

Enigmatic city

In contrast to the contemporaneous Maya, Teotihuacán lacked a well-developed writing system, so little is known of its dynastic histories. The cause for Teotihuacán's abandonment remains one of the great mysteries of the ancient capital. Theories include climatic change, invasion and even internal unrest, but so far the precise reason for the city's demise is unclear.

ritual processions to the many important religious buildings that flanked the avenue.

The largest and most impressive monument was the Pyramid of the Sun, which measures about 280m (918ft) wide at the base and soars to a height of about 65m (213ft). It would have been surmounted by a temple made of perishable materials, which would have extended it much higher. Excavations carried out directly under the pyramid in 1971 revealed a ceremonial cave.

At the northern extreme of the Avenue of the Dead is the equally impressive Pyramid of the Moon. Excavations carried out at the pyramid since 1998 by a team of archaeologists led by Saburo Sugiyama have revealed a great deal of material, including human burials. The Pyramid of the Moon is fronted by a large plaza surrounded by administrative platforms and the Palace of the Feathered Butterfly (Quetzalpapalotl), perhaps the most extravagant of the residential palaces.

The names and significance of these pyramids are unknown – and in fact the actual language of the inhabitants of Teotihuacán remains a source of scholarly debate – but again we owe the names to the Aztecs who continued to worship at these shrines when they were encountered and recorded by the Spanish.

Right A human burial discovered at the Pyramid of the Moon revealed human skeletons, along with thousands of pieces of mortuary offerings, including jade ornaments and shells.

The Moche

Beginning in the first century AD a civilization known as the Moche emerged on the north coast of Peru that could rival any in the world for wealth and power. The Moche were skilled craftsmen who, among other things, created wonderful pots that record many aspects of their way of life.

The major Moche settlements were located in the massive river valleys that cut through the desert coast. Here they farmed vast tracts of land, harvested huge quantities of resources from the ocean and controlled herds of camelids. Large numbers of specialized labourers produced pottery, metalwork, textiles and other luxury items. The Moche constructed enormous adobe (mudbrick) pyramids and developed sophisticated irrigation systems and road networks.

Moche religion and ritual life were spectacular, filled with pageantry, drama and violence. Ritualized warfare, the capture and display of prisoners, and human sacrifice were its hallmarks.

Moche society

Each major Moche settlement was ruled by a set of hereditary rulers who held political and religious power. At one of the settlements, San José del Morro, studied by archaeologist Luis Jaime Castillo, women held the most important religious posts, although elsewhere it was men. Below the rulers in this hierarchical society was a vast group of retainers and administrators, who held many specific roles in religious, political and economic life. Thousands of commoner families supported the Moche state with their agricultural work, or by fishing or herding. Upon their deaths Moche people were buried in cemeteries or elaborate tombs, with their placement determined by their social and economic positions in life.

Below Despite its history of erosion and destruction during the colonial period, the monumental stepped Pyramid of the Sun (Huaca del Sol) still towers above the surrounding plain. Overlooking the Pyramid is the Temple of the Moon (Huaca de la Luna).

Moche artisans were highly skilled, living in segregated sections of major settlements or in their own towns. One set of specialists were the potters, who produced a huge range of moulded, sculptural pottery bottles depicting animals, plants, buildings, scenes from everyday life and, most famously, people. They produced pottery known in Peru as the *huacos eroticos* (erotic pots) that show men and women engaged in a wide range of sexual acts and related activities, as well as many other types of pots. Fineline pottery, with detailed drawings of Moche rituals, is among the rarest and has been important in revealing details about Moche religion and ritual.

The Moche artisans were also expert metalworkers. Jewellery and other ornaments of gold, silver, copper and alloys were often inlaid with turquoise and lapis lazuli. They also crafted metal tools, such as chisels, spear points and fishhooks.

Warriors held a special position in Moche society, living well until at least some of them suffered a gruesome end. We know this because of careful study of Moche pottery and other art, especially the ceramic vessels known as portrait pots. These three-dimensional sculptured images of the faces of Moche warriors and others on the outside of mould-made

Below A gold funerary mask with lapis lazuli eyes was found in one of the royal tombs.

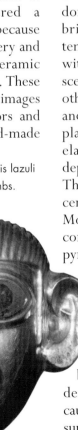

Above A depiction in copper and gold shows the sacrificer god holding a knife in one hand and the head of one of his victims in the other.

ceramic bottles have provided important clues about the lives of ancient Moche warriors.

Building works

The major Moche settlements were dominated by huge adobe (mud-brick) pyramids with platforms, temples and huge spaces, decorated with friezes depicting Moche deities, scenes of processions of prisoners and other huge murals. Tombs of rulers and other important people were placed inside the pyramids in elaborate ceremonies that are depicted on Moche fineline pottery. The residences, workshops and cemeteries of the vast majority of Moche people were situated in compounds adjacent to the major pyramids and in towns up and down the river valleys.

The Moche built huge complexes of canals to irrigate the vast agricultural fields required to feed their people. However, catastrophic rains brought on periodically by El Niño destroyed the irrigation systems, causing widespread disruption in food supplies that may have had long-term consequences for the Moche economy.

They also appear to have prompted the Moche to sacrifice groups of young men, probably in the hopes of appeasing the gods who they believed brought on the devastating rains. The recent discovery by archaeologist Steve Bourget of the skeletal remains of at least 34 sacrificed adult males resting in layers of mud on the edge of the Pyramid of the Moon attest to the Moche practice of large-scale human sacrifice.

Pyramid of the Sun

Moche archaeological studies have advanced greatly in the last two decades, but there is still much to learn. The spectacular wealth of the ancient Moche has been one of the biggest challenges, because Moche sites have been subject to 500 years of looting. When the Spanish arrived in

Below The facial features and expressions depicted on portrait pots are so lifelike that they probably represented real Moche people. Musicians were a popular subject for moulded pots.

Below Although they had no written language, many aspects of the Moche culture are depicted in their pots, including ritual human sacrifice, as shown here.

Peru they looted all the gold and silver they could extract from the Inca Empire, but they also turned their attention to Moche Pyramids containing rich tombs. The most spectacular and tragic example is the Pyramid of the Sun along the Moche river, the focus of a recent long-term study project. This truncated pyramid structure was made of some 140 million adobe bricks, most of them imprinted with the mark of the community that provided them in some form of tribute. The Pyramid of the Sun was the largest adobe structure ever built in the Americas, but only an estimated one-third of it remains today. During the Spanish colonial era the Moche river was actually diverted in order to wash the structure away so that the treasure inside could be mined. The Spanish were after gold and silver, which they melted down and shipped back to Spain.

We will never know what was inside the destroyed portions of the pyramid, or what clues about

Above Archaeologists have been working on the excavation of the temple tomb at Sipán.

Moche civilization were lost forever. Looting still continues today, and archaeologists and Peruvian officials are engaged in a constant battle to preserve Moche sites as tourist destinations and as repositories of information and local heritage.

Moche mummy

In 2005 archaeologists discovered the mummified body of a young Moche woman at the El Brujo archaeological site on Peru's north coast near Trujillo. The mummy, which was dated to around AD 450, had complex tattoos and was remarkably well preserved. A young girl with a rope around her neck had been buried alongside her. The presence of gold jewellery and other artefacts, including a headdress, indicated that the woman had been a member of the Moche elite. Archaeologists also excavated various military artefacts, including war clubs and spear throwers.

Sipán's tombs

The dramatic story of the discovery of royal tombs at the Moche site of Sipán began on the night of 16 February 1987. Walter Alva, the archaeologist in charge of what was then a small regional museum on Peru's north coast, was awakened by a call from local police. A group of local looters had been digging illegally at Sipán and began to fight over the rich spoils of their labours. One or more of them went to the local police, who recovered a few spectacular gold objects and asked Alva to inspect them. Alva confirmed that they were pre-Columbian objects and, on a tip-off from one of the looters, he went to Sipán to search for their source.

Over the course of the next few months, and under constant threat of attack from the looters, Alva studied the site, confirming that the confiscated items had been taken from Sipán. He then mounted a project that was eventually to uncover the most magnificent burial ever found in the Americas. The tomb contained the remains of a man wearing spectacular ritual regalia, including textiles, featherwork, beaded items, gold and silver necklaces, staffs and hundreds of pottery vessels. The items had been layered on top of the body of the man who had been buried deep inside a huge mud-brick pyramid. This was the first scientifically excavated tomb of a Moche ruler. The painstaking excavation, which took months to conduct, would be the key to huge advances in our understanding of the ancient Moche.

Christopher Donnan, an archaeologist who had spent decades amassing an illustrated archive of Moche pottery, had published a number of papers on the scenes depicted on Moche fineline pots. These rare vessels were completely covered with elaborate drawings of rituals, such as burial ceremonies and sacrifice. Although Donnan and his colleague Donna McClellan had identified a series of figures that appeared repeatedly in the scenes found on the pottery, they had never seen evidence that such figures had actually existed in Moche society. The newly excavated Sipán tomb provided such evidence. Donnan was able to identify object after object found buried in the tomb as the same items depicted in the drawings of the costume and paraphernalia associated with one of the figures from the pots. This finding revolutionized the study of the ancient Moche, and subsequent finds at Sipán and other major Moche sites confirmed that the rulers of different Moche settlements had been the figures in the fineline drawings on the pottery. The fineline drawings depicted gruesome scenes of ritual sacrifice, and the discovery of one of the key figures in the drawings suggested that these rituals had actually occurred.

The ability to match iconographic scenes to the bodies of real individuals who lived nearly 2000 years ago was an incredible advance in archaeology. Since that first discovery, Moche studies have proliferated up and down the north coast of Peru. The remains of Moche rulers have been found at several other sites and have led to a much more in-depth understanding of Moche political economy and ritual organization. Archaeologists now believe that hereditary rulers of each of the major Moche cities came together periodically to perform the spectacular rituals depicted on the fineline pots.

Below The central coffin containing the body of the Lord of Sipán is surrounded by the bodies of sacrificed retainers.

Chichén Itzá

The importance of Chichén Itzá as a Maya ceremonial centre is reflected in its architecture, which includes a massive stepped pyramid, an observatory, a great ballcourt and the Sacred Cenote, which was a natural well into which offerings and human sacrifices were made.

Chichén Itzá is located in the state of Yucatán in Mexico, far to the north of the Classic Maya heartland, which contained cities such as Calakmul and Tikal. Chichén Itzá was occupied during the Terminal Classic and Early Postclassic periods (around AD 800-1200), flourishing at a time that roughly coincided with the collapse of the large centres of the southern and central Maya lowlands. Once one of the largest cities of Mesoamerica, today the ruins extend over an area of 5 sq km (2 sq miles).

The American John Lloyd Stephens visited the ruins in 1840 and published an account of his findings. From 1895 Edward H. Thompson began a 30-year exploration of Chichén Itzá, which included dredging the first artefacts out of the Sacred Cenote. The Carnegie Institution and the government of Mexico began a 20-year restoration and excavation project in 1924. Further work has been carried out at the site since the 1980s.

Architecture

The architecture at Chichén Itzá is organized around a series of ambient outdoor spaces, called plazas, in a pattern that is seen throughout the Maya area. Chichén Itzá is divided into two main areas of settlement, one of which is traditionally considered to be Terminal Classic (*c*.AD 800-900) Maya, while the other is ascribed to an Early Postclassic (AD 900-1250) Maya-Toltec hybrid culture. The earlier settlement, located on the south of the site, contains architecture that is traditionally associated with the Maya,

whereas the architecture in the newer part shows strong influences from central Mexico, with buildings reminiscent of those at Tula (the Toltec capital). However, the cultural and

Above Two pillars in the form of a feathered serpent stand at the entrance to the Temple of the Warriors. At the top of the stairway in front of the two serpent statues is a reclining *chacmool* figure.

Above The interior of the Castillo houses King Kukulcán's Jaguar Throne, which is made of stone and painted red with jade spots.

chronological distinctions between these two areas of the site are becoming increasingly blurred as new research is conducted on the site.

The Castillo

One of the site's most important monuments, in the 'Toltec' part of the city, is the Castillo. This square-based, stepped pyramid is about 25m (82ft) high and each of its four sides has a staircase of 91 steps. The Castillo is decorated with snake iconography, most notably along the balustrades of the staircases. Scholars Linda Schele and Peter Mathews have suggested that the structure might represent a 'snake mountain', an important location in Mesoamerican religion. At the spring and autumn equinoxes the sun's shadow creates the illusion of a serpent

moving down the pyramid. Excavations at the Castillo has revealed evidence of an earlier construction.

The Great Ballcourt

There are other smaller ballcourts at Chichén Itzá, but the Great Ballcourt is the largest in Mesoamerica, measuring about 166 x 68m (545 x 223ft). It is also notable for its well-preserved murals and elaborate architecture, with temples at either end. The sides of the

Below Astronomers made observations of the stars from the tower of the Caracol.

interior of the ballcourt are lined with sculpted panels depicting teams of ball players. While the actual rules of the ballgame are still shrouded in mystery, it appears to have been an activity steeped in both political overtones and religious imagery.

The observatory

The astronomical observatory, known as the Caracol ('snail' in Spanish) in reference to its spiral staircase, is the only round structure at Chichén Itzá. It features an observation tower built on two rectangular platforms.

Chaco Canyon

A thousand years ago, Chaco Canyon in New Mexico was home to a remarkable prehistoric society that lived in multi-storey villages, developed irrigation systems that enabled them to grow crops in the desert environment, and built an extensive road system.

Chaco Canyon National Historical Park is, with Mesa Verde, one of the most important archaeological sites in North America. The canyon is a seasonal wash that cuts through the dry deserts of northern New Mexico. Its dryness, coupled with long winters and a short growing season, hardly made it a promising location for the flowering of such a remarkable culture. And yet, between around AD 850 and 1250, the Ancestral Puebloan (Anasazi) Indians built several large villages here, with buildings designed for residential, ceremonial and public use.

As at Mesa Verde, Chacoan potters produced beautifully painted and technologically sophisticated ceramic vessels. As well as pieces of pottery, excavations have also unearthed other examples of their craftsmanship, including baskets and turquoise jewellery.

Chaco Canyon reached the height of its influence in the 11th century AD. After this it declined, and was finally abandoned in the middle of the 13th century AD.

Apartment living

The sites in Chaco Canyon were first viewed by Europeans in the mid-19th century, and excavation began at the end of the century. A series of large and smaller villages are scattered through a section of the canyon, approximately 20km (12 miles) in length. The largest, of which there are 13, are known as great houses. Each consists of several hundred inter-connected rooms built on several levels, arranged around public plazas. Some housed families, while others were used as storerooms.

The buildings were constructed using timber, sandstone and adobe, and are interspersed with roughly cylindrical masonry structures known as kivas. These chambers, which are partly sunk into the ground, were

Below This Chacoan white-ware pitcher is decorated with a typical geometric design, which was applied with a yucca brush. The colours were achieved using plant dyes.

used for meetings and ceremonies, as similar chambers are by Puebloan Indians today. The canyon also contains larger versions of the kiva, called great kivas, which have astronomical significance. Casa Rinconada is the best example.

Archaeologists have found evidence of well-engineered water-diversion systems such as dams and ditches. These collected as much run-off water from the cliffs above as possible and transported it to fields in the canyon around the great houses, where crops such as corn and squash were grown.

Sections of the canyon walls still contain rock art, and carved handholds and steps that the inhabitants would have used to climb to the mesa tops above. Although most archaeologists believe that the canyon was occupied all year round, some have speculated that it was used only at certain times of the year, perhaps in the cycle of some religious ceremony.

Pueblo Bonito

The largest and best-known great house in Chaco Canyon, known as Pueblo Bonito ('pretty village' in Spanish), was excavated by Neil Judd on behalf of the National Geographic Society during the 1920s. Arranged in a 'D' shape, the buildings originally stood four to five storeys high and were built of high-quality, shaped masonry that has withstood the test of time remarkably well. Analysis of tree rings in the wooden beams has revealed that construction

began in the 900s, with the major work being carried out between 1075 and 1115. Pueblo Bonito comprises over 300 individual rooms at ground level; some estimates put the total number as high as 650. It also contains at least 32 kivas and two great kivas, the biggest almost 20m (66ft) across.

Ancient networks

Chaco was at the centre of a network of over 645km (400 miles) of well-constructed roads that fanned out over the surrounding countryside for as far as 160km (100 miles). Many of the roads connected the canyon to more than 150 so-called Chacoan outliers — smaller habitation and ceremonial sites that were part of the overall Chacoan network. The roads facilitated trade but may also have connected individual ceremonial sites into the wider network. One example is Chimney Rock, 150km (93 miles) north of the canyon, in the pine forests of southern

Above An aerial view of the Chaco Canyon ruins shows Pueblo Benito in the foreground. The connecting road network is clearly visible.

Colorado. Some archaeologists have suggested that Chimney Rock served as a centre for harvesting lumber, meat and hides, which were then transported back to Chaco for use there or for redistribution. Others have suggested that because Chimney Rock was probably built in the 11th century AD, at the time of a lunar standstill, its purpose was primarily religious.

Artefacts, such as copper bells and macaw skeletons, have been discovered at Chaco Canyon, suggesting trade connections with other contemporary Mesoamerican cultures. However, the intensity of this trade connection is not clear. The presence of these items might be the result of sporadic contact, rather than the existence of a formal trading and exchange system between the two areas.

Satellite images

In the 1980s NASA conducted a series of infrared satellite scans of Chaco Canyon, and these revealed a remarkable feature that was undetectable by conventional archaeological methods at ground level or from aerial photography. They showed an extensive network of roads with the canyon at its centre. The most surprising feature of these roads was that they are absolutely straight, even going across obstacles in the terrain rather than around them. The reason for this uncompromising straightness is not known, but it could have been practical: as the Chacoans went everywhere on foot, and did not use pack animals or vehicles, they could take the most direct route. Alternatively, it could have had a symbolic significance.

Mesa Verde

Located in south-west Colorado, Mesa Verde National Park contains some of the best-preserved archaeological sites in North America. Chief among these is an incomparable collection of sites where the Ancestral Puebloan (Anasazi) Indians lived, dating from approximately AD 600-1300.

Mesa Verde, which means 'green table' in Spanish, is a series of flat-topped mountains (mesas) – a common feature of the western United States. Although there is evidence of human occupation in the area from as early as 10,000 years ago, the most remarkable remains are those associated with the Ancestral Puebloan Indians – so called because they were the ancestors of the modern Pueblo people.

The archaeological remains were first brought to public attention in 1888 by Richard Wetherill, a young Colorado cowboy. An early visitor to the site was Gustaf Nordenskjöld, who in 1893 published *The Cliff Dwellers of*

Below Cliff Palace is the largest of the cliff dwellings, built into an alcove 27m (89ft) deep and 18m (59ft) high. The circular kivas can be seen in the foreground.

the Mesa Verde, the first scholarly study of the site. In 1906 the area was established as a national park to preserve the extensive remains, which had been ransacked and damaged by looters. It was designated a World Heritage Site in 1978.

Thousands of different sites have been discovered, including semi-subterranean pithouses and masonry roomblocks, both of which were

the complex contains some original plaster, which had been painted with abstract designs.

Abandonment

The Ancestral Puebloans occupied these cliff dwellings for only the last 75 to 100 years of their occupation of the Mesa Verde region, and archaeologists speculate that they may have been located where they were for defensive purposes. Their inhabitants abandoned the region over the period of a couple of generations at the end of the 13th century, possibly forced out by drought.

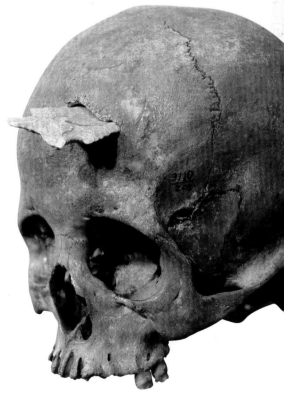

places where people lived. There are also circular, underground kivas, which were used for ceremonial purposes. Extensive masonry water reservoirs were part of the complex water irrigation systems that the Ancestral Puebloans built in this arid region. They also grew corn and produced beautiful pottery of different shapes and designs.

Cliff Palace

The most spectacular sites at Mesa Verde are the multi-storeyed, many-roomed pueblos ('villages' in Spanish) that were built into the natural cliff alcoves on the sides of the mesas. Of these, the most famous is Cliff Palace,

Above The cliff dwellings feature distinctive key hole doors.

which contains upwards of 200 rooms and 23 kivas. The primary building materials were sandstone slabs, mortar and wooden beams. Dwelling rooms were lined with plaster, which was often painted. Specially cut stairs allowed the inhabitants to reach their fields on the mesa top. There are several multi-storey round and square towers at Cliff Palace. The interior of a four-storey tower at the south end of

Right The skull of a 20-year-old woman was excavated at Mesa Verde. The flint that killed her is still lodged into the front of the skull.

241

L'Anse aux Meadows

When Norwegians Helge and Anne Stine Ingstad excavated L'Anse aux Meadows in Newfoundland in 1961, they found astonishing proof that the first Europeans to settle in the New World were Scandinavians in the 11th century AD – some 500 years before Columbus.

Ancient Norse sagas told of the Viking hero, Erik the Red, who was banished from Norway in AD 982 and ultimately established a series of colonies in a forest-covered land called Vinland. Later generations identified Vinland with North America. However, there was no evidence of Viking occupation there until the Ingstads, tipped off by a local fisherman, started work on L'Anse aux Meadows, which lies on Epave Bay near the northernmost tip of the island of Newfoundland. For the next nine years the Ingstads led an international team of archaeologists in the excavation of the site. Major excavations were continued by Parks Canada from 1973 to 1976.

These excavations unearthed the remains of eight houses (of wood and sod construction), smaller buildings, a smithy and a charcoal kiln. The buildings were of the same kind as those used in Iceland and Greenland just before and after the year AD 1000. Artefacts found in the ruins of these buildings included typical Viking objects of the 11th century AD, such as iron rivets, a bronze pin and a spindle whorl. Radiocarbon dates supported the artefact chronology.

Viking settlement

In every characteristic the site differs from contemporary American Indian settlements in the area, and it can be plausibly linked to the story of Erik the Red in the so-called Vinland Sagas. The climate was too severe for cultivating grapes, so the term Vinland may refer to the making of berry wine from the numerous wild berries found nearby.

The shallowness of the middens indicates that the site was only occupied for a relatively brief period of time, perhaps about 30 years. It is unclear why it was abandoned so soon after it was settled. The climate may have been unsuitable for long-term reliance on agriculture. Or perhaps its isolation simply made it too dangerous.

Below Three Norse sod houses have been reconstructed at the site.

Cahokia

During the 11th century AD a great metropolis arose on the fertile flood plain of the Mississippi River. A major centre of the Mississippian Culture, Cahokia is a leading candidate for a true pre-Columbian city in North America. The site is the focus of ongoing archaeological research.

Cahokia is located just east of St Louis, Illinois, in an area known as the American Bottoms, where the confluence of the Missouri, Mississippi and Illinois rivers has created one of the most fertile regions on the continent. The site, which was inhabited from AD 700-1400, covers an area of about 15 sq km (6 sq miles).

In the early 19th century journalist and explorer Henry Marie Brakenridge studied the site and described it in a letter to Thomas Jefferson. His findings aroused little attention, however, for although Cahokia is named after the local Indian tribe, for most of the 19th century Euroamerican settlers refused to believe that a site as complex as this could have been built by ancestors of contemporary American Indians. Many fanciful stories circulated as to who had built this and other mounds, including the lost tribe of Israel, the Egyptians, even a band of Welshmen. Early relic-hunters and archaeologists did not realize the significance of their finds, and full-scale scientific excavation did not begin until the 1960s.

A well-planned city

Excavations at the site have revealed a 3km- (2 mile-) long wooden stockade encircling the inner part of the site, which almost certainly served as a defensive wall. Inside the stockade are the remains of plazas, earth mounds and communal buildings. Houses were built around the plazas and arranged in rows within the stockade. The remains of suburbs outside the stockade and satellite villages have also been found.

Above Monk's Mound is the largest man-made mound in North America.

The largest structure at the site is Monk's Mound, a rectangular, terraced earth mound that overlooked a large plaza at the centre of the city. Carbon dating has revealed that this mound was started in around AD 950 and took over 200 years to reach its current size. Its base covers 6ha (15 acres), and it reaches about 30m (98ft) high. The flat top of the mound originally supported some sort of wooden structure, possibly a chieftain's house or a religious building. Smaller mounds at the site were used as burial sites for prominent individuals.

During excavations of one burial mound (Mound 72), archaeologists found the body of an important man in his 40s, along with a cache of arrowheads from different parts of the region buried nearby. Over 250 other skeletons were also found in Mound 72, many in mass graves and some with their heads and hands missing.

At its peak Cahokia was at the centre of a wide-reaching trade network that extended from the Gulf of Mexico to Hudson Bay and from the Atlantic coast to the Great Plains. Archaeologists are unclear as to why the city fell from power, but AD 1200 marked the arrival of a period of severe drought, which may have undercut the population's ability to produce food.

Woodhenge

In the early 1960s archaeologist Dr Warren Wittry identified some large pits at the site that seemed to be arranged on the arcs of circles. Noting that wooden posts set in these pits would have been oriented to the rising sun, he suggested that the circular structure served as a calendar, and named it Woodhenge. Further excavations revealed that there were as many as five post circles at the site.

Great Serpent Mound

Winding along the crest of a ridge overlooking Bush Creek Valley in southern Ohio is a giant earthwork construction. Aerial views of the site show the unmistakable shape of a spectacular serpent curving for some 400m (1300ft).

Great Serpent Mound (or Serpent Mound) is the world's largest extant example of the so-called effigy mound, the term given to prehistoric earthen constructions that represented animals and which are found throughout the American Midwest.

The mound is constructed from earth built onto a clay and rock base; it is about 6-7.5m (20-25ft) wide and, on average, about 1.5m (5ft) high. Its creators worked with artistry and skill to create a sinuous snake whose three

Below The mysterious oval mound at the serpent's head can be seen in the top right-hand corner of this aerial photograph.

coils appear to be evenly sized and spaced, as if representing a symbolic pattern. Some archaeologists interpret an oval mound at the head end as an egg in its open mouth. Others see it as the eye of the serpent.

Dating

The site was first recorded by Ephraim Squier and Edwin Davis in *Ancient Monuments of the Mississippi Valley*, their monumental study of the earthen mounds of the Midwest published in 1848. The first excavations were undertaken by archaeologist Frederic Putnam of Harvard University in the late 1880s. In 1901 an engineer named Clinton Cowan mapped and carried out geographical surveys of the site. This work, along with Putnam's excavations, have been the basis for modern investigations of the mound.

Archaeologists have found the mound difficult to date accurately because so far no artefacts or human remains have been found in it. The historical view was that it was created during the so-called Adena Culture – a predominantly hunter-gatherer society that inhabited present-day Ohio, Kentucky and West Virginia between 500 BC and AD 200. Burial mounds in the surrounding area have been definitely attributed to the Adena people, so the connection seems plausible. However, it is possible that the Serpent Mound is much later. A burial mound and village site close to the serpent's tail date to about AD 1000, which places them within the Mississippian Culture. And pieces of charcoal recently recovered from a previously undisturbed part of the Serpent Mound have been radiocarbon-dated to the same time.

As with so much prehistoric imagery, it is almost impossible to determine exactly what the mound meant to its builders, or how it fitted into contemporary religion and iconography. Burial data from Adena and Mississippian contexts provide some insights into prehistoric religion and iconography, so if a firmer date could be determined for the Serpent Mound, archaeologists would have greater leeway in trying to understand its purpose.

Chan Chan

Until the 15th century AD Chan Chan, on the north-west coast of Peru, was the impressive capital of the Chimú civilization. Today, the ruins of the enormous pre-Inca city make up one of the largest and most important archaeological sites in the New World.

Chan Chan is the largest known adobe city in the Americas and it was named a UNESCO World Heritage Site in 1986. It has also been listed as one of the world's most endangered archaeological sites because of natural and human threats posed to the site.

Much of what we know about Chan Chan today is due to the massive archaeological research project directed by Michael E. Moseley and his colleagues during the 1970s, known as the Chan Chan-Moche Valley project. This project, which included archaeological surveys and excavations, as well as environmental studies, produced huge amounts of archaeological data. In addition, a number of now well-known North American archaeologists conducted their graduate research on the project. Ongoing research at Chan Chan and throughout the north coast of Peru continues to produce new discoveries and to build on the foundations laid by the project.

Adobe city

Chan Chan covers an area of roughly 6 sq km (2 sq miles) along the Moche River Valley. The city comprises at least nine huge compounds, known as *ciudadelas* (citadels), that contain the remains of palaces and administrative complexes. The huge decorated adobe walls of the compounds are 10m (33ft) high and protected vast networks of storage rooms, as well as courts, royal residences, a reservoir and burial chambers. Each compound was accessible only through a single

doorway. There are also vast areas of residences, workshops and cemeteries. The city was supported by a huge complex of irrigated agricultural fields, as well as by fishing and herding.

Left A statue stands sentinel in the Tschudi Complex, which is the best preserved of the city's *ciudadelas* and also features friezes, courtyards and some original walls.

Chan Chan was meticulously planned and built by the ancient Chimú civilization, which controlled much of northern Peru before the Inca conquest. The Chimú civilization arose beginning around AD 1000 and became increasingly powerful until the mid-15th century, when they were conquered by the Inca. Chimú statecraft, engineering and religion were incredibly advanced, and they greatly influenced the technology and culture of Inca civilization.

Below A view of part of the core of the city shows fragile adobe ruins. They are vulnerable to natural erosion, as they become exposed to air and rain, and require careful conservation.

Tenochtitlán

Excavations under present-day Mexico City have periodically uncovered the remains of Tenochtitlán's walled precinct, including the Great Temple, which was the ceremonial heart of the once vast capital of the Aztec empire from AD 1325 to the arrival of the Spanish in 1521.

Located on an island in the lake system of the Basin of Mexico, Tenochtitlán grew rapidly to become the largest city of the ancient Americas, a thriving hub of political, economic and religious activity with a population of 250,000.

Following the Spanish conquest, however, much of the the ancient city was destroyed to make way for the capital of New Spain. Fortunately, much is known about the Aztecs and their capital city from the colonial period histories collected by Spanish chroniclers using native informants. The most important of these was the *General History of New Spain*, compiled by Fray Bernardino de Sahagún in the mid-16th century. Other useful sources of information include legal documents from land disputes in the early colony, and pictorial manuscripts produced by indigenous scribes.

Most of the city remained buried until the year 1790, when excavation for water pipes uncovered two Aztec sculptures. A few sections of the city's Great Temple, or Templo Mayor, were unearthed in the first half of the 20th century. However, it was not until the 1970s that a major excavation project was undertaken.

Expansion

The city was founded in the 14th century by Nahuatl-speaking migrants from the north, who settled on an unpopulated island. The Aztecs met the challenge of island life by constructing causeways to the mainland. They also expanded their space by building floating gardens (*chinampas*) of reed mats covered with a thin layer of lake silt and anchored into the shallow lakebed by the roots of corn plants. Over time, these floating gardens became increasingly solid, to the point where they could be used for housing.

After the initial years as poor fishermen and mercenary soldiers employed by more powerful city-states, in 1420 the Aztecs formed an alliance with neighbouring groups to conquer and control the Basin of

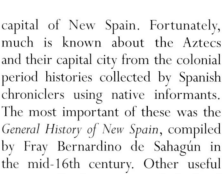

Left While it suffered cataclysmic destruction during the Spanish conquest, the rapid metamorphosis into Mexico City has in some ways preserved the foundations of the Aztec city, with remarkable finds such as the Great Temple still awaiting discovery.

Above A symbolic sculpted eagle was found within the sacred precinct.

Mexico. This alliance quickly grew through military conquest and coercion until it commanded tribute from throughout the central highlands and the Gulf Coast.

The Great Temple

Tenochtitlán's ceremonial precinct of monumental buildings was dominated by the Great Temple, a massive dual pyramid dedicated to both the Aztec patron deity Huitzilopochtli, and the storm god, Tlaloc.

Archaeological excavations at the base of the temple demonstrate that it was built as a symbolic re-enactment of the birth of Huitzilopochtli. According to myth, the pregnant goddess Coatlicue was attacked by her jealous daughter, the moon goddess Coyolxauqui, while on Serpent Mountain (*coatepec*). Decapitated, Coatlicue still gave birth to her son, Huitzilopochtli, who dismembered Coyolxauqui, whose body rolled to the base of the mountain.

When, in 1978, workers employed by the Electric Light Company discovered the huge Coyolxauqui sculpture – depicting a naked, dismembered woman – archaeologists knew that they had found the base of Serpent Mountain and the ritual centre of the Aztec empire.

Right The base of the skull rack (*tzompantli*) is decorated with sculpted skulls. The rack would have been used for the public display of human skulls, typically those of war captives or other sacrificial victims.

The mammoth excavation project, headed by the Mexican archaeologist Eduardo Matos Moctezuma, required the demolition of several city blocks in the centre of Mexico City, adjacent to the Cathedral and National Palace. Clearing the architectural rubble caused by the destruction of the temple by the Spaniards revealed six stages of construction, as the temple was sequentially expanded, perhaps by each Aztec ruler.

The second stage of the Great Temple pyramid was small enough that it survived, even preserving some of the stone temple structures on the pyramid base. A multi-coloured *chacmool* sculpture of a reclining warrior was found in the Tlaloc temple, and a sacrificial stone was unearthed in the Huitzilopochtli temple. Additionally, serpent heads decorate the preserved pyramid and the surrounding walls, to represent the mythical Serpent Mountain.

Over 100 caches of valuable and symbolically charged objects have been found buried in and around Tenochtitlán's Great Temple, including artefacts of gold, jade and other precious materials.

Also of note are the hundreds of animal skeletons from sea, land and sky, along with artefacts from previous Mesoamerican civilizations, which were buried in an attempt to make the Great Temple a symbolic *axis mundi*, or world axis of creation.

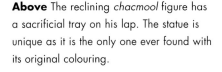

Above The reclining *chacmool* figure has a sacrificial tray on his lap. The statue is unique as it is the only one ever found with its original colouring.

In addition to the Great Temple itself, archaeologists have also uncovered a warrior's compound and a *tzompantli*, or skull rack, in the ceremonial compound. Other construction excavations have yielded remnants of the ancient city, including the famous Calendar Stone, which is decorated with calendrical signs representing the sacred cycle of time.

During the building of the Metro system, archaeologists accompanied construction teams to recover and preserve evidence of the ancient city wherever possible. One area that has been extensively excavated and preserved is the city's Tlatelolco district, where Aztec pyramids, colonial cathedrals and modern high-rises are juxtaposed in what is known as the Plaza of the Three Cultures.

247

Little Bighorn

On 25 June 1876, General George Armstrong Custer rode to his death against a force of Sioux and Cheyenne Indians. Custer's Last Stand passed into American legend, but many of the details of the battle remained a mystery until archaeologists started working on the site in 1983.

Custer and 647 men of the 7th Cavalry were taking part in a US army campaign to force Sioux and Cheyenne Indians back onto the Great Sioux Reservation of South Dakota. On 25 June they inadvertently stumbled onto a mass Indian village of as many as 7000 inhabitants, located along the banks of the Little Bighorn River in Montana.

Unaware of, or perhaps deliberately ignoring the size of the force confronting him, Custer charged the village. At the end of that day, he and 210 men under his command lay dead. About 60 Indians had died. However, perhaps because the dead tell no tales, and the Sioux and Cheyenne were never asked, for over

a century little was known about the actual sequence of events. We still don't know with certainty, for example, how Custer died.

Below The site was first preserved as a national cemetery in 1879. In 1890, the marble blocks that dot the battlefield were added to mark where the soldiers fell.

Revealed by fire

It was not until 1983, when a grassland fire bared the prairie, that archaeologists were able to unravel many of the battle's secrets. From then until 1996, archaeologists, led by Dr Douglas Scott of the National Park Service, have conducted surveys of the land. Scott's team visually identified the physical remains of the battle and used metal detectors to locate spent bullets and other metallic objects (ten iron arrowheads were also found).

Careful analysis of the artefact distribution showed that Custer split his command into three elements. This was an accepted tactic when cavalry attacked a village, but it may have been a factor that hastened his defeat.

Scott's groundbreaking work encouraged others. For example, one of Scott's colleagues, Dr Richard Fox, identified individual combat positions and plotted the movements of both soldiers and Indians as they moved across the battlefield. Fox concluded that the location of Custer's so-called 'last stand', Custer's Hill as it is called today, was not actually the last place where fighting took place. Rather, the last American casualties came after the soldiers had fled the hill.

Fox concluded that although the Americans had arrived at the battle well-organized and tactically prepared to fight, as the battle progressed they gradually lost discipline, ultimately succumbing to a fatal panic that destroyed their cohesion as a fighting unit. It seems that archaeology has destroyed at least one segment of the Custer legend. The excavations carried out by Scott and his team have also pioneered the archaeological investigation of battlefields in other parts of the world.

Right A pile of bones is all that remains on the battlefield of Little Bighorn in this photograph looking towards the Indian village, taken around 1877.

Skulls

Of great interest are the forensic studies commissioned by Dr Scott on the skeletal remains of some of the troopers, who fell and were subsequently buried on the battlefield itself. Analysis revealed that skull fragments had been smashed while the body was still alive, or very soon after death – confirmation of Indian accounts of the troopers being finished off with clubs and axes. Other remains showed evidence of mutilation. One individual aged about 25 had been shot in the chest by a repeating rifle. He had then been shot in the head, had his skull smashed in, been pierced with arrows and then had his front and rear torso slashed. Other skeletons tell of similarly grisly ends.

GLOSSARY

Absolute dating A date for an object, structure or occurrence that is accurate to a specific year. Absolute dates for some archaeology can be secured using scientific techniques such as radiocarbon dating.

Acheulian A tradition of tool-making associated with *Homo erectus* in the Lower Palaeolithic period.

Acropolis From the Greek meaning 'the high point of the city', the upper, fortified citadel of an ancient Greek city.

Adobe Mudbrick made by drying mud in the sun and used for building.

Adze A stone tool made of flakes or pebbles used for woodworking.

Agora An open public space at the centre of an ancient Greek city.

Amphora A large storage jar.

Anthropology The biological and cultural study of humanity.

Apadana The pillared audience hall of an ancient Persian palace.

Aurignacian Cultural assemblages associated with *Homo sapiens sapiens* as they replaced *Homo neanderthalensis* lasting about 12,000 years from around 40,000 years ago.

Australopithecine A general term for the species that make up the pre-human hominid genus *Australopithecus* found in Africa between 4 and 1 million years ago.

Barrow A mound of earth and/or stones over a grave or graves. Also known as a tumulus.

Biface A stone tool that has had flakes removed from both faces.

Bronze Age The second age of the Three Age System in which bronze was the primary material for tools and weapons.

Canopic jars Clay containers used to hold the internal organs removed from a body when it was mummified in ancient Egypt.

Caryatid A column in the form of a female figure. The male equivalent is a telamon.

Cenotaph From the Greek meaning 'empty tomb', cenotaphs were tombs built for ceremonial purposes but which were never intended to hold the human remains.

Cenote A naturally formed well.

Codex A manuscript formed from leaves bound together on one side recording historic, political or religious information.

Cuneiform An early script developed by the Sumerians in about 3000 BC. It was written using a wedge-shaped tool known as a stylus which was impressed into wet clay.

Cylinder seal A Mesopotamian carved seal that was rolled across a clay seal producing an impression of the design.

Dendrochronology A method of dating based on the analysis of tree-ring sequences.

Effigy mound A prehistoric mound in the form of an animal.

Egyptology The study of ancient Egyptian archaeology and artefacts.

Faience A non-clay ceramic glaze used for figurines and jewellery in ancient Egypt and the Near East.

Hellenistic The period between the accession of Alexander the Great and the establishment of the Roman empire.

Hieroglyphs A form of writing using pictographic and ideographic symbols used in ancient Egypt and Mesoamerica among other places.

Henge A usually circular ritual enclosure consisting of a bank and ditch system sometimes enclosing a circle of stones or wooden posts.

Hydria A type of three-handled Greek jar used for carrying water.

Hypostyle hall From the Greek meaning 'bearing pillars', a hall with a flat roof supported by pillars.

Iron Age The third age of the Three Age System in which iron became the main material for tools and weapons.

Kiva A circular underground room in a Pueblo Indian village.

Kouros From the Greek meaning 'a youth', a standing nude male statue. The female (fully clothed) equivalent is called a kore.

Lararium A household shrine in ancient Rome.

Linear A The syllabic script used by the Minoans of Crete.

Linear B The syllabic script used by the Mycenaeans and Minoans.

Mahat Mudbrick shrines that held limestone stelae found at the ancient Egyptian site of Abydos.

Mastaba tomb An ancient Egyptian royal tomb consisting of a freestanding, rectangular mudbrick superstructure over a burial chamber.

Megalith A large stone. A megalithic monument, such as Stonehenge, is one that is made from large stones.

Megaron A rectangular, freestanding hall usually with a centrally located hearth entered through a two-columned porch. Associated with Aegean architecture.

Menhir A single standing stone.

Mesoamerica Term for different civilizations in the region between central Mexico and Northern Honduras characterised by shared cultural phenomena.

Mesolithic Middle Stone Age.

Mesopotamia The region between the rivers Tigris and Euphrates.

Midden A rubbish dump or accumulation of human, domestic waste products.

Moche Pre-Columbian culture of the Moche Valley, Peru.

Mousterian A term for stone tool assemblages associated with the Neanderthals in the Middle Palaeolithic.

Mummification A technique developed by the ancient Egyptians to maintain the lifelike appearance of a dead body.

Necropolis A cemetery, from the Greek meaning 'city of the dead'.

Neolithic New Stone Age.

Obelisk A four-sided stone pillar that tapers towards a pyramidal point. Usually carved from a single piece of stone (a monolith).

Obsidian A sharp volcanic glass used to make tools and jewellery.

Ossuary A container such as a chest for the bones of the dead.

Palaeoanthropology From the Greek meaning 'study of ancient man'. The multidisciplinary study of human evolution focusing on examination of the fossil record.

Palaeolithic Old Stone Age.

Papyrus An early form of paper made from the pith of the papyrus plant.

Passage tomb A tomb that is approached by a narrow, tunnel-like passage.

Petroglyph A piece of rock art consisting of a carving made into a rock face.

Pictogram A system of writing using pictures to represent words.

Pithos A large jar used in ancient Greece for storing oil and wine.

Pleistocene A geologic period denoting the most recent Ice Age that began about 1.8 million years ago and ended about 10,000 years ago.

Polychrome pottery Pottery decorated with more than two colours.

Prehistory The period of human history before written records.

Punic Of or relating to Carthage, its people and language.

Radiocarbon dating A method of dating carbon-bearing materials including wood, plant remains, bone, peat and calcium carbonate shell based on the radioactive decay of the Carbon-14 isotope.

Relative dating A system of dating archaeological remains in relation to each other which does not produce an absolute date for objects.

Relief A carved stone slab with projecting decoration. Also bas-relief (low relief).

Sarcophagus A stone chest used to contain a corpse.

Scarab An ancient Egyptian seal type that was shaped like a dung beetle and incised with a design that was stamped onto the seal.

Stela An upright slab of stone, often carved with funerary reliefs and used as a grave marker.

Stone Age The first age of the Three Age System covering the period from the first production of stone artefacts to the first production of metal artefacts.

Strata Layers of earth or levels on an archaeological site.

Stratigraphy A method of dating that involves placing archaeological deposits in sequence according to the stratified layer in which they are found.

Stupa A Buddhist monument or shrine.

Stylistic dating A method of dating that involves placing artefacts in a sequence according to a perceived development in form or decoration.

Tesserae The basic units that make up a mosaic.

Tholos A round tomb with a rectilinear entrance passage.

Tumulus An artificial mound, usually covering a burial or burials.

Ziggurat A stepped temple tower in ancient Mesopotamia. Shrines to the gods were built on their summits.

INDEX

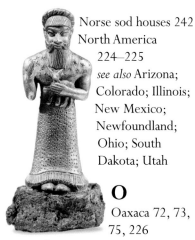

This edition is published by Hermes House, an imprint of Anness Publishing Ltd, Hermes House, 88–89 Blackfriars Road, London SE1 8HA; tel. 020 7401 2077; fax 020 7633 9499

www.hermeshouse.com;
www.annesspublishing.com

© Anness Publishing Ltd 2007

Produced for Hermes House by Toucan Books.
Managing Director: Ellen Dupont

Anness Publishing has a new picture agency outlet for images for publishing, promotions or advertising. Please visit our website www.practicalpictures.com for more information.

ETHICAL TRADING POLICY
Because of our ongoing ecological investment programme, you, as our customer, can have the pleasure and reassurance of knowing that a tree is being cultivated on your behalf to naturally replace the materials used to make the book you are holding. For further information about this scheme, go to www.annesspublishing.com/trees

For Anness:
Publisher: Joanna Lorenz
Editorial Director: Helen Sudell

For Toucan Books:
Editor: Jane Chapman
Designer: Elizabeth Healey
Picture researcher: Wendy Brown
Maps: Julian Baker
Indexer: Michael Dent
Proofreader: Marion Dent

Contributors: Dr Paul Bahn, Dr Caroline Bird, Dr Peter Bogucki, Jane Callander, Dr Philip Duke, Dr Chris Edens, Dr David Gill, Dr Geoffrey McCafferty, Dr Jane McIntosh, Dr Margarete Prüch, Dr Anne Solomon, Dr Joyce Tyldesley, Dr Karen Wise

10 9 8 7 6 5 4 3 2 1